European Studie

Rob Sibley

Stanley Thornes (Publishers) Ltd

Dedication

To Deb for her patience, and to Wendy for her valuable assistance.

First published in 1993 by:
Stanley Thornes (Publishers) Ltd
Ellenborough House
Wellington Street
CHELTENHAM
GL50 1YD
UK

A catalogue record for this book is available from the British Library.
ISBN 0 7487 1609 2

Photoset by Northern Phototypesetting Co Ltd, Bolton.
Printed and bound in Great Britain by The Bath Press.

Contents

Introduction

This book has been written to help you to meet the requirements of the BTEC National units *European Studies* and *Business European Studies*. It will also be of use to those students starting the new BTEC GNVQ – in both the mandatory units *Understanding Business* and *Business Performance*, and the option *European Business*. I hope it will also be of interest to students on the increasing number of courses that have a European dimension to them – such as Travel and Tourism or Social Care. For many of you, European Studies will be a new topic and this book should help to develop an understanding of the importance of the European Community in the world today and how it works, and offer an insight into the countries and peoples that are members.

The book adopts the conventional format of headed chapters which, as you will see, run parallel with the outcomes for the current *Business European Studies* unit. **Activities** are incorporated into the text and each chapter concludes with longer **assignments**. This means the book is very useful as either a class text in conjunction with college tuition, or for independent study. **Appendices** at the back of the book will provide you with useful sources of information about the European Community.

Although chapter headings closely follow BTEC outcomes, the book is designed to allow topics to be studied in any order. To assist this, cross-references have been made where necessary.

The philosophy of BTEC courses is reflected in this book – namely that students learn best by 'doing'. Consequently, the activities and assignments are central to the book itself. Activities are designed to reinforce understanding of points made in the text, and the assignments allow you to demonstrate the skills and knowledge that you have developed.

Assignments may be used by college lecturers for assessment purposes, safe in the knowledge that BTEC outcomes will be adequately covered.

1 The idea of Europe

Aims

- To introduce the European Community and note its importance today
- To assess our views and those of others on Europe
- To note the specific 'language' of the Community
- To identify sources of information on the Community.

What is the European Community?

1.1 The 12 EC member states

Today's European Economic Community (EEC or more commonly, EC) is a unique combination of 12 member states – Belgium, The Netherlands, Luxembourg, France, Germany, Italy, UK, Ireland, Denmark, Greece, Spain and Portugal – who have all pledged to aim for economic, political and social integration. The vast population of 344 million makes the Community the world's largest trading grouping. In terms of the size of the domestic home market, and the volume of trade, the EC already rivals the USA and Japan together, making it very significant economically. Japanese companies, wishing to gain a foothold in the EC have been preparing for some time, setting up motor car and electrical manufacturing sites in the UK and other EC countries. This illustrates the importance which they place on the EC. In addition to this economic role, the EC also has an important influence in promoting peace and democracy.

Community aims

The main aims of the Community, detailed in the legal treaties setting up the EC, are based upon chiefly economic principles. The major principle is the promotion of an economic area in which goods, services, people and capital can move freely – in the same way that they would within usual national state boundaries. This economic area, known as the Single Market, came into effect on 1 January 1993. The Community is also trying to achieve 'ever closer union' between its member states by encouraging political integration. As we move towards the 21st century, the Community intends to promote further economic and political union.

Why European studies?

You may well be asking 'What has Europe to do with me?' All too often people in the UK view the idea of Europe with a good deal of suspicion, perhaps claiming that we have nothing in common with our European neighbours. But, as well as being part of Western Europe, we share many things with our fellow Community members. For instance, we all are subject to various laws and regulations that are made in Brussels that sometimes our national governments disagree with. It is now extremely difficult for businesses in the UK to operate without allowing for the impact of the Single Market. If businesses wish to remain competitive they must respond to the European environment. Learning and studying about Europe, its peoples, cultures, geography and business habits will inevitably help future generations to conduct their business operations more efficiently and successfully within the European context.

The common currency

Part of the new European environment may well be a common currency – the ECU (European Currency Unit). This would replace the British pound, the German mark, the Dutch guilda and all the other European currencies. It is this sort of development that often makes the whole issue of Europe a very controversial one.

ACTIVITY

Read the extract below (from *European Unification* published by the European Commission):

> Within the system the 'ECU' plays a central role. (The name has a dual parentage: it stands for 'European Currency Unit'; at the same time it also revives the name of a 13th-century French gold coin) . . . The exact value of the ECU in terms of each currency is fixed every day by the Commission and the rates are published . . .
>
> In private transactions the ECU offers businesses, workers and the ordinary citizen protection against sudden fluctuations in exchange rates. For banking purposes it already operates as a fully-fledged Euro-currency, being used for private and business savings and overdrafts, especially by small and medium-sized firms and independent operators. The hope is that people will ultimately be able to use the ECU in any member state as an acceptable alternative to the national currency. But this goal is a long way off, and economic and monetary policies will have to grow much closer before it becomes a practical proposition.

1 What justifications are offered for the existence of the ECU?
2 What is meant by the term 'Euro-currency'?
3 How would you react to the ECU replacing sterling in the UK? What are the advantages of such a currency?

The European idea

Europe is important for a number of reasons.

- For many years, central Europe has been the dividing line between East and West. This, up until recently, was symbolised by the imaginary Iron Curtain and the very real Berlin Wall.
- The two world wars of the 20th century were started and largely fought in Central Europe.
- For a long time, Western Europe has been considered as the model of democratic government that developing states should be encouraged to copy.
- A large geographical area like Europe has many different natural resources to offer.
- Europe has had an important impact on the rest of the world in terms of industrialisation and development.
- Europe is virtually a super-power.
- Europe is now the world's largest trading bloc.

The reasons for integration

The idea of a united or integrated Europe is certainly not a 20th-century one – it existed in the days of the Roman empire, 15 centuries ago. However, the motivation to unite Europe became very strong in the wake of the destruction caused by the Second World War. All the countries involved suffered much human loss, experienced acute shortages of food and many saw the destruction of their homes and cities. It was out of this horrific experience that a real will to unite Europe came about. In particular, certain forces combined to make the idea of a united Europe seem very attractive to European governments.

Although the idea of a united Europe had been voiced before, the post-war years saw this call being made again, but this time much more loudly. In particular, there was a feeling among all states that such a devastating war should never be allowed to happen again, and that rather than oppose one another, there should be a move towards co-operation in Europe.

Integrated Europe?

Today many of the dreams of the early 'Europeanists' have come true. What we have today is a European Community which is integrated in many ways, but which also allows individual states to retain their own, specific identity. On many occasions the Community speaks with one voice (for example, when negotiating with the USA in the GATT – General Agreement on Tariffs and Trade, see Appendix 1 – talks), but on other matters individual states offer their own distinct opinions and views (for example, over the acceptance of the Maastricht Treaty). The Community can never take away the cultural identity that each member state possesses and it does not want to. By retaining our national cultures and identities, the Community will continue to be a vast resource, and even those among us who may consider ourselves one day to be 'European' will still owe much of what we are to our nation states – whether it be Germany, Portugal, Denmark or any other of the member states.

▶ *1.2 The EC symbol*

Culture and the Community

The fact that the Community is made up of different cultures and business practices makes the running of the EC difficult because all views have to be taken into account. Consider, for example, how English culture differs from that of Ireland, Scotland or Wales. Having noted the differences between these cultures, you can perhaps start to appreciate how difficult it is to marry European cultures within the Community.

ACTIVITY

The purpose of this activity is to explore your own attitudes and those of the rest of your class towards Europe.

1 With a partner, discuss whether you see yourself as being British first of all, or European. How do the two differ? What characteristics do you have as a British person that you might not have as a European?
2 In a class discussion, try to suggest ways in which our European Community neighbours differ from ourselves. Are there any similarities between us?
3 Based on your discussion, try to draw up a profile of a typical British person and a profile of a European (in the broad sense of the term). Compare your profiles with other people in your group.

Different people, different views

People have strong views on the European Community, especially when it comes into direct contact with them. For example, many see the new burgundy-coloured European passport as the result of a meddlesome EC, while others may decide that it brings a much-needed identity to the Community. We have already noted the intention to introduce a common EC currency – some view this as a means of smothering national identities, while others see it as an important step in the right direction for further European integration. Many misunderstandings about the Community exist – some are rooted in reality, while others are the result of rumour. One purpose of this book and of your European Studies course, is to make you aware of this and other issues. This should encourage you to think more about the Europe that we are all part of.

ACTIVITY

Below is an extract of part of a discussion on Europe that took place. In it, people offer their opinions and views on the European Community. Read the extract.

Sally: 'Why should we need to associate with Europe at all – we can stand up for ourselves. I've never really liked foreigners anyway . . .'

Jim: 'It's not just about associating with Europe – it's a question of what can be done in numbers, rather than as individuals. We can achieve much more if we are part of a larger, unified Europe . . .'

Helen: 'Well, I can't see what all the fuss is about . . . 1992 and all that. Things will be exactly the same in ten years' time – the EC can't do anything about it . . .'

Yakub: 'I think it's an exciting prospect for people of our generation – we'll be able to travel all over Europe and be eligible for jobs . . .'

Mac: 'The EC has a lot to answer for if you ask me – we've got petrol in litres, vegetables in kilos and what have you. The longer it all goes on, the greater the chance of losing our British identity once and for all . . .'

Gill: 'But Mac, what about the environment? Anything that the EC can do here is fine by me – English beaches badly need tidying up . . .'

Mac: 'That's as maybe, but soon I'll be paying for my beer with flaming ECUs! I ask you – what a stupid name for a currency! Whatever happened to good old pounds and pence? . . .'

Jim: 'It's no good crowing about the ECU – that's coming anyway. What you should be thinking about is how it will help us when we go on holiday abroad . . .'

Sally: 'Well that's the least of our worries – with all those foreigners coming into the UK after 1992, we won't have jobs, so we won't be able to afford to go abroad . . .'

Yakub: 'But it's important that we go along with this European thing – if we don't, we'll get left behind! . . .'

Mac: 'They *can* leave us behind for all I care – Great Britain is an island and has nothing in common with the rest of Europe. End of discussion!'

1 Using the headings set out below, draw up a table on which to list the main points and opinions offered by the speakers. You should have about ten points or opinions.

ATTITUDE BATTERY TOWARDS THE EUROPEAN COMMUNITY					
Statements	Agree strongly	Agree	Neither agree nor disagree	Disagree	Strongly disagree

Indicate, with a tick, the attitude that you have towards the point or opinion offered. What does your attitude battery reveal about your underlying attitudes towards the EC?

2 In a group discussion, share your attitudes with other members of the group. Are there any issues or points that the group can form a consensus upon?

A supranational or intergovernmental approach?

Since the birth of the Community in January 1958, one of the major issues that has consistently been discussed is to what extent the Community should become a **supranational** body. The term 'supranational' means something that goes beyond the limits of national boundaries. Within the Community, this means allowing law-making, authority and power to be the responsibility of a body that acts only for the interests of the whole Community, and not for individual member states. For instance, the Community could impose a decision on member governments and they would be compelled by European law to abide by this or face the consequences. Already, British citizens can take a case beyond the British courts and on to the European Court of Justice (for example, on human rights issues). To many, this raises the controversial issue of the erosion of national sovereignty (the power to rule the UK, for example).

We shall see later how the European Commission attempts to look after the Community interest, while the Council of Ministers tends to adopt the *intergovernmental* approach. Here, the term 'intergovernmental' means following purely *national* interests, but agreeing to Community-wide measures if those national interests are not threatened in any way.

The difference between supranational and intergovernmental is important because this has helped to shape the past history and development of the EC. Indeed, some argue that only when member states are prepared to accept greater supranational measures, will the Community move ahead as a really united body.

The Maastricht Conference, held in The Netherlands in December 1991, assisted the move towards more supranationalism by agreeing to a common currency for the EC by 1999 at the latest. In other areas, such as political union, the trend seems to be for member states to retain a certain degree of intergovernmentalism, at least for the moment. The way that the Community develops in the future will very much depend upon the balance between supranationalism and intergovernmentalism, and upon the amount of national sovereignty that each member state is prepared to give up.

Eurospeak – a new language!

In the course of your study of Europe and the European Community, you will come across many abbreviations and shortened forms which are often referred to as **acronyms**. An acronym is a word formed from the initial letters of other words. For example, EEC is an acronym of European Economic Community and CAP is an acronym of Common Agricultural Policy. You will eventually come to recognise some of these shortened forms instantly, while others will be unfamiliar. To help you further a 'Glossary of EC acronyms' is included in Appendix 1 of this book.

Sources of information

There are many sources of information which help us to learn more about Europe and how the Community works. Many Community publications are issued free to encourage people to expand their knowledge.

Sources of European Community information

Information source	
Community publications	The Community publishes a whole range of booklets, leaflets and papers in many different series. A catalogue of publications is available from the Commission of the European Communities. You should make contact quickly as many publications are offered free of charge. In addition, the Community issues a weekly broadsheet – *The Week in Europe*, which is free of charge. This will keep you up to date with all the latest news on the Community's activities and Europe in general.
Government departments	Many government departments issue advice in the form of brochures and leaflets, depending upon the topic that you are studying. In particular, the Department of Trade and Industry (DTI) should be able to help you.
Libraries	An obvious starting point for those commencing a course in European Studies! As well as books, libraries also keep back copies of newspapers, magazines and journals, and you should ask librarians for assistance in seeking the information that you require. Some libraries also stock photographs.
European Documentation Centres (EDCs)	Many universities throughout the UK have European Documentation Centres attached to them. These contain much information on Community proceedings – but normally you cannot take items out and there is the problem of having so much information to consider. Such places should be used with care and advice from the experts. (See list of EDCs in Appendix 2.)
Newspapers	Again, an obvious source of information on the Community but one worth noting. Publications like *The European* are specifically produced for those with an interest in Europe and are useful in keeping you up to date. However, any 'quality' newspaper will carry news and articles of interest too.
Private companies	Some private companies issue booklets and information sheets on the activities and economic performance of the Community. The high street banks regularly publish information which can be obtained by making contact with the relevant head office.
National tourist boards	Information about member states can usually be obtained from national tourist boards, most of which have their headquarters in London. However, it should be noted that many of these now ask for donations towards the cost of postage when dispatching information.
National embassies	These are also a good source of information on member states and will often accommodate requests where possible.
Local authorities	Many local authorities (especially the larger county councils) have officers who offer advice to local businesses about Europe. These often stock the type of publications available from government departments like the DTI.

Television programmes The Community is very rarely out of the news and many documentary programmes deal with topical issues that arise. Programmes like the BBC's *Money Programme* regularly carry items or features on the Community (usually viewed from an economic perspective). Other companies offer, from time to time, series that deal with certain aspects of the Community or its people – for example, Channel 4's *The Germans*.

MPs and MEPs Members of Parliament and Members of the European Parliament may also be considered as sources of information on Community matters, although actually getting to see them might be another matter!

An action checklist

To make the most of the available information sources on the Community, it is a good idea to make contact with some of the agencies above as early as possible. You might decide to do some of the following:

- Get your name included on the mailing list for the broadsheet *The Week in Europe*
- Request the catalogue of publications available from the Community (this might be best approached as a group activity, so as not to flood agencies with requests!)
- Survey your college and local libraries for information on the Community that is held
- Find out where your local EDC is situated
- Contact private businesses to see what information they can offer
- Find out whether your local authority has an officer specifically appointed to deal with European matters
- Find out who your local MP and who your local MEP is.

ACTIVITY

1. With other members of your group, set up a resource file or data base for your European Studies course. This might contain useful publications, leaflets and information sheets. Request information on behalf of your group.
2. Ask your college librarians to set up a file of press cuttings concerning the EC. Alternatively, do this yourself, using copies of cuttings taken from issues of newspapers and magazines.
3. Throughout your European Studies course, keep a diary of the main events, issues discussed and decisions taken at Community level. Periodically, present an item or article to the rest of the group, which sums up the issue in question offering your own views.

Review your progress: 1

1. What does EEC stand for?
2. What is an ECU?
3. Name the 12 member states of the EC.
4. Explain the difference between 'supranational' and 'intergovernmental'.
5. List six different sources of information on the EC.
6. Give three reasons why Europe is important.

Summary

- The European Community has an increasing and important role in the world today, with some suggesting that it has assumed super-power status. This is one reason why European Studies should be part of the curriculum.
- Europe is significant for a number of historical reasons.

- The Community is made up of many different cultures and one of the problems that it faces constantly is how to bring together these unconnected (and largely unfamiliar) backgrounds and traditions.
- A long-running tension within the Community has been the extent to which it should become supranational or intergovernmental.
- We can learn, and keep up to date with, the Community from a wide range of sources that are generally widely available to the public.

Assignment 1 — Local community survey

Task 1 Conduct a local community survey on the European Community, by use of a questionnaire which seeks to discover, from a cross-section of the population, local awareness on the issue. Aim to produce 12 – 15 questions in your questionnaire which might include the following.

- Do you know how many Community members there are?
- Can you name any of the members?
- When did the UK join the EC?
- What is the symbol of the EC?
- Can you name any of the Community policies?
- Do you consider yourself to be a) British or b) European first and foremost?

Remember that the above are only suggestions – you might want to devise other questions that assess the awareness of local people.

Task 2 Using the results of your survey, produce a written report for your European Studies tutor, which draws conclusions about the level of 'European' awareness in your local community.

Task 3 Append to the written report, graphical interpretations of some of your results. It is suggested that you produce at least three different diagrams or charts to illustrate your results.

Task 4 Produce an article (no more than 350 words in length) for the local chamber of trade quarterly magazine, *Trade Counts*. You may use up to two illustrations to support your article.

Assignment 2 — Raising the European profile

Task 1 In groups, contact various agencies for information on the European Community. Restrict the information that you gather to introductory or general information about the EC. Collate the information for Task 2.

Task 2 Set up a display in your college foyer or library, or in a local building society or bank window, which advertises the European Community. The display should seek to raise the profile of the Community at the local level, and to answer some of the general questions that people might ask.

Task 3 Arrange to visit a local primary school to inform young school children about the Community. Give a 'presentation' to the children which might involve different foods, costumes and cultural items. Support the presentation with activities for the children to complete (e.g. word-searches, flag recognition and so on).

Task 4 In a group debriefing session, discuss what was learned about the level of awareness of young children of the European Community in your area and what might be done to raise the profile of the EC in the local community as a whole.

2 The international environment of business

Aims

- To develop familiarity with the political and geographical maps of Europe
- To consider and compare the aims, reasons for and consequences of, a policy of protectionism and a policy of *laissez-faire*
- To develop awareness of the major international trade agreements
- To develop an appreciation of the 'Trade versus Aid' debate in relation to less developed countries.

Relevant BTEC Outcome Performance Criteria

1a Familiarity displayed with world map

1b Major international trade agreements identified

1c Different government approaches to business and trade identified

The 'new face' of Europe

Over the past few years, the face of Europe has changed dramatically with new states being formed from old ones and a host of new names to contend with – Bosnia, Herzegovina and Azerbaijan are random examples. Many would argue that the catalyst for all these changes was the demolition of the Berlin Wall, culminating in the unification of East and West Germany, and the consequent breakdown of the Communist bloc in Eastern Europe. There have been many changes – Eastern Germany has been absorbed into a greater German state, the Soviet Union has divided into component parts including Russia and Byelorussia all coming under the collective umbrella of the CIS, and the former Yugoslavia is currently still ravaged by civil war as its component states, Bosnia, Serbia, Montenegro and so on, all try to establish themselves as independent states. The previously unchanged map of the continent has now been transformed into the new face of Europe.

The political map of Europe

Until the unification of Germany in 1991, the political map was distinguished by the imaginary Iron Curtain dividing East and West – the mass of territory to the east of the Berlin Wall being under the control of Communist Russia, while the western European powers were characterised by democracy. However, the great changes afoot in Eastern Europe may mean that future maps of Europe will indicate many more democratic states based on the Western-style model. During this time of political upheaval, students of Europe should be aware that changes are occurring all the time – there is therefore a need to keep up to date with alterations to territories and countries' names.

The new Europe

Since the end of the Second World War, and up until the demolition of the Berlin Wall, the world was viewed as two distinct halves – the East and the West. The political difference between the two resulted in the Cold War, with periods of hostility followed by co-operation, depending upon who was in power. The major actors in this war of words were the USA and the Soviet Union, opposed to one another for many reasons but largely because of political beliefs: in the East, the belief in Communism with the state controlling all factors of production and an apparently harsh way of life for citizens with many basic human rights denied; in the West, the belief in democracy, allowing citizens to have their say, promoting free markets, and providing social welfare and benefits for the population. Both sides saw their method as correct and were opposed to that of the other. This did not just involve the USA and the Soviet Union because both blocs had political allies: the East with its control of the countries surrounding the Soviet Union; the West with the relationships between the USA and other democracies such as France and the UK. The increase in the number of nuclear weapons available to each side made the situation so much more potentially deadly and there were a number of very close calls – for example, the Cuban Missile Crisis of 1961. It seemed that there would never be a 'thaw' in the Cold War, and that East and West would always be enemies.

The tearing down of the Berlin Wall altered the situation, however, and it set in train events that led to a very different world today. It triggered off the breakup of the Soviet Union into the component states that existed before the Russian revolution and, perhaps more importantly, it brought about a new phase of co-operation between East and West that was signalled by Soviet President Gorbachev's *glasnost*. Relations improved considerably between East and West, although the world now looked to other regions where conflict was occurring – the former Yugoslavia and the component states of the Soviet Union, where the call was for independence. As new states have been proclaimed in the light of these changes, the political map of the world has altered. Just how much this has happened can be seen by reference to the map below.

The geographical map of Europe

▶ *2.1 Geographical features of Europe*

Europe is the smallest continent of the northern hemisphere. It stretches westward from the Ural Mountains and is surrounded on three sides by sea. In the north-west of the continent are old mountains consisting of hard rock – these make up most of the Scandinavian Peninsula. Much of the area is covered by barren rocks and moorland. The larger part of it is divided from the North European Plain by the North and Baltic Seas.

The North European Plain stretches from England and France, across the north of the continent to Finland and Russia, as far as the Black Sea. For the most part, the plain is well watered and very fertile with a varied climate and vegetation – meadows and deciduous woodland in the west, and much coniferous forest in the east. Across the plain are scattered deposits of coal, oil and natural gas.

Southern Europe is hilly or mountainous with the exception of two plains – a triangular-shaped area in Northern Italy and a broad area in the Middle Danube region. From west to east is a chain of mountain ranges – the Pyrenees, the Alps and the Carpathians – while facing southwards are the Apennines and the range known as the Balkans.

Although the mountain ranges form natural barriers, so many rivers and valleys exist that, in fact, no part of Europe is completely isolated. In the south, a Mediterranean climate providing mild winters and hot summers exists, allowing for the cultivation of vines, olives and citrus fruit. However, the soil is is generally too dry for extensive grain cultivation. The far south of the continent is often volcanic, notably Mounts Etna and Vesuvius, located in Italian territory.

European land features

Land feature	*Description*
The Alps	A range of mountains extending in a crescent shape from south-east France, through Switzerland and Italy, and into Austria, for a distance of almost 970 km. Their great height results from an upward earth movement occurring before the last Ice Age. Glaciers cut out the valleys, blocking some with debris to form the Swiss and Italian lakes. Highest peaks include Mont Blanc with many areas reaching over 3500 m. Above 1830 m, snow lies for six months of the year and, on the high peaks, all year round. The main through valley is the Brenner Pass, connecting Italy with Austria towards the east.
The Pyrenees	Three ranges of mountains on the French – Spanish border. They extend for over 400 km between the Bay of Biscay and the Mediterranean. About 100 km wide, the western and eastern parts are lower than the central range, which rises to 3404 m. Iron ore, zinc, bauxite and talc are all found below the permanent snow-line (around 2000 m).
The Balkans	An area forming the great peninsula of south-east Europe, bounded by the Adriatic, Aegean and Black Seas. It is a very mountainous area with the Dinaric Alps of the former Yugoslavia, the Pindus Mountains of Greece and the Rhodope Mountains of Bulgaria, all barriers to the mild Mediterranean climate. Thus, winters can be extremely cold. The scenery varies from barren countryside to wooded slopes and to the flat River Danube plains. Earth tremors are frequent, especially in the west and south.
The Carpathians	These mountains extend sickle-shaped for 1400 km around the north and east of Central Europe's Danube Plain. The highest peaks are in the north – Tatras in Czechoslovakia (2663 m) for example. In Romania, the system becomes several ranges with the highest being the Transylvanian Alps.
The Caucasus	A series of high, parallel mountain ranges extending for almost 1200 km, south-eastward from the Black Sea to the Caspian Sea. Permanent snow lies above the 3000 m line. Large deposits of iron, manganese and oil exist. The range, more than 160 km wide at some

	points, contains lakes, plateaux, narrow gorges and broad valleys. Several good passes exist, offering access from the north into Georgia and Azerbaijan.
The Urals	A long chain of mountains extending for over 2100 km. Stretching north to south, they separate European Russia from Siberia in the east. A high point of 1894 m is reached in the north. Extreme climatic conditions apply – the north is seldom free of frost, while the south may see parched summer months. Winters everywhere in the region are long and severe.
Scandinavia	The western mountains of Norway rise to a height of 2470 m (the Glittertind) with fiords cutting deeply into them. A ridge of mountains run down the spine of the Scandinavian Peninsula. The area is rich in copper and iron.
Iberia	Two-thirds of the Iberian Peninsula is a plateau known as the Meseta and it contains several rugged mountain ranges, drained by several major rivers.
The Ukraine	Situated in the European region of the old USSR, the Ukraine stretches from the Carpathians to the Donetz River and is bounded in the south by the Black Sea. In the north, it consists of the low plains, woods and marshes of Byelorussia, while to the south, it is a vast, treeless *steppe* (a plain of rich, black soil). In the extreme south is the Crimea, a peninsula with a milder climate than the steppes. Coal and iron ore, salt, mercury, bauxite and manganese are the natural resources.

European rivers and lakes

River Volga this is Europe's longest river and Russia's most important waterway. Navigable for almost all of its 3700 km, the Volga rises in the Valday Hills of north-west Russia and flows into the Caspian Sea.

River Danube the second longest river in Europe at a total length of 2820 km, the Danube rises in the Black Forest of Germany, and winds through Austria, Hungary, the former Yugoslavia and Romania, and finally into the Black Sea. In some places the current is so strong that navigation upstream is very slow.

River Dnepr this flows through the European part of the former USSR and is Europe's third longest river at 2300 km. Its source is in the Valdai Hills of the Smolensk region, and it flows southerly towards the Black Sea. It is navigable for most of its length.

Lake Ladoga this is Europe's largest lake, extending for over 200 km and some 130 km wide. It is frozen from December to March and navigation is hampered at other times by fogs and storms.

Lake Onega second largest in Europe with a total area of 8030 square km. It has canal links with the White Sea and the Baltic (via Lake Ladoga).

Lake Vanern the third largest lake on the European continent. It is located in southern Sweden.

ACTIVITY

Using an atlas or encyclopedia, find out the following about the geography of Europe:

1 The total area of Europe (in square km)
2 The total population of Europe
3 Europe's five largest cities (in terms of population)

The European Community

The European Community is an example of an economic customs union which has opted to pursue a policy of free trade within its boundaries. Under the terms of the Rome Treaty, the 12 states trade freely while a Common External Tariff (CET) surrounds the EC. The imposition of this CET means that goods coming into the Community from non-member states are subject to tariffs (taxes) that products traded between member states are not subjected to. The advantages of a customs union can include:

- the stimulation/encouragement of trade within the customs union area;
- the establishment of a much enlarged 'home' market – that is, the whole EC rather than just member states;
- greater efficiency, for states that are good at producing certain goods will concentrate on these with the hope that others will be allowed to produce their speciality;
- greater co-operation between the member states than would be the case if they acted and traded independently of each other.

There are disadvantages in establishing a customs union however, and the usual criticisms include:

- loss of economic independence by individual member states;
- trade diversion.

International trade options

In conducting trade with other countries, any nation state has to choose between the options available in order to secure the best situation. Basically, two major trade options exist:

- a policy of protectionism;
- a policy of *laissez-faire* or free trade.

These policy options require some further explanation.

Protectionism

Some would argue that if international trade were allowed to operate unhindered, it would benefit all those nations who are involved. However, complete freedom of trade does not exist in the world economy because countries impose restrictions which mean that trade is hindered. But why do countries decide to impose such restrictions on trade?

Arguments for protection

Several arguments are usually given for a policy of protection. The major ones are as follows.

- The need to protect essential industries – some governments feel that they need to protect certain industries due to their *strategic* importance to the country. An example often given is domestic agriculture in war time – protection is needed in order to ensure a supply of food for the population.
- The need to protect 'infant' or developing countries. Any industry that is in the early stages of development may well be threatened by already well-established foreign competitors. Therefore, governments provide protection to such infant industries allowing them to develop normally. When this has happened, the protection can be removed. A drawback here is that many industries do not own up to having developed or 'grown up'.
- The need to protect domestic industry from 'low-wage' countries. Some of the poorer countries of the world operate their economies on such a low wage structure that they are able to compete on an unequal basis with the more developed countries.

- The need to protect against 'dumping'. This refers to the situation when a foreign producer has a surplus of produce which it does not want to sell in its home market because it would cause prices to fall. So, the produce is 'dumped' on another country at very low prices. Here it is argued that domestic producers should be protected against this unfair competition.
- The need to protect against unemployment. In times of depression, a policy of protection can cause demand to be diverted from foreign goods to home-produced goods (because they are cheaper), thus protecting jobs in the industries producing these goods. However, retaliation can result, exaggerating the problem.
- The need to improve the balance of trade. Here, if the number of imports persistently exceeds the number of exports, protection should be used by the government in order to restrict the number of imports and, therefore, improve the balance of trade.

ACTIVITY Protection

1 What are 'infant' industries? Why do they need protection?
2 In 'low-wage' countries, other factors may contribute to goods costing less. What might these other factors be?
3 Explain what is meant by 'dumping'.
4 Does a *positive* balance of trade mean that a country has more exports than imports or vice versa?

In order to protect domestic industries in any of the situations that were considered above, national governments have a range of methods which can be used.

Methods of protection available to governments

Method	*Description*
Imposition of tariffs (taxes on goods entering a country)	Tariffs will cause the price of imported goods to rise, leading to a reduction in demand for these goods. A further possible effect is a rise in demand for similar home-produced goods.
Imposition of quotas (limits set upon the quantities of products allowed into a country)	To limit the number of foreign goods entering the country for domestic purchase – eg limits on the number of imported Japanese cars. The hope is that the demand for home-produced cars would be stimulated.
Imposition of exchange controls (limiting the availability of foreign currency with which imports can be bought)	Limits can be imposed because, when exchange control is in use, foreign currency received by a country's residents must be given to the central bank in exchange for home currency. Also, any foreign currency required by residents (to purchase imports) can only be obtained with approval of the central bank. This can have the effect of limiting imports, by restricting use of foreign currency.
Imposition of strict standards on imported goods	This acts as a restraint on the quantity of imports allowed into the country, by imposing higher standards to ensure quality.
Discrimination in favour of home producers	Governments can do this when buying supplies, even though they may be cheaper from other countries. The hope is that imports will be limited. Grants may also be given to home producers to help them compete more effectively against foreigners.
Voluntary export restraint agreements	Worked out by the two countries involved (that is, *bilaterally*), where each agrees to limit quantities of particular goods exported to each other.

ACTIVITY

In a class discussion, consider the following questions:

1. Under what circumstances do you think the EC should employ any of the above methods of protection? Give your reasons.
2. Should countries who are members of the EC be allowed to use protective methods? Why?

Laissez-faire (free trade)

The term *laissez-faire* means 'leave alone' and in this sense it refers to allowing commodities to circulate freely. This policy, when applied to international trade, means that the state should not intervene at all in economic affairs – in other words, the opposite of protection, and therefore also known as free trade. This policy does not protect home industries against foreign competition, allowing free import and export of all goods.

The argument for free trade is convincing if it is believed that unhindered international trade will benefit all involved. In addition, many observers believe that free trade is a desirable option because it demands no interference from governments, and allows business to seek and establish its own markets.

The economic development of the UK supports this idea – the gradual removal of all protective customs duties in the UK between the 1820s and 1870 is closely associated with an enormous expansion of trade and industry.

Within the EC, free trade largely operates and this is one of the objectives of the Single Market of 1992. However, some may argue that the EC is an exclusive economic club with imports entering from outside, only after they have been subject to taxes or duties.

There are many potential dangers with free trade however – an individual state may be too weak economically to compete with cheap imported goods for example, and then a government may feel compelled to use some of the protective measures outlined earlier.

ACTIVITY

Consider the following situations and decide which would result from a) a policy of free trade, b) a policy of protectionism:

1. Less variety of goods available to consumers
2. Imported goods compete with home-produced goods in terms of price
3. A wider range of goods is available for consumers
4. Exported goods can be sold at prices fixed by the producer
5. Consumers are more likely to purchase home-produced goods
6. A company decides to concentrate on the domestic rather than overseas market.

Major international trade agreements

The European Community is extremely dependent on trade – imports and exports – and Figure 2.2 illustrates this. In fact, the value of EC external trade is equal to about 20 per cent of its GDP. The USA is the Community's most important trading partner, providing over 16 per cent of its imports and taking over 20 per cent of EC exports. The Rome Treaty allows EC states to develop a common commercial policy, to establish and maintain relations with international bodies, and to make tariff and trade agreements, both on a multilateral (with many states taking part) or a bilateral (just two states taking

Breakdown of world trade* (%, 1989)

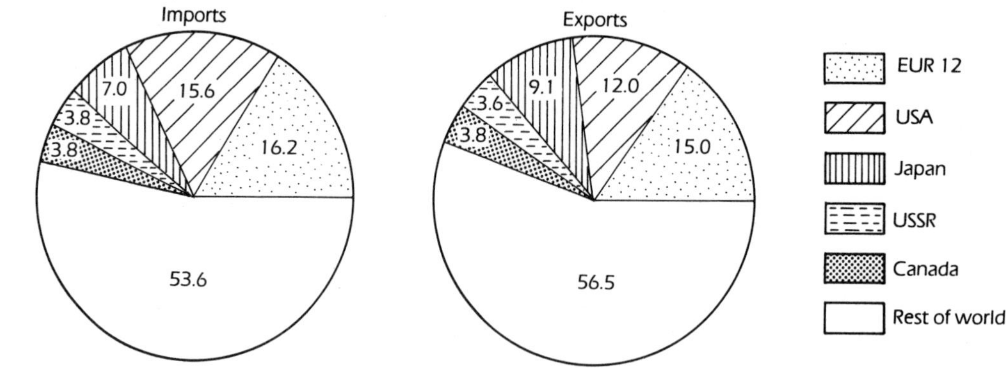

*Excluding trade between Community countries

Shares of world trade in agricultural products* (%, 1989)

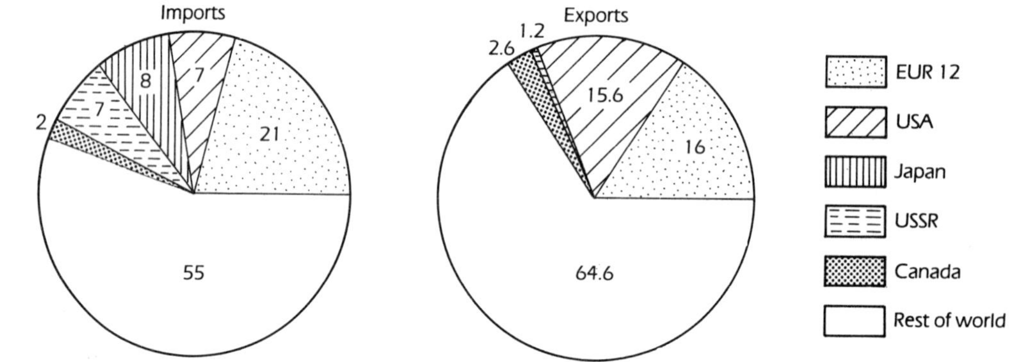

*Excluding trade between Community countries

Source: Eurostat

▶ *2.2 The EC as a world trade leader*

part) basis. As a result, the EC has reached trade agreements or co-operation agreements with many countries across the world.

In the main, international trade agreements have been agreed between different states in order to secure the various benefits of free trade. As the EC has expanded, its role in the forging of these agreements has increased. The US Marshall Plan to revitalise Europe after the Second World War included clauses that would encourage the development of economic co-operation between European states. In American eyes, this has happened perhaps *too* successfully, for the US economy is threatened by the strength of trade from the EC, resulting in lengthy and inconclusive discussions about future trade agreements – in particular, those concerning the General Agreement on Tariffs and Trade (GATT). The chief international trade agreements concluded by the EC include the following.

General Agreement on Tariffs and Trade (GATT)

Established in 1948, GATT aimed at providing a code of conduct for international trade and the reduction of barriers to trade. The agreement currently covers over 120 countries.

A major principle of the agreement is the clause which deals with the 'most favoured nation'. Here, if a member state wants to offer a particular concession (such as a reduction in tariffs) to another country, then it must provide a similar concession to all other member states.

The agreement contains 38 articles, along with many additions (in the form of schedules and annexes) in respect of the many thousands of trade concessions that exist. The agreement is based on four main principles:

1 Non-discrimination – the 'most favoured nation clause'. This does not apply to a full customs union (like the EC) or free trade areas (like EFTA)
2 No quotas are allowed – in trade processes, no restrictions or quantities can be fixed
3 Developing countries enjoy special provisions and exemptions from tariffs
4 Regular negotiation of tariff reductions with regular conferences. This has run into difficulty lately with the current Uruguay Round still not having been concluded after five years.

ACTIVITY

GATT Progress

EC and US GATT negotiators said they had made 'good progress' in narrowing down their differences over EC farm subsidies following talks in Brussels at the weekend. Commission Vice-president Frans Andriessen said afterwards that the aim had been to make a serious effort to 'assemble the elements for a final settlement'. He said that the meeting had provided 'elements' only and not a complete agreement. The issue of EC subsidies to oil seed producers remains unsolved. Technical discussions continued overnight to prepare for a further EC – US round of talks on the fringes of a trade ministers' meeting in Canada at the weekend.

Source: *The Week in Europe*, 15 October 1992

EC – US GATT talks stall

EC negotiators are expressing regret and apprehension following the latest breakdown in talks to solve the oil seeds dispute with the United States. The US had demanded deeper cuts in support for EC oil seed production as a price for restarting the GATT talks involving most of the world's trading nations over the past five years. EC's external trade negotiator, Commission Vice-president Frans Andriessen, confirmed in Brussels yesterday that the EC would have to consider retaliation if the US carried out a threat to impose sanctions on about 1 billion dollars' worth of EC exports to the EC, mostly food and alcoholic drinks. But he hoped talks with the US negotiators could meanwhile continue in the hope of resolving the dispute.

Source: *The Week in Europe*, 5 November 1992

Read the above articles and then answer the following questions:

1 For what reasons did the GATT talks break down between 15 October and 5 November 1992?
2 Why do you think the US had been calling for deeper cuts in EC support for oil seed production?
3 What form might EC 'retaliation' against the US take, if needed?
4 Why do you think the GATT talks have lasted so long? What external factors have contributed to the lack of agreement?

EFTA and the EEA

Apart from the US and Japan, the countries of the European Free Trade Association (EFTA) – namely, Iceland, Norway, Finland, Sweden, Switzerland, Austria and Liechtenstein, are the major export markets for the European Community. Within the developed world, the EC's relationship with the EFTA states is an important one. EFTA is a free trade area for states who are members. From 1993, a new European Economic Area (EEA) aims to strengthen trade and economic relations between the EC and EFTA states. This is an important development in terms of international trade for the EC because the EEA will become the world's largest single market, allowing increased opportunities for

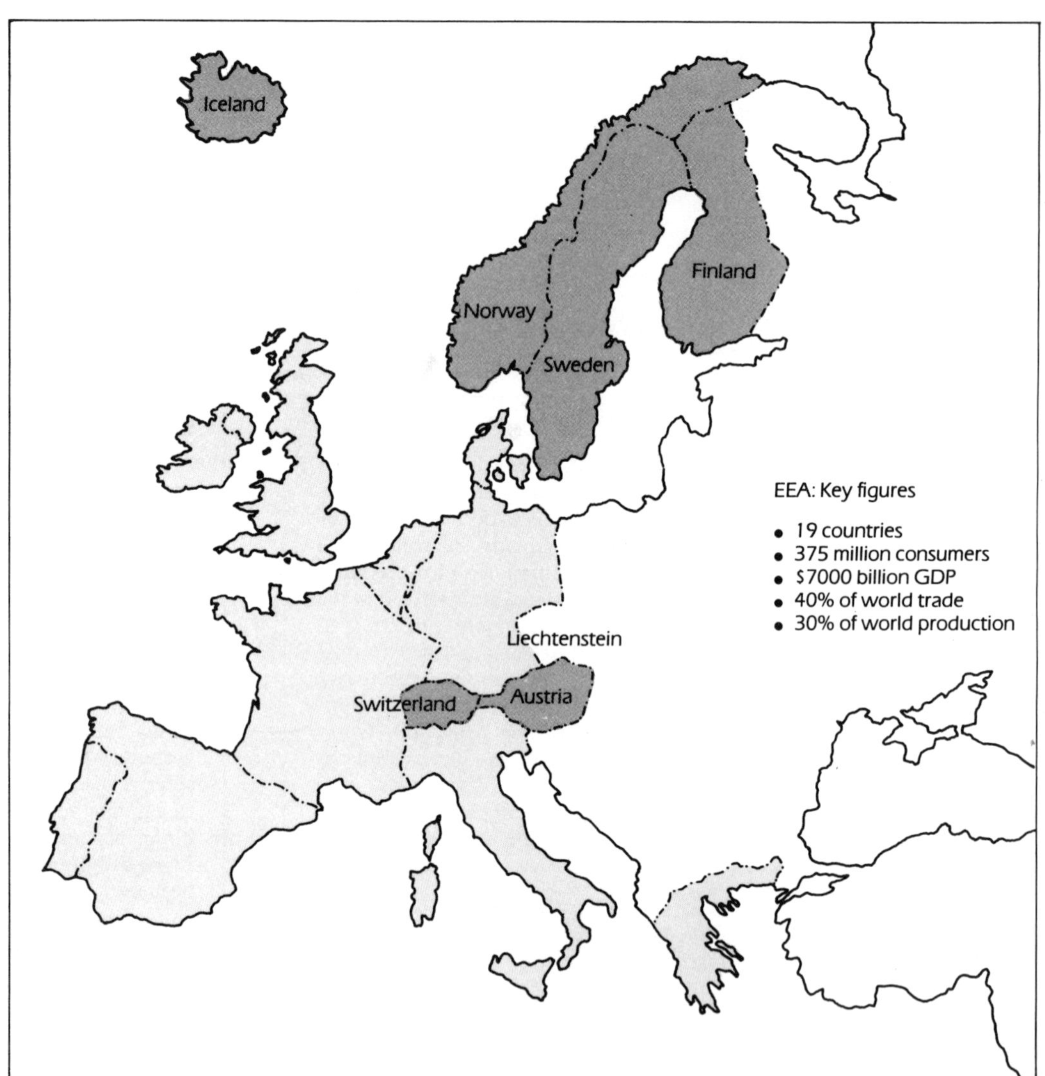

▶ *2.3 The EEA*

businesses and the stimulation of growth. In practice, the EC Single Market will be extended to the EFTA states with some legislation also being extended – basically that concerning the 'four freedoms' (free movement of goods, services, capital and persons). EC competition rules will also apply to EFTA states.

Agreements with the Third World

Agreements with the developing countries of the Third World have really arisen from the individual policies of EC member states. Some favoured a more 'regional' approach, targeting specific areas, while others took a more 'global' view. To start with, co-operation tended to be with countries with which the EC had historical links, for example the former colonies of member states like France, Belgium and The Netherlands.

EC policy towards development in the Third World consists of a combination of trade concessions and aid granted to LDCs (less developed countries).

EC trade initiatives with Third World

Agreement	*Description*
Generalised System of Preferences (GSP)	Introduced in 1971, the GSP covers a range of industrial and agricultural products. The main beneficiaries have been the former Yugoslavia, Malaysia, Hong Kong, South Korea and Brazil. Generalised preferences are tariff preferences, giving the states receiving them an advantage over products exported by other industrialised states. They are known as generalised because they are granted to developing countries by industrialised states and because they involve all industrial products as well as many agricultural goods. The main purpose of the GSP is to increase the export income of poor states, to assist their industries and to help speed up their rates of economic growth.
Global Mediterranean Policy (GMP)	A series of preferential trade agreements between the EC and countries of the Mediterranean area – includes Tunisia, Algeria, Lebanon, Syria, Israel and Turkey. GMP agreements tend to be more generous than the GSP.
Lomé Conventions	The most significant part of EC policy towards Third World states. These agreements were named after the capital of Togo where they were signed. They deal with both trade and aid and, so far, four have been concluded, each covering five years, apart from the current one which runs for a period of ten years (until 2000). Under the agreements, all African, Caribbean and Pacific (ACP) states' products are allowed to enter the EC without tariffs or quotas. Some restrictions, however, have been applied on agricultural goods such as sugar and beef, because these compete with EC products!

ACTIVITY

Decide whether you think the EC should be responsible for preferential trade agreements with the Third World. Give your reasons.

Agreements with Eastern Europe

The EC has started to put into place policies that will grant the countries of Eastern Europe better access to its own market. However, although the EC has concluded new trade agreements with Poland, Hungary and Czechoslovakia (known as the Visegrad states), and Bulgaria, Romania and the former Soviet Union, these are limited in their scope. Thus, negotiations on free trade with the EC have begun. In moving towards the objective of free trade, the EC has pledged to reduce its tariffs and other import barriers.

ACTIVITY

Visegrad Summit

UK prime minister John Major and Jacques Delors, president of the European Commission, hosted a meeting of the prime ministers of Poland, Hungary, and the Czech and Slovak republics, the so-called Visegrad group of countries, at a summit in Lancaster House, London, on Wednesday. In a joint statement afterwards, Major and Delors said they welcomed the meeting as a demonstration of European Community support for all the newly democratising countries of Eastern and Central Europe. The summit agreed to encourage intensified, practical co-operation between the Community and the Visegrad countries. To follow up the European Agreements which envisage eventual accession to the EC, four areas were marked out: more open and liberal markets; local and democratic links; training and education; and parliamentary links. Major and Delors welcomed the moves towards powerful Association Agreements linking the Visegrad group with the EC. They also looked forward to the development of ever closer co-operation, although Major told a press conference later that there was no fixed timetable for full accession to the EC.

Source: *The Week in Europe*, 29 October 1992

Read the article 'Visegrad Summit' and then answer the following questions:

1 Which Eastern European states make up the Visegrad Group?

2 What do you think is meant by the term 'newly democratising countries'? Why is the EC keen to assist them?

3 What difficulties might there be for the Visegrad states if they wished to join the EC now?

4 An increasing number of Eastern European states may wish to join the EC in the future. What effects do you think this will have on the Community?

The trade versus aid debate

In relation to the less developed countries, much debate and discussion surrounds the question of whether the EC should encourage trade in order to assist economic development or whether it should offer aid which may not actually stimulate development at all. There are a number of advantages and disadvantages put forward in relation to trade and in relation to aid.

The advantages and disadvantages of trade and aid

TRADE *Advantages*	*Disadvantages*
Allows LDCs to find markets in which to sell their products	Developed states, by trading with LDCs, may be furthering worker exploitation (long hours, low wages, poor work conditions)
Assists the stimulation of the economy by the collection of export revenues by LDCs	The quality of goods from LDCs may be inferior to those of industrial states, due to lack of technology and expertise
Assists the general economic development of LDCs	Cheaper imported goods from LDCs may threaten the domestic market, leading to loss of profit and jobs at home

AID *Advantages*	*Disadvantages*
Aid is one way in which developed nations can assist LDCs, by supplementing their sparse sources of domestic finance/ income	Aid tends to weaken the need for self-reliance and the need to tackle problems without reliance on the easy option of external help
Aid can be used to target specific projects in LDCs – irrigation, infrastructure etc., which may not otherwise be targeted	The possible concentration of aid on urban-based rather than rural-based projects
Where short-term measures are needed, aid may be the best policy	Aid is given to governments, which may strengthen their positions, but may not be used for the intended purpose
Aid is generally immediate, but the positive effects of trade take time to filter through to the economy of an LDC	Aid programmes can be cut by developed countries as a means of making economies in an ailing balance of payments

ACTIVITY

In a class discussion, consider the following:

1 On balance, would you agree that trade is more desirable than aid to LDCs? Why?

2 'The public should purchase goods from LDCs (wherever possible) rather than from the richer developed nations.' How far do you agree with this statement?

3 Charitable appeals for people in LDCs are a feature of modern life. Many people contribute to these appeals, with vast sums of money raised. Why do they seem to make little or no impact on the situation in many poor countries?

European Community Aid

Aid is granted to ACP states under the Lomé Conventions and this is allocated usually via the European Development Fund (EDF). In some cases, it takes the form of loans to LDCs.

Part of the Lomé regime has been the introduction of the STABEX and SYSMIN schemes. Both of these are trade-related assistance schemes which are designed to stabilise the earnings that ACP states derive from their exported goods.

STABEX – this provides compensatory payments to exporters of a limited range of products, subject to conditions. It originally covered 29 products although others have now been added.

SYSMIN – this was introduced under the second Lomé Convention and basically extends the STABEX principle to ACP mineral exports not covered by STABEX. It covers bauxite, copper, cobalt, iron ore, manganese, phosphate and tin.

ACTIVITY Review your progress: 2

1 Name five new states that have emerged in Europe since the demolition of the Berlin Wall.
2 Europe is the second largest continent in the world. True or false?
3 State the geographical locations of the following:
a) the Pyrenees?
b) the Balkans?
c) the Urals?
d) Iberia?
e) the Ukraine?
4 Which is Europe's third largest river?
5 Explain what is meant by the Common External Tariff (CET).
6 a) How does protection differ from free trade?
b) State three methods of protection available to governments.
7 What do the following stand for:
a) GATT?
b) GSP?
c) EEA?
d) GMP?
Briefly explain the purpose of each of the above.
8 Explain what is meant by the trade versus aid debate.
9 Give two advantages and two disadvantages of trade and of aid to LDCs.
10 What are the STABEX and SYSMIN systems designed to do?

Summary

- The political map of Europe has undergone a number of important changes recently and may alter again in the near future.
- The continent of Europe has a varied set of geographical features, coupled with important natural resources.
- Options for international trade open to national governments include policies of protection and free trade. Those governments opting for protection have a range of measures at their disposal.
- Several international trade agreements exist and the EC is a key actor in these.
- A common dilemma in relation to less developed countries is whether to encourage trade or assist them with aid. There are advantages and disadvantages connected with both courses of action.

Assignment 3 The Third World charity delegation

You are employed by a charity that does valuable work in the Third World, ranging from famine relief to providing funding for infrastructure projects in less developed countries. The manager of your branch has been asked to attend a conference in London, on the effects of international trade on the economies of Third World countries. He has been invited to speak on the trade versus aid debate, along with other guest speakers from the US delegation of GATT, the Finnish delegation to EFTA and various EC delegates. In order to be well prepared for the conference, he asks you to give him some assistance by carrying out the following tasks.

Task 1 Prepare a set of detailed notes on the trade versus aid debate that your manager could make use of when delivering his speech to the conference delegates. In particular, he wants the notes to distinguish clearly between the advantages and disadvantages of trade and aid to Third World states.

Task 2 As part of the background to his speech, he asks you to spend some time preparing a formal report which deals with the following issues:

- the role of the EC
- the role of GATT and
- the role of EFTA and the proposed European Economic Area

in international trade.

Task 3 When conducting your research for the manager, a discussion develops in the office over the protection versus free trade debate. Reconstruct this discussion in your college in a formal debate, which argues the following proposition: 'Protection is the best trade policy for the UK, but is fatal for the less developed countries.'

You should generally argue **for** or **against** the proposition.

3 How the European Community works

Aims

- To explore the status of EC legislation
- To explain the legal framework under which the EC operates
- To introduce the Community institutions
- To consider the relationship between the EC institutions
- To consider the EC budget and other financing mechanisms
- To review EC links with other economic groupings.

Relevant BTEC Outcome Performance Criteria

1b Major international trade agreements identified
2a Main organisational structure of EC set out
2b Workings of formal bodies clarified
2c Nature and use of directives explained
2d Budget and funding mechanisms identified
2e Links with other groupings identified

The legal framework of the European Community

The Treaty of Rome

The European Community came into legal force on 1 January 1958. The document establishing the Community was the Treaty of Rome, signed by the six founder members – Belgium, The Netherlands, Luxembourg, France, Germany and Italy – in 1957. The Treaty resulted from much discussion between the interested parties as to the specific direction of the new Community. The resulting document made provision for Community institutions such as the European Commission, Council of Ministers and European Parliament – these were mirror images of bodies established under the European Coal and Steel Community (ECSC), the forerunner of the EC set up by the Treaty of Paris in 1951. In addition to the Treaty of Rome, a separate treaty established the European Atomic Energy Community (Euratom), permitting the six members to combine their efforts in the development of atomic energy.

The Rome Treaty enabled the setting up of the EC, and this was intended to be an economic union that would remove the obstacles preventing the free movement of people and resources within the Community. At the same time, the general objective of economic growth was to be pursued. To assist this process, trade tariffs would be maintained against non-members (a common external tariff), but even these would be less than those employed before the EC. The Rome Treaty also made reference to the improvement of living and working conditions, assisting the development of the world's backward areas, the safeguarding of peace and liberty, and the pursuit of 'an ever closer union' of European peoples.

Key aims of the Treaty of Rome

The articles of the Rome Treaty aimed to:

- remove customs duties, taxes or quota restrictions on goods moving from one state to another;
- establish identical customs duties in the six states for goods entering any of them from outside the Community. This was to prevent non-member states taking advantage of lower rates of duty in one state in order to flood the market of another member state that had higher rates of duty;
- allow every citizen in each member state to work in any of the other member states while also enjoying the same pay, social security benefits and working conditions of the people to whose country the citizen had moved;
- establish the right of any firm to set up in a member state to operate in any of the others, while being subject to the same legislation and taxation as firms originally set up in that member state;
- set up a body of rules governing preferential treatment of a member state's own citizens over other member states' citizens in business;
- remove restrictions on transfer of funds from one member state to another. This aim requires a common currency (such as the ECU) to allow it to work effectively.

ACTIVITY

1 Consider the six key aims of the Treaty of Rome and rank them in order of importance as you see them, rating the most important as Number 1 and so on. Be prepared to offer reasons for your rankings.
2 How do your rankings compare with others in your group? Which key aim would have been most important to the founders of the EC do you think? Why?

The Maastricht Treaty

Before the Treaty was agreed upon in December 1991, few people would have been aware of the Dutch town of Maastricht. Now, most people have heard of Maastricht – not because of the town itself but through the controversy surrounding the Treaty that resulted from the EC summit held there.

Discussions at Maastricht lasted for two days, with the result that many national governments received part of what they wanted. An important result of the Treaty has been the ratification required of all member states – this is the process by which national parliaments agree to the details of the Treaty. The fact that the Danes rejected the Treaty in a national referendum (although later accepted it in a second referendum) and the French only narrowly accepted it has meant that the Maastricht issue remains controversial.

The Treaty was an important development for the European Community. The main provisions included:

- agreement on EC member states adopting a single currency by 1999. The UK government negotiated an opt-out over this important issue;
- the removal of the Social Charter. This partly resulted from the UK's refusal to go along with its provisions. It was agreed that a special protocol for the Social Charter should be established, which would allow the other member states to continue with the type of social issues contained in the Charter, while the UK would be able to opt out;
- the promise of more EC money for Spain and Portugal;
- provisions which may allow the creation of a common foreign and security policy;
- an increased role for the European Parliament;
- other measures, including education, training, the environment, trans-European networks, health, industry, consumer protection and culture.

Legal status

In many ways, the provisions of the Maastricht Treaty were forged from compromise and this is a feature of the way the EC conducts its business – ground lost in one policy area can often be regained in another by national governments. This method of decision-taking seems to be favoured by most (if not all) EC member states. The ratification process means that once accepted, national states have to abide by the treaties and therefore their legal status is applicable in all states that have agreed to the clauses contained in them.

ACTIVITY

Several EC member states conducted referendums to determine whether national populations agreed with the Maastricht Treaty. The UK refused to use this method of ratifying the Treaty. How far do you agree with this decision? Should people in the UK have had the opportunity to express their views on Maastricht? Give your reasons in a class discussion.

The Community's image

Since the birth of the Community in 1958, it has often suffered from an unfavourable image in the media, especially in countries like the UK which was reluctant initially to become a member. This 'bad' image is sometimes the result of Community-wide policies, set up by the European Commission, for implementation in all member states. Budd and Jones, in *The European Community – a guide to the maze* (4th edn, 1991), have pointed out that many view the 'Brussels bureaucracy' as trying to create misery in our daily lives by either 'banning' something, making it more expensive or financially ruining some groups in society (whether they be farmers, brewers or steelworkers). Some of the misunderstandings about the EC have made the headlines in our daily newspapers and so become cause for concern.

ACTIVITY

1 What do you think is meant by the 'Brussels bureaucracy'?
2 Why might people have a hostile attitude towards this bureaucracy?

ACTIVITY

'NOT CONTENT WITH BANNING THE VINEGAR WE PUT ON OUR CHIPS, THEY'RE TRYING TO BAN THE NEWSPAPER WE WRAP THEM IN'

'NOW THE IDIOTS ARE TRYING TO STANDARDISE STINK BOMBS, ITCHING POWDER AND SNEEZING POWDER'

'FOOTBALL STARS WHOSE CONTRACTS HAVE EXPIRED CAN PACK THEIR BAGS AND JOIN A TEAM IN ANY EC COUNTRY, WHETHER THEIR OWN CLUB LIKES IT OR NOT, BECAUSE OF AN . . . EC RULING'

'HEARD THE LATEST EEC DAFTNESS? THEY WANT US TO RENAME WATERLOO STATION!'

Source: Budd and Jones, *The European Community – a guide to the maze*

1 What attitudes about the Community are conveyed in the four newspaper headlines?
2 What effect do you think such headlines have on the public?

3 What words would you use to describe the image of the EC as portrayed by these newspaper headlines?
4 During the coming week, collect headlines from newspapers that deal with EC issues. Do these differ from the above in the way that they portray the image of the Community?

The structure of the European Community

It is difficult to draw comparisons between the Community institutions and national governmental bodies such as the British House of Commons. In addition, the geographical location and the 'spread out' nature of the EC institutions have helped to underline the distance from them that is felt by many, and to reinforce unfamiliarity with such bodies.

It should be pointed out here that power is *shared* among the three main EC decision-making institutions and the member states. Power is distributed among:

- the European Commission;
- the Council of Ministers;
- the European Parliament.

This arrangement is deliberate in order to provide a series of 'checks and balances' within the European system. Important in this balance are the individual national interests of member states which have to be considered against the 'supranational' or Community interests.

Power sharing arises from the fact that European integration has always been seen as a **gradual process** with member states agreeing to pool more and more of their resources as times goes by, in the move towards 'ever closer union'. Here, it was always hoped that the Commission would take more responsibility as the Community developed, while the Council of Ministers was seen as the champion of national interests. In this role, the Council has the ability to veto proposals. Within the relationship between Commission and Council, the move towards genuine European unity would be marked by a shift to majority voting in the Council of Ministers (see page 30).

The European Commission

The Rome Treaty (notably Article 155) spells out the role of the European Commission. It is really the executive arm of the Community and answers to the European Parliament when carrying out its function of designing new Community policies. In fact, the Commission is the only institution that is able to draw up Community law. It issues proposals for policy on areas such as agriculture, energy and regional development. Largely based in Brussels, the Commission has offices in Luxembourg, along with information offices in all member states and delegations in many of the world's capitals. Of all the Community institutions, the Commission is considered to be the most unusual and distinctive in its make-up. This is because it is composed of commissioners who serve the Community interest first, rather than national interests.

Composition
The Commission consists of 17 Commissioners. Other officials support the Commissioners. These Commissioners are appointed for a period of four years. It is important to note that national governments often view their right to nominate Commissioners as an opportunity to limit the independence of the Commission, perhaps preventing further integration.

National composition of Commission

Member state	*Number of Commissioners*
France	2
Germany	2
Italy	2
Spain	2
UK	2
Belgium	1
Denmark	1
Greece	1
Ireland	1
Luxembourg	1
Netherlands	1
Portugal	1
Total	17

Organisation

The Commission is headed by a president who is appointed, like the Commissioners themselves, by agreement among the 12 member states. The presidency lasts for two years and is rotated among the member states. The current president is the Frenchman, Jacques Delors, who was reappointed to the position. Current UK commissioners (1993) are Sir Leon Brittan and Bruce Millan.

Once Commissioners are appointed, they have to swear allegiance to the Community. This means that they have to act as a unified body despite them having very different cultural and political backgrounds. They must not seek or receive instructions from any government. The effect of this is to underline the basic 'Europeanness' of the Commission and of its proposals. An example of this allegiance to the Community as a whole is illustrated in a short news item taken from *The European Times* (22 May 1992).

Mack the Knife wins the day

Not for nothing is Raymond MacSharry known as Mack the Knife in Brussels. The agreement by EC farm ministers last night to curtail the chronic over-production of food owes much to the dogged persistence of the man from Sligo.

When Mr MacSharry, from the Irish Republic, took up the post of European agriculture commissioner in 1989, few imagined that a man from a country that had done so well out of the EC's . . . common agricultural policy would be prepared to press for far-reaching reform.

Flawed as the final package of measures may be, Mr MacSharry can claim to have administered the biggest shake-up to the agricultural status quo in the EC's history and to have moved it away from food price rigging.

The Commission usually meets on Wednesdays. Decisions are normally taken by a simple majority and, in theory, Commissioners are collectively responsible for Commission activities and decisions.

Like the UK civil service, each Commissioner has a 'cabinet' of six or more permanent administrators along with secretarial support. Most of the cabinet staff are of the same nationality as the Commissioner. These staff help keep the Commissioner up to date on all aspects of Community policy. The main bulk of the Commission personnel are referred to as 'services' and it is their role to prepare technical aspects of legislation, and to implement it.

The Commission is served by a staff of more than 12 000, divided into 23 separate departments or 'Directorates-General' (DGs). The DGs are the responsibility of individual Commissioners – for instance, there is a Commissioner responsible for DG VI (Agriculture). The UK Commissioner Sir Leon Brittan is currently responsible for External Economic Affairs. The staff who work in the DGs are recruited from all of the Community's member states.

Directorates-General of the Commission

DG I	External Relations
DG II	Economic and Financial Affairs
DG III	Internal Market and Industrial Affairs
DG IV	Competition
DG V	Employment, Social Affairs and Education
DG VI	Agriculture
DG VII	Transport
DG VIII	Development
DG IX	Personnel and Administration
DG X	Information, Communication and Culture
DG XI	Environment and Nuclear Safety
DG XII	Science, Research and Development
DG XIII	Telecommunications, Information Industries and Innovation
DG XIV	Fisheries
DG XV	Financial Institutions and Company Law
DG XVI	Regional Policy
DG XVII	Energy
DG XVIII	Credit and Investments
DG XIX	Community Budgets
DG XX	Financial Control
DG XXI	Customs Union and Indirect Taxation
DG XXII	Co-ordination of Structural Instruments (used for structural funds)
DG XXIII	SME (Small and Medium Sized Enterprises) Task Force

ACTIVITY

Look at the table showing the different Directorate-Generals of the European Commission and decide which DG would be responsible for:

- trade with non-EC members;
- industrial pollution;
- fixing milk production;
- recognition of qualifications across EC member states;
- helping small businesses in the Single Market;
- helping to reduce unemployment in depressed areas of the EC.

Role and functions

The Commission has several important tasks.

- The introduction of all policy, including detailed drafting of proposals for Community legislation. Here, a balance has to be struck between national interests and the interests of the EC as a whole. Ultimately, the Commission has to protect and promote the Community interest. This sometimes involves 'trading off' national interests one with another. In the introduction of policy, the Commission must seek the opinions of member states before submitting proposals to the Council of Ministers.
- The Commission is also responsible for putting Community policies into practice, once they have been agreed upon. It is also the duty of the Commission to supervise the day-to-day running of policies.
- The Commission acts as the 'conscience' of the Community, making sure that Community obligations are met. In carrying out this 'guardian of the treaties' role, the Commission can refer member states to the European Court of Justice, should they fail

to carry out certain Community policies. This, combined with the role of introducing policy, helps the Commission to be an important motor in driving forward integration, often being able to set the pace.

- The Commission has powers set down by the Treaties in the area of competition policy and control of government subsidies. For example, companies that breach the rules of competition can be referred to the European Court of Justice which could then take action against those companies.
- The administration of Community funds is also one of the functions of the Commission. Funds include:
  - the European Regional Development Fund
  - the European Social Fund
  - the European Agricultural Guarantee and Guidance Fund.
- Responsibility for the drawing up of the draft annual budget and of directing investment to different parts of the Community via the grants and loans sections of the above funds, is also an important role. The Commission represents the Community in trade negotiations of the General Agreement on Tariffs and Trade (GATT), and in consultation for those states seeking EC membership.

ACTIVITY

1. Some would say that the Commission is a unique institution within the EC. From your own viewpoint, draw up a list of the arguments that might be put 'for' and 'against' the Commission.
2. Decide which of the arguments in your list you agree with. Share these with your fellow students in a class discussion on whether the Commission has too much power.

The Council of Ministers

Apart from when it holds its meetings in Luxembourg (in April, June and October), the Council of Ministers is based in Brussels, and is located in the Charlemagne building. The Council allows the governments of member states to take part in decision-making within the EC and it is the major decision-making body.

Advice and support is offered to the Council of Ministers by the Secretariat, also based in Brussels. The Council is responsible for setting down policy in all areas of the EC's activities – it adopts legislation based on proposals suggested by the European Commission.

Composition

The Council of Ministers consists of one minister from each of the 12 member states. The ministers who participate in meetings are decided by the specific topic being discussed – for example, if the Common Agricultural Policy was under discussion, then agricultural ministers from the governments of member states would attend. For this reason, the Council will have different members at different times (dependent upon the topic) – these different compositions being known as 'specialist' councils. The main specialist councils are:

- Foreign Affairs (including trade policy and general issues)
- Agriculture
- Community Budget
- Finance
- Industry
- Internal Market
- Research.

It is usual for foreign ministers of member states to hold responsibility for the overall co-ordination of Community policies.

Organisation

The Council of Ministers holds its meetings in private, with its presidency rotating every six months between the member states in alphabetical order. The national ministers from the member state holding the presidency chair their respective Councils, and their officials chair the Councils' other bodies and working parties.

The importance of the presidency role has increased over the years, with respect to the EC decision-making process. The six-month period in office has allowed member states to bring particularly favoured policies to the fore. Presidency of the Council also involves representing the Council at meetings of the European Parliament, answering parliamentary questions and reporting on meetings. The president also represents the Community in dealing with third countries (non-members), along with the president of the European Commission.

An important feature of the Council is the method by which it arrives at decisions. All EC decisions of any importance are taken by the Council, with the European Commission taking part in the discussions only on a non-voting basis.

The decision-making method of the Council is laid down by the Treaty of Rome. The Treaties actually provide for three different methods of decision-making by the Council.

Methods of decision-making by Council of Ministers

Method	*Meaning*
1 Unanimity	No member state votes against the proposal(s). Those that abstain (decide not to vote at all) do not prevent unanimity. For example, 10 states vote for a proposal and 2 abstain. This means the proposal would be adopted by unanimity.
2 Simple majority voting	At least 7 out of the 12 (a simple majority) are in favour of the proposal. For example, 8 states vote for a proposal, 3 states vote against and 1 state abstains. This means the proposal would be adopted by a simple majority.
3 Qualified (weighted) majority voting	Based on the relative size and weighting of votes of the member states (see below). For example, if 55 votes are in favour of a proposal and 21 votes are against, this means the proposal is adopted by a qualified majority.

Before the Single European Act (which allowed for a wider area of majority voting), measures to establish the internal market, for example, were taken by unanimity. The possibility of majority voting in those areas not referred to in the original treaties was extended by the Single European Act. Here each member state's vote is weighted in relation to its size and importance.

Majority voting in the Council of Ministers

Member state	*No of votes*
France	10
Germany	10
Italy	10
UK	10
Spain	8
Belgium	5
Greece	5
Netherlands	5
Portugal	5
Denmark	3
Ireland	3
Luxembourg	2
Total	76

Most proposals regarding the Single Market are subject to qualified majority voting. For a measure to be adopted by the Council, 54 out of the possible 76 votes are needed. A 'blocking minority' is 23 votes (where a qualified majority is not possible). The qualified majority voting procedure prevents smaller member states from being outvoted by the larger ones and it has helped to promote decision-making based on consensus.

A major problem with qualified majority voting in the Council is the existence of the 'veto', provided by the 'Luxembourg Compromise'. This was supposed to be used only when vital national interests of a government were at stake – but, it has been used as a political device. One of the implications of the Single European Act is that majority voting would become more widely used. Although major decisions will still need to be taken unanimously, and the veto will continue to safeguard threatened national interests, the legislation should help to reduce the holding up of decisions by governments who feel that the time is not right for a certain proposal or policy. For example, if the UK government was not prepared to accept the setting up of a European Community army, it could use the veto, claiming that it was not in the best interests of the UK.

ACTIVITY

1. Draw up a pie chart to illustrate the number of votes allocated to each member state for majority voting in the Council of Ministers.
2. Discuss with a partner why you think the larger states (France, Germany, Italy and UK) have more votes than the other states. What reasons do you think can be offered for this apparent unfairness?
3. Devise a short list of factors to take into account when allocating the number of votes to new members of the EC.

ACTIVITY

Record presidency

As the single market programme moves into the final straight, it is now clear that the recently ended Dutch presidency did some excellent work in marshalling the field round the final corner. During the second half of 1991, the Dutch reached agreement on 25 measures from the Commission's 1985 White Paper and 74 single market measures overall. This second figure is a record for any presidency. 232 of the 282 measures in the White Paper have now been agreed, which takes the Community past the 80% mark.

Tax
The Dutch registered good progress on the tax aspects of the single market. Finance ministers agreed in October the system for the collection of VAT after 1992, including a decision to retain duty-free shopping till 1997. In December they agreed the rules for the movement of goods subject to excise duty after 1992.

Transport
Transport ministers also moved matters along smartly. The December Council made a first step towards opening up the Community's bus and coach transport market, with a commitment to further liberalisation at a later stage . . .

Pharmaceuticals
Pharmaceuticals were a bright feature of the Dutch presidency. In July agreement was reached on the classification of medicines, on the labelling of medicinal products, on the wholesale distribution of medicines, and on the advertising of medicinal products. In December, the Council also agreed common standards for homoeopathic medicines. Now only the main proposal on a Community system for the authorisation of medicines remains for the single market in medicines to be complete.

Financial services
Steady progress was made towards a single market in financial services. Agreement was reached on the consolidated supervision of credit institutions . . .

Agriculture
The Dutch made less progress than expected on agriculture, agreeing two measures on the plant health regime and ornamental plants, and a number of animal welfare measures.

Other items
The Internal Market Council on 19 December worked through a lengthy agenda. Agreement was finally reached on three vehicle type approval directives, on masses, tyres and glazing, so opening the way to a single EC vehicle type approval. The *Second Diplomas Directive* provides for the mutual recognition of qualifications requiring less than three years' study. A political agreement was reached on public procurement rules for services.

Source: DTI *Single Market News*, Issue 14, Spring 1992

Read the article 'Record presidency' and then answer the following questions:

1 How do you think the Dutch might have benefited from their 'record presidency'?
2 What factors do you think led to the decision to retain duty free shopping until 1997?
3 Why were the agreements reached on pharmaceuticals a 'bright feature of the Dutch presidency'?
4 What reasons might there be for the Dutch making less progress than expected on agricultural measures?

Role and functions

We have identified the significant role of the Council of Ministers as the major decision-maker of the Community. Without this function, the EC would find progress difficult. It should be pointed out that the Commission takes part in the work of the Council and may, at any time, amend or withdraw its proposal for discussion and decision.

In many ways, the incomplete nature of the Commission and the Council means that they are forced to co-operate with one another. In Council meetings, the Commission has a 'go-between' role, trying to match, in some way, the different interests.

Functions of the Council of Ministers are:

- the right of initiative (to propose solutions and decisions to problems);
- legislative powers (to make decisions on policy and legislation);
- supervision of the Commission (by considering proposals and amending them if necessary);
- the right to appoint members of other institutions (such as the Economic and Social Committee and the Court of Auditors).

In some policy areas, the Council has to seek prior consultation with the European Parliament and the Economic and Social Committee.

The European Parliament

The phrase 'European Parliament' is not mentioned in the Rome Treaty. The term 'Assembly' was used and the Council of Ministers still largely uses this. However, the Commission and the Parliament tend to use 'European Parliament', and this partly results from the fact that the Parliament is the only directly elected (elected by the citizens of member states) institution of the Community. The European Parliament was directly elected for the first time in 1979.

Composition

Since 1986, the European Parliament has consisted of 518 MEPs. These MEPs are elected every five years, with the next European Parliamentary elections due to take place in 1994. The number of MEPs allocated to each member state reflects the size of its population.

Organisation

In the European Parliament, MEPs arrange themselves in specific political groupings, rather than according to their respective nationalities.

The MEPs and their political groups are supported by a secretariat of 3500 staff (normally housed in the Kirchberg, outside Luxembourg City). This secretariat moves to Strasbourg whenever the European Parliament meets there.

The Parliament is not in permanent session and the plenary sessions (attended by all members) last for five days, once a month (apart from August), and are held in Strasbourg. In between plenary sessions, specialist committees usually meet in Brussels.

Much of the detailed work of the Parliament is completed in the 18 specialist committees. These committees prepare for the five-day plenary sessions and are divided by subject areas. They examine closely Commission proposals before submitting them to the Parliament as a whole.

Source: European Community

▶ *3.1 Number of MEPs for each EC state*

Distribution of seats by political groups*

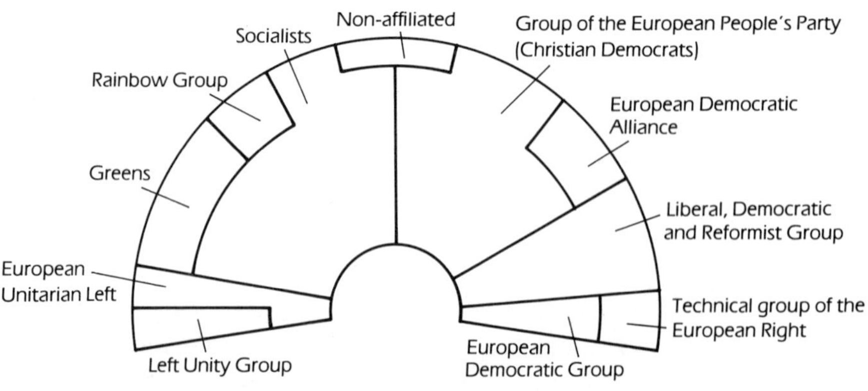

*Position on 18 February 1991

Source: European Community

▶ *3.2 The European Parliament: the voice of the people*

The specialist committees of the European Parliament are as follows:

- Political
- Agriculture, fisheries and food
- Community budgets
- Economic, monetary, industrial
- Energy, research, technology
- External economic relations
- Overseas development
- Budgetary control
- Procedure, petitions
- Legal, citizens' rights
- Social and employment
- Regional policy and planning
- Transport
- Environment, health and consumers
- Youth, culture, education, information, sport
- Women's rights
- Institutional affairs
- Members' credentials.

When the European Parliament is consulted on a proposal, it refers this to one of the specialist committees listed above. The Committee then appoints a *'rapporteur'* for the proposal (an MEP charged with preparing a report on the proposal). The specialist committee then discusses that report and might decide to amend it. Each report includes a *draft opinion* on the Commission's proposal – this opinion is put to the Parliament by the specialist committee and is adopted as the Parliament's opinion.

ACTIVITY

1 Suggest reasons why it is more desirable for MEPs to arrange themselves in European political groupings rather than according to their nationality.
2 What problems might exist with this arrangement?

Role and functions

The European Parliament is an advisory body with no power to legislate (or make laws), except on some budgetary items. It has a number of important roles and functions set down by the various EC treaties.

1 Legislative role

Unlike traditional national parliaments such as the UK Parliament, the European Parliament does not actually make laws. However, it has an important role in the formulation of EC Regulations, Directives and Decisions by offering its opinion on Commission proposals, and by asking the Commission to amend these proposals when it feels it is necessary. The Single European Act introduced the 'Co-operation Procedure', offering this amending role to the Parliament, enabling it to influence European legislation.

2 Budgetary role

The European Parliament formally adopts (or rejects) the Community budget. On two occasions, the Parliament has exercised this right to reject the budget. When this occurs, the whole budgetary process starts again.

In the case of 'compulsory' expenditure (basically, that spent on agriculture), the Council of Ministers has the final say, but with respect to 'non-compulsory' expenditure, the Parliament has the final word and here it can modify expenditure proposals.

3 Role as a political driving force
This is an important part of the Parliament's function. As a directly elected body, it represents nearly 344 million people. In this capacity, the Parliament can ask for policies to be either developed or modified. For example, the Parliament might ask the Commission to introduce a policy to control animal experiments.

4 Supervisory role
The Parliament has the power to dismiss all of the Commission, providing it is able to obtain a two-thirds majority. In practice, this power has never been used. Some would argue that this is a misdirected power, as the Parliament and Commission tend to see themselves as 'natural allies' against the Council of Ministers. Despite having the power to dismiss the Commission, the Parliament does not take part in the appointment of Commissioners.

In its supervisory role, the Parliament also checks to see that Community policies run smoothly, usually with reference to reports from the Court of Auditors. The Parliament puts written and oral questions to the Commission and Council of Ministers in this capacity.

Furthermore, Community Ministers for Foreign Affairs reply to questions from MEPs too, and the President of the Council informs the Parliament of the outcomes of each meeting of the European Council.

Finally, the Parliament plays an important role in maintaining and promoting links between the Community and the many developing states that are associated with it.

ACTIVITY

1. In consultation with your tutor, write to your MEP to invite him or her to come and talk to your group about the activities of the European Parliament, and his or her own role in particular.
2. Prepare a set of questions that you could ask your MEP when he or she visits your college.
3. Imagine you are an MEP. Decide on the different influences you would have to consider in this role. For instance, you might consider your responsibility to your voters, your political party, your country, the Community.
4. Write to the European Parliament office in London to find out more about the activities of the institution. Set up a display in college to inform staff and students about the role of the Parliament.

The European Court of Justice

It has been suggested that the European Court of Justice (ECJ) is the most supranational of all the Community institutions, given the type of authority that it has over the 12 member states. Located on the outskirts of Luxembourg City, the ECJ is adjacent to the European Parliament. The Court of Justice rules on the *interpretation* and *application* of Community legislation with the judgments of the Court being binding on all member states. Hence the claim 'most supranational'.

Composition

The Court of Justice consists of 13 judges and 6 advocates-general, appointed for 6 years by agreement among the 12 member states. Of the 13 judges, 1 is appointed by each of the 12 members with the 13th judge usually appointed by one of the large member states, in rotation.

The members of the Court of Justice come from widely differing backgrounds – thus, judges, politicians, diplomats and academics give the Court a wide experience.

Organisation
Every three years, there is a partial replacement of the Court's membership, when six or seven judges and three advocates-general are replaced alternately. This helps to ensure *continuity* in the decisions of the Court, especially as most judges have served more than one term of office.

The treaties state that Court judges be selected 'from persons whose independence is beyond doubt and who possess the qualifications required for appointment to the highest judicial offices in their respective countries . . .'.

From their 13 members, the judges elect a president of the Court who serves for 1 year. An important role of the president is to allocate cases to chambers, appointing a *judge-rapporteur* for each case, and setting the schedule for the various stages of the procedure and dates of hearings.

The six advocates-general attached to the Court have no equivalent in English law. Their role is to sum up in public the cases before the Court, giving expert legal advice before the Court's judges make their decision.

The Court of Justice has its own permanent staff. However, this is so small that it tends to 'borrow' interpreters from the European Parliament, just as the Council of Ministers does from the Commission.

Role and functions
When legislation is passed by the Council of Ministers, it becomes part of national law – it is then the duty of national governments to uphold this law. The Court of Justice helps to do this.

The Court is only able to rule on Community legislation – however, its rulings are final on matters of European law and this takes *precedence* over national law. In this role, the independence of the judges is important. In particular, the Court has six major areas of responsibility and it rules in disputes:

- between member states;
- between the Community and member states;
- between Community institutions;
- between individuals and the Community;
- offering opinions on international agreements;
- it gives preliminary rulings. These are frequent occurrences for they represent the only way that an ordinary firm or organisation can really get a decision against its own government or against a rival firm.

The Court ensures general compliance with the Treaties and with the Community's own legislation (Regulations, Directives and Decisions).

Any member state, institution or individual can appeal to the European Court of Justice. The Court investigates such cases with complete impartiality and hands its findings to the Council of Ministers. The decisions of the Court are taken in secret by a simple majority (at least seven votes).

In coming to decisions, the Court's judges may request the alteration of national decisions and laws which do not comply with the provisions of the treaties.

Via its judgments and interpretations (in 1990, the Court heard 380 cases, passing 225 judgments), the Court of Justice has built up a body of Community law which applies to all. The Court has heard cases brought by individuals where member states, for example, have failed to meet their obligations on issues such as equal pay for men and women. In addition, companies that have broken Community law (over levels of pollution for example) have been fined by the Court.

The European Court of Justice is another important force pushing forward the process of European integration – in this, its workload over the years has increased significantly. It is also important in that generally, when called to interpret the *intentions* of the Treaties, the Court has favoured interpretations which help to promote further integration and the extension of the authority of the Community institutions.

ACTIVITY

A woman cook is worth her salt – and that's law

Julie Hayward, a highly qualified cook at Cammell Laird's shipyard, Birkenhead, considered that her work was of equal value to the firm as that done by their male joiners, painters and insulation engineers, and that she should be paid as highly as them.

Until the beginning of 1984, there was no legal way in which she could make her claim. But, in January, amendments to the Equal Pay Act 1970 came into force – legislation required as a result of a ruling by the European Court of Justice in July 1982.

The original Act allowed for equal pay for women when it could be shown that they did the same or similar work to a man. But it did not take account of European Community Directive 75/117, which requires equal pay for work of *equal value*, even if the jobs are different.

Julie Hayward, therefore, saw her chance. Backed by her trade union and by the Equal Opportunities Commission, she applied to the Industrial Tribunal.

Although the Act lays down no formal rules for investigations, the Tribunal accepted the conclusion that the work of a canteen cook was of equal value to the men's jobs. Julie, who had been earning £99 per week, was awarded a £31 rise to bring her up to the men's £130 a week.

The EOC sees the case as a challenge to the traditional assumptions that male skills should be more highly regarded than female skills. It hopes that employers will take note, make suitable pay adjustments, and avoid lengthy legal cases. Julie Hayward has at least proved that the Act works.

Source: *Europe 85*, January/February 1985

Read the article 'A woman cook is worth her salt – and that's law', and then answer the following questions:

1 What was the role of the European Court of Justice in the case of Julie Hayward?
2 How far do you think this case illustrates the 'supranational' nature of the Court of Justice?
3 Do you agree with the eventual decision of the Industrial Tribunal? Give your reasons.
4 What implications for employers do you think the case of Julie Hayward held? In general, have employers responded to these implications since the case?

Community legislation

Community legislation can only be based upon those areas included in the treaties – for instance, the Council of Ministers could not rule that the UK should change to driving on the right. However, in some areas, joint action between member states may be agreed – the Schengen Agreement between France, Germany and the Benelux states allows for a large measure of co-operation in the tracking down of terrorists.

It is important to remember that the national parliament of each of the 12 member states has a part to play in the process of legislation. Any proposals for policies or new laws are considered carefully by national parliaments before the process in Brussels gets under way. For example, copies of proposals are sent to the UK Parliament – these are then examined closely in committees in the House of Commons or House of Lords. Individuals can attempt to alter or amend the proposals by contacting their MP.

The process of legislation

Community laws and policies are very often the result of a lengthy and complicated procedure of consultation and negotiation. Remember that it is up to the European Commission to propose or suggest new laws and policies for the EC.

Usually the first step in the process of legislation is for the Commission to talk to experts from member states about its ideas for a new policy or law. At this stage, individuals or businesses who might be affected by the proposals try to make their voices and opinions heard. For example, the proposal to have just one frontier document when goods are passing from state to state would have been commented on by businesses affected.

Any new proposal for a policy or law must have a statement or *'Fiche d'Impact'* attached to it. This document tries to consider the impact on businesses or affected groups of the proposed changes, for example, how a policy aimed at improving drinking water standards would affect member states.

The formal process then starts with proposals being *adopted* (taken on board) by the Commission. These proposals or ideas are then put to the Council of Ministers, which generally consults with the Economic and Social Committee and the European Parliament.

Many proposals are covered by the 'Co-operation Procedure'. Here, the European Parliament gives two opinions:

1 when the Commission's proposal is put forward to the Council;
2 after the Council has reached an agreement in principle – or what is known as a 'Common Position'.

In both cases, the Parliament can suggest amendments to the original proposals.

The Council of Ministers then receives the proposals – it has the right to:

- adopt the proposals;
- request alterations;
- amend the proposals itself;
- reject the proposals;
- take no action.

In practice, the Commission proposals are considered by all 12 Council members – here the Council's president may exercise influence. The Council can reach a decision by weighted majority (54 out of 76), but most recent decisions have been taken unanimously.

Commission proposals are considered by:

- a working group of officials from member states;
- COREPER (or COREPER deputies) – the Committee of Permanent Representatives which assists the Council in decision-making;
- ministers of member states in the specialist Council – the aim being to iron out remaining problems and take the final decisions.

Community legislation, once adopted, will be published in the *Official Journal of the Communities* as a draft Regulation or Directive. The status and implications of these instruments are considered in the table on page 41.

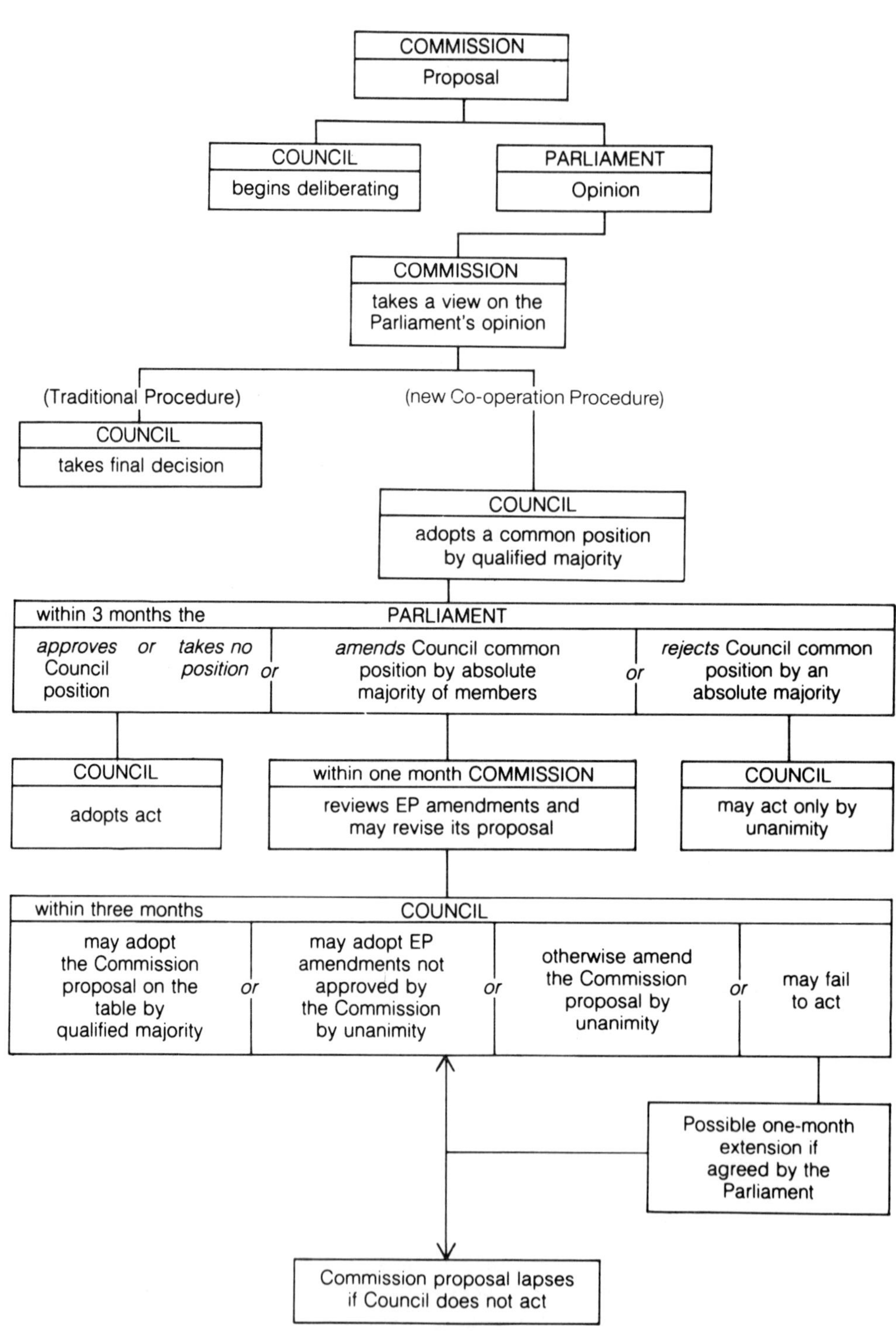

Source: Department of Trade and Industry

▶ *3.3 Community legislative process: news co-operating procedure*

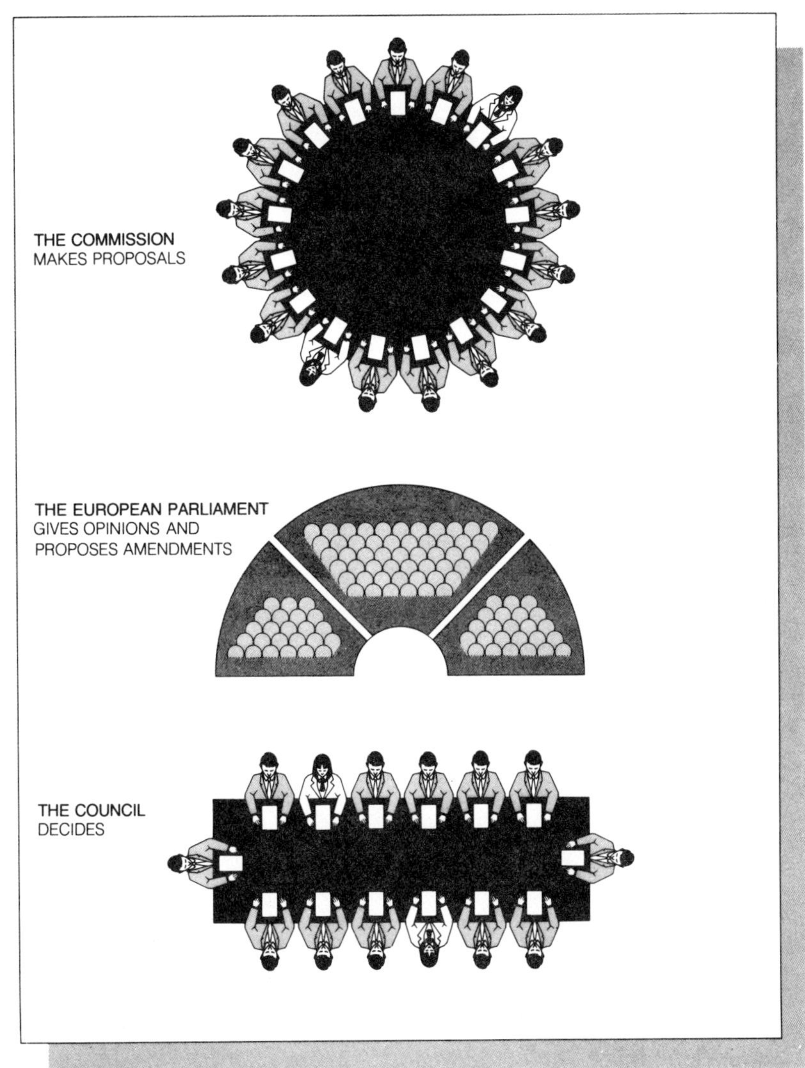

Source: Department of Trade and Industry

▶ *3.4 The process of legislation summarised*

Community Instruments used by the Commission

Instrument	*Scope*
Regulation	Once adopted by the Council, all parts are binding and it applies to all member states. For example – if a new Regulation about the maximum number of working hours in a week is agreed by the Council, it will immediately become part of national law in all member states.
Directive	This is binding on member states with regard to the *results* required, but the method of achieving these results is left to the individual member states to decide upon. For example, all states may decide to try to end social security fraud. Although all agreed to be involved, the methods used may differ in each member state.
Decision	Similar to a Regulation, but it *may* not apply to *all* member states, but perhaps to one or more individual members. An example is the Council agreement to allow Greek membership of the EEC which was a Decision.
Recommendations and opinions	Recommendations and opinions are exactly that – they are not binding on member states and they do not form part of Community law. In some cases, however, the Court of Justice may refer to them so their legal status is not always clear.

ACTIVITY

1 Consider the issues in the table below and decide whether you think 'Yes – the EC should have a say in this issue' or 'No – the EC should not have a say in this issue'. Copy down the table and then tick the relevant column in each case, giving reasons for your choice.

Issue	'Yes'	'No'	Reasons
a The introduction of death penalty for murderers			
b Compulsory registration of pet dogs			
c The cleaning up of British beaches			
d The fixing of fines for firms guilty of industrial pollution			
e The setting of a minimum wage for all workers			
f The stationing of UK soldiers in an international trouble spot			

2 Compare your answers with those of a partner. Together, try to decide on the five most important issues that the EC should have a say in. Why have you selected these issues? What do your answers suggest about the role of the EC in relation to individual member states like the UK?

ACTIVITY

The ounce bounces back from the brink

Brussels bureaucrats yesterday dropped plans to ban pints, inches, pounds and ounces from 1999.

The EC wanted only metric measurements to be allowed on packaged goods. But Britain refused to go along with the change.

Consumer Affairs Minister Edward Leigh argued that many consumers who only understand imperial units would suffer.

The decision is also good for news for British exporters who will be able to continue using single production runs for sales in the EC and in countries which still use imperial measurements such as the US and Canada.

Britain could be pressed to introduce compulsory identity cards when the European Single Market comes into effect at the end of this year, the EC Commission said.

Passports will no longer be required to travel within the EC. But some standard identification will be required to assist police carrying out spot checks.

Citizens of all EC countries except Britain and the Irish Republic already have to carry such cards.

Source: *Daily Mail*, 26 February 1992

Read the article 'The ounce bounces back from the brink' and then answer the following questions:

1 What does the article suggest about the relationship between the EC Commission and the UK government?
2 For what reasons has Britain refused to accept metric measurements on all packaged goods?
3 In your opinion, how would the British public react to compulsory identity cards?
4 Draw up a list of the advantages and disadvantages of a compulsory identity card system.

The Community budget

The European Community budget differs from national government budgets in many ways. The most important difference is that, under the Treaty of Rome, Community revenue and expenditure must balance. This is not the case in individual member states. For the Community, this means that neither a deficit nor a surplus is allowed within the budget.

The Community has the power to spend money in its own right and the budget is financed entirely by 'own resources' – partly from revenue paid to the EC by the 12 member states along with other sources. In particular own resources is made up of:

- customs duties levied on goods coming into the Community from outside (from non-member states);
- agricultural levies (placed upon imported agricultural products to bring prices up to the level of EC prices);
- a proportion of VAT collected in member states, calculated according to a uniform assessment method;
- a 'new resource' (or Fourth Resource) created in 1988. Here contributions are made by member states adjusted to their share of EC Gross National Product (GNP). GNP is the total output from resources owned by the residents of a country, wherever these resources are located.

The Community budget lays down amounts of money that can be spent on the various EC policies such as the Common Agricultural Policy (CAP) and Social Policy. Community expenditure is labelled either 'compulsory' or 'non-compulsory'. Compulsory expenditure is that which *necessarily* arises from the Rome Treaty or other legislation associated with the Treaty and includes money spent on agricultural support and overseas aid. Non-compulsory expenditure includes spending on regional and social policies. By far the largest item of expenditure in the EC budget is agricultural price support, under the Common Agricultural Policy. This is discussed in more detail in Chapter 5.

Funding mechanisms

The Community budget makes provision for several funding mechanisms that are central to the operation of the EC.

EC budget funding mechanisms

Funding mechanism	*Purpose*
European Agricultural Guidance and Guarantee Fund (EAGGF or FEOGA)	The EC supports farmers by setting a floor for prices they receive for farm produce. If prices fall below this level, the EC buys up produce offered to it by farmers, stores and then resells it. This is the *guarantee* section of the Fund. The much smaller section (in expenditure terms) is the *guidance* sector which is used to help farmers move into new areas of production or to assist in retraining, for example.
European Regional Development Fund (ERDF)	The second largest area of expenditure from the EC budget. This mechanism helps to promote the development of economically less-favoured areas (defined by the EC), and includes provision for road improvement and water supply improvement schemes, as well as other infrastructure projects such as telecommunications networks.
European Social Fund (ESF)	This mechanism is concerned with training, retraining, resettlement and job creation schemes. Social Fund money is in the form of non-repayable grants, which basically match financial costs made by national governments or other public authorities. This fund is heavily over-subscribed.

The guidance section of EAGGF, the Regional Development Fund and the Social Fund are collectively known as the 'structural funds' because they seek to deal with the improvement of the infrastructures of member states such as retraining and transport networks.

Other funding mechanisms provided for in the Community budget are concerned with the following areas:

- joint action in research, energy, industry, the environment and transport;
- co-operation with Third World countries;
- co-operation with the countries of Central and Eastern Europe.

ACTIVITY

1 Do you believe it is important for the EC to have its 'own resources'? With a partner, list reasons why it might be important.

2 Study the pie charts illustrating revenue and expenditure within the 1991 EC budget.

a) Identify the largest items of income and spending for the EC.

b) What proportion of revenue is received from VAT and financial contributions?

c) From whom are customs duties collected?

d) Why do you think agricultural price support is the largest item of expenditure?

e) What proportion of expenditure is taken up by the Social Fund and the Regional Development Fund?

f) What items of expenditure might administration consist of?

Revenue (billion ECU)

Agricultural levies 2.3[1]

Fourth resource payments 8.5

Customs duties 12.0

VAT/financial contributions 30.5

[1]Also includes levies raised on sugar and isoglucose

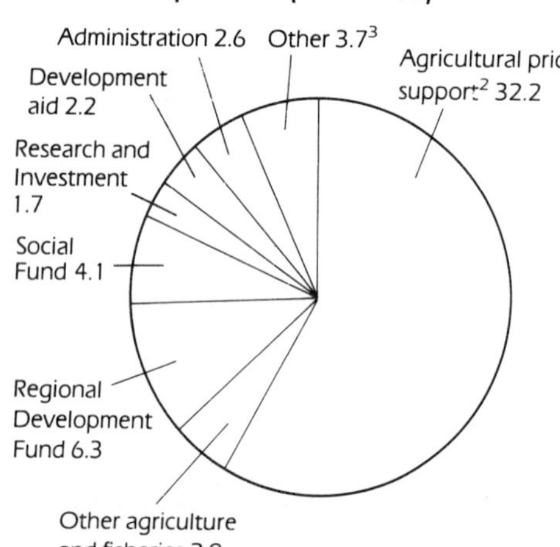

[2]Includes allowance for depreciation of produce held in storage

[3]Includes 1 billion ECU monetary reserve to allow for the effects of exchange rate fluctuations between the ECU and the US dollar

Source: *Statement on the 1991 Community Budget*

▶ 3.5 *1991 Budget: revenue and expenditure by type*

European Community links with economic groupings

The European Community has links with particular economic groupings. The key groupings are as follows.

European Free Trade Association (EFTA)

The European Free Trade Association was formed in 1959 with the UK as one of its founder members. Current members are Austria, Finland, Iceland, Liechtenstein, Norway, Sweden and Switzerland.

The basic objectives of EFTA – to establish free trade in industrial products between member states and the conversion of Western Europe into a free trade area for industrial goods – have largely been achieved. To this end, the proposed European Economic Area (EEA), an agreement between the EC and EFTA, reinforces this. A number of other important points can be made about EFTA:

- relations between the EC '12' and the EFTA '7' are generally close, though not necessarily balanced;
- the institutional structure of EFTA is weaker than that of the EC;
- many EFTA members also belong to the Organisation for Economic Co-operation and Development (OECD) and the Council of Europe. In addition, Finland, Iceland, Norway, Sweden and Denmark make up the Nordic Council (a body set up to encourage and further co-operation and development in areas such as social and economic policies, cultural links and legislation);
- the development of the European Economic Area, and the weaker position in relation to the EC that EFTA experiences, is encouraging many EFTA states to seek full EC membership (especially Austria, Norway and Sweden). The EEA agreement is in some ways seen as the first step in EC membership for such states.

European Economic Area

The European Economic Area agreement was formally signed in Oporto, Portugal on 2 May 1992. It was due to come into force on 1 January 1993, the same date that was set for the completion of the Single Market, but it was put forward to 1 July 1993.

ACTIVITY

Agreement on EEA reached!

Agreement on the creation of a new European Economic Area (EEA) has finally been reached. This economic area will consist of the 12 EC member states and the 7 EFTA member states. This agreement will establish a market of 380 million consumers, stretching from the Arctic to the Mediterranean.

The new EEA is due to come into force in 1993 and it is estimated that it will account for more than 40% of world trade. The EC president, Jacques Delors, predicted that the agreement would offer valuable experience to those EFTA states, such as Austria and Sweden, who may be considering EC membership.

The EEA took more than two years to be negotiated and its key points include:

- free movement of products in the EEA;
- EFTA states to take on board some of the EC rules, particularly those relating to company law and social policy;
- the establishment of an independent joint court to deal with EEA-related disputes;
- mutual recognition of professional qualifications;
- a review of the agreement every two years.

The EEA, which will create an economic grouping of 19 states, has to be approved by the European Parliament and then ratified by each member state's national parliament. In 1990, EC imports from EFTA states amounted to ECU 108.6 billion (£76 billion), while exports to EFTA states from the EC totalled ECU 111.37 billion (£77.9 billion).

Source: *The Week in Europe*, 24 October 1991

Read the article 'Agreement on EEA reached!', and then answer the following questions:

1 Why do you think agreement on the EEA has taken over two years to negotiate?
2 How will those states seeking EC membership in the future benefit from the creation of the EEA?
3 What implications are there for the UK for a) the free movement of products in the EEA and b) mutual recognition of professional qualifications? Give your reasons.
4 What objections to the EEA, if any, might EC member states' national parliaments raise before agreement is finally reached?

European Economic Interest Groupings

In 1985, the Council of Ministers approved a Regulation which established, from 1989 onwards, the provision to set up European Economic Interest Groupings (EEIGs). This is an arrangement whereby firms or companies in different member states may enter into agreements governing the sharing of technology, and research and development under the protective framework of European Community law. For example, if a British company wishes to team up with a Danish company to pursue the development of a new product, and agreement is reached, the resulting EEIG would pool technology, and research and development resources in order to develop that new product.

ACTIVITY

1 With a partner, list the advantages and disadvantages of two firms teaming up to form an EEIG.
2 In what circumstances might the forming of an EEIG between two companies be considered as undesirable?

ACTIVITY **Review your progress: 3**

1 Which institution:
   a) takes decisions for the EC?
   b) makes EC policy?
   c) interprets EC legislation?
   d) can reject the EC budget?
2 How many of the following are there:
   a) Commissioners?
   b) Members of the Council of Ministers?
   c) MEPs?
   d) judges?
3 What is the difference between a Regulation, a Directive and a Decision?
4 How often does the presidency of the Council of Ministers change?
5 Decide which method of Council decision-making has been used in the following cases:
   a) 9 states voted against Proposal X
   3 states abstained.
   RESULT: Proposal X was not adopted.
   b) 70 votes were in favour of Proposal Y
   6 votes were against Proposal Y.
   RESULT: Proposal Y was adopted.
   c) 7 states voted for Proposal Z
   2 states voted against Proposal Z
   3 states abstained.
   RESULT: Proposal Z was adopted.
6 When are the next elections to the European Parliament?

7 Where is the European Court of Justice located?
8 What is a *'Fiche d'Impact'*?
9 How can national parliaments affect the EC decision-making process?
10 What is the main difference between the EC budget and national government budgets?
11 Distinguish between 'compulsory' and 'non-compulsory' expenditure.
12 Why was EFTA formed? What is its current relationship with the EC?

Summary

- The EC institutions have specific roles allocated to them by the treaties.
- The EC decision-making process is based on the sharing of power between the institutions.
- The decision-making process in the EC involves a complex and lengthy procedure.
- EC policies and laws can only be based upon those areas stated in the treaties. Regulations and Directives are used by the EC to clarify the status of different pieces of Community legislation.
- The EC budget differs from national government budgets and contains provision for various funding mechanisms.
- The EC has made specific economic arrangements with EFTA and the EEA.

Assignment 4

The Brussels trip

You work as a research assistant for a well-known firm of publishers. One morning you receive the following memorandum from your manager:

DART PUBLISHERS PLC

Memorandum

To:

Date: 23 May 1993

From: Overseas Manager

Ref: OM/EC

Subject: Trainee visit to Brussels

As you will be aware, this year's batch of trainees have now been with us for over six months. It is now time for them to make the usual visit to our European office in Brussels. This time, I thought it would be a good idea if they visited some of the Community institutions – it would help to raise their awareness of the EC. The Managing Director informed me that you have some 'specialist' knowledge in this area and I thought, therefore, that it would be useful if you prepared a package for the trainees which includes the following:

a) a guide to the EC institutions – include location, composition, organisation and the functions of each institution plus any illustrations or diagrams.

b) a short glossary of EC abbreviations.

In addition, I would be grateful if you could prepare:

- a press release for the local newspaper detailing the trainees' trip to Brussels and the EC institutions. Make sure you get something in about our forging links with Europe – you know the sort of thing!
- a set of short notes on the EC institutions for a presentation that I have to give to the trainees before they leave for Brussels!

For this individual assignment, you are required to produce the following:

Task 1 A 'Guide to the EC Institutions', suitably illustrated.

Task 2 The short glossary of EC abbreviations.

Task 3 The press release to the local newspaper.

Task 4 The set of notes on the EC institutions for the presentation.

Assignment 5 — The oral report

In groups of three or four, choose one of the following EC institutions:

- the European Commission
- the European Parliament
- the European Court of Justice
- the Council of Ministers.

Task 1 For a period of two weeks and using suitable information sources, follow the activities of your chosen institution. Record major decisions taken and other events in a group diary.

Task 2 Prepare a group oral report on your selected institution. The presentation should make use of suitable audio-visual aids and might consist of the following:

- location
- composition, organisation and functions
- recent activities of the institution.

Task 3 Prepare a handout for use during your presentation which deals with one aspect of your institution.

Task 4 As a whole group, evaluate each oral report given using appropriate assessment methods.

Assignment 6 — The great European board game!

Few people know about how the European Community works, let alone the names of the institutions that exist. In groups of three or four, design a unique board game that could be used to educate people about the European Community. The board game should be fun and informative, and aimed at adults. The presentation of the game will be very important.

The board game should have a number of features which deal with the following areas:

- recognition of the world political map
- identification of the main institutions of the EC and their functions
- a basic appreciation of the decision-making process of the EC
- the Community budget and funding mechanisms
- EC links with EFTA and the EEA
- the possible formation of European Economic Interest Groupings (EEIGs).

4 European Community policies: 1

Aims

- To explore the EC's approach to social policy, regional development, the Single Market, and monetary and political union
- To examine the impact of the Social Charter on the individual and on organisations
- To examine Community funding in the social and regional policy areas
- To consider the impact of the above policies on the individual, the organisation and member states.

Relevant BTEC Outcome Performance Criteria
3a Main aims and provisions of major EC policies identified
3b Action and support of policies accurately noted and commented on
3c Potential and actual effects of policies identified and assessed

Social policy

An important area of concern for the European Community is social policy. Out of this developing policy the Social Charter has emerged. This was debated during the Maastricht Conference in December 1991 and some of the provisions were so controversial that the UK government negotiated an 'opt-out' clause on certain aspects of its contents.

What is social policy?

In most member states of the EC, government social policy covers such areas as health care, education, housing, social security benefits, the care of vulnerable groups in society (such as young, elderly and disabled people) and various facets of working life (health and safety at work, for example).

For the most part, the development of social policies has been a 20th-century phenomenon and largely the result of the process of industrialisation in most Western states, which highlighted the social needs of the working population. For instance, in the UK, the National Health Service and provision of Social Security benefits only commenced in the late 1940s, when the state began to take on more responsibility for its citizens.

With the free movement of labour that the European Community stresses, there has been concern that the EC should provide for its population with some form of social protection. This raises the question as to who is responsible for certain aspects of social policy – the EC, national governments or a combination of the two.

ACTIVITY

Consider the areas of social policy in the following table and tick whether you think they should be:

a) the concern of national governments only
b) the concern of the EC only
c) the concern of both national governments and the EC.

Policy area	*National government*	*EC*	*Both*
Maximum working week (hours)			
Health care of citizens			
Health and safety at work			
Stock of housing			
Consumer protection			

You may have found, in completing the above table, that your opinions differ from those of other people in your group. These differences are a reflection of what happens when the EC wishes to legislate on some aspect of social policy – some governments welcome an initiative while others view it as another example of the EC meddling in what should be national government concerns. This was the case when the UK government negotiated an 'opt-out' clause from the maximum working week measure included in the Maastricht Treaty. UK Prime Minister John Major argued that imposing a maximum number of hours to be worked in a week on UK firms would destroy their competitive edge and have a detrimental effect on the UK economy.

ACTIVITY

1 In groups of three or four, discuss why a maximum working week might have a detrimental effect on the UK economy.
2 For what reasons do you think the EC wanted to impose a maximum working week on member states?
3 Produce a short article (no more than 400 words) on the advantages and disadvantages of the maximum working week, for a local trade newsletter, *The Traders Gazette*.

The development of EC social policy

Early EC social policy did little more than promote the free movement of labour and provide assistance to migrant workers. Although the Rome Treaty had set up a **European Social Fund** (ESF), this was small in cash terms and it only had a minor role. By the early 1970s, however, there was concern among EC members that the Community should have a more 'human face'. This meant that more resources should be allocated to social policy and it was recognition by the EC that consideration should be given to the social as well as economic factors surrounding economic growth in the Community.

The development of EC social policy

Date	*Policy development*
1971	Increase in the size of the European Social Fund.
1973	Social Action Programme introduced. This aimed to: a) provide full and better employment in the EC b) improve living and working conditions c) develop participation by the two sides of industry by increasing worker participation in the decision-making process of companies.
1983	Changes made to the European Social Fund to make it more responsive to needs – in particular, vocational training for 'special' groups.
1987	Single European Act introduced. This gave wider powers to the Commission to implement aspects of social policy.

ACTIVITY

The Social Action Programme of 1973 aimed to develop and encourage participation by both sides of industry – in other words, the workers as well as management.

1 With a partner, list the advantages and disadvantages of allowing workers to participate more in the decision-making of a company.
2 For what reasons do you think the EC decided to take action in the area of worker participation?
3 What form(s) might worker participation take?

The EC's role in social policy

EC social policy is concerned with employment and working conditions (hence the measure on maximum working hours), rather than the wider aspects of what is usually considered to be social policy, such as health care, education and housing. These areas remain the responsibility of national governments, while the Community focuses upon the following areas:

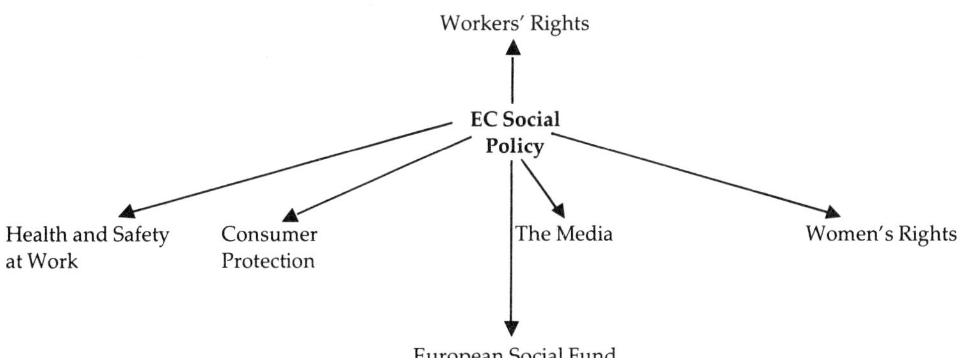

ACTIVITY

Papandreou on International Women's Day

Commissioner Vasso Papandreou, in a declaration to coincide with International Women's Day, pointed out that despite legislation and positive action programmes, unemployment amongst women in the Community was running at 11.6% as against 7.7% for men, while the difference between pay for men and women was as high as 30%. Low levels of vocational training, inadequate child-care facilities and unequal sharing of the burdens of raising a family were all factors which prevent the best use being made of the potential represented by women.

Source: *The Week in Europe*, 12 March 1992

Read the article 'Papandreou on International Women's Day' and then answer the following questions:

1 What is the main point being made in the article?
2 What measures do you think could be taken by a) the EC and b) companies and organisations, to iron out some of the differences between male and female workers?
3 As a group, debate the following statement: 'Men make the best managers and women are best suited to subordinate roles. Any significant change in this situation would seriously damage UK business.'

ACTIVITY Case studies

Air hostess wins equal pay for women

A Belgian air hostess struck a major blow for sexual equality. About 10 years ago she sued the airline that had employed her on the grounds that it discriminated between its male and female employees. By winning her case she won a victory for all working women in Europe.

When she was 40, Gabrielle was forced to retire from her job of chief stewardess, under the terms of her contract. Immediately afterwards, she started a series of legal proceedings against her former employer, on the grounds that she and other female employees had suffered a triple discrimination compared to their male colleagues. Their wages were lower, they had to retire earlier and because of this their pensions were smaller, she claimed. The courts rejected the case, but a judge agreed to examine the issue of wages in greater detail. He put the facts before the European Court of Justice and asked whether the Treaty of Rome directly guaranteed equal pay for women or whether they had to wait until national legislation was drafted. In the course of the hearings a number of member states contributed to the debate. One of them pointed out that if firms had had to introduce equal pay on the day that their country joined the EC, several would have gone bankrupt.

The judges ruled that any woman being paid less than a man for doing the same work could directly seek redress from any national court under European law.

Source: *European Community*

Disabled rights

An Italian family moved to France and the father found a job. But problems lay ahead. The authorities to whom they turned for help said that they were not entitled to state benefits. However, thanks to the father's tenacity, social legislation in Europe took another major step forward.

Mr C was living in Lyons with his family. One of his children, Bernard, was seriously mentally handicapped. When he reached his 20th birthday, he technically became an adult, but in order to qualify for a disability allowance, he needed to be a French citizen.

The French social security system would not help because he was Italian. His father, Mr C, appealed through the courts and was turned down. He protested, claiming that Community legislation gives equal protection to all workers in the EC, regardless of their national identity. But the problem was that Bernard had never worked. The social benefits on which he relied were at the discretion of the individual member state concerned. Finally, a high court appeal referred the case to the European Court of Justice.

The European judges agreed that, because of his handicap, the young man would never work and therefore could not be subject to the same protection offered to European workers. But because a denial of benefits might cause his parents to leave France and go back to their country of origin, the money should be made available on the principle of free movement of labour, they argued. Mr C had won.

Source: *European Community*

Read the case studies 'Air hostess wins equal pay for women' and 'Disabled rights', and answer the following questions:

1 Which basic rights, enshrined in the Treaty of Rome, are illustrated in the two case studies?
2 For what reasons do you think the Belgian air hostess was forced to retire earlier than her male colleagues?

3 On what grounds did the air hostess claim discrimination?
4 What implications does the case study on 'Disabled rights' have for the free movement of labour within the EC?
5 Do you agree with the outcome of the 'Disabled rights' case study? Be prepared to give your reasons.

In addition to the areas of social policy mentioned earlier, an increasing role for the EC has been in the field of education. Specific programmes promoting particular aspects of education have been developed by the EC including:

ERASMUS a programme encouraging student exchanges from different member states of the EC

LINGUA a programme encouraging the improvement of language skills among students of EC member states.

The European Social Fund

The common market has brought economic changes to many parts of the Community. These changes may have caused difficulties for certain social groups – for example, youth and the long-term unemployed. The role of the European Social Fund (ESF) is to compensate for some of these problems.The Commission administers the ESF and there are a number of features associated with it.

- The Social Fund is concerned with training, retraining, resettlement and job creation schemes. Very little cash is actually available for *social work*.
- Social Fund cash is allocated in the form of non-repayable grants. It helps to fund training and employment schemes, matching the financial contribution made by the national government or other public authority involved. For example, if the Dutch government wishes to set up a youth training scheme costing 500 000 guilders, it can claim 250 000 guilders from the ESF if it provides the remainder itself.
- The Fund has particular priorities including training and retraining of the long-term unemployed, disabled people capable of working, migrant workers and their families, and small and medium-sized firms (those with fewer than 500 employees) who require training in new technology – for example, computerised machinery.
- Unfortunately, the demand for cash from the ESF heavily outweighs the supply. This means that the Commission has regularly to revise its priorities, offering flexibility so as to respond to the changing needs of the labour market.
- Certain rules regarding the operation of the ESF are unlikely to change. These include the fact that the Fund cannot be used to pay for social security schemes and that schemes claiming cash must be in receipt of support from national governments.
- Generally, aid is granted for one year at a time.
- When a scheme is approved, 30 per cent of the ESF grant is paid when the scheme gets under way, 30 per cent at the half-way stage and 40 per cent on completion.
- Any private or public organisation can apply for ESF cash. The first stage in the process is usually an initial consultation with the Social Fund Unit of the Department of Employment.

ACTIVITY

1 Why do you think the European Social Fund provides very little cash for social work?
2 What do you think is meant by the terms 'retraining' and 'resettlement'?
3 The ESF cannot provide cash for national government social security schemes. List the reasons why you think this is so.
4 Suggest why contributions from the ESF are allocated 30 per cent at the beginning, 30 per cent in the middle and 40 per cent at the end of a scheme.

ACTIVITY

Read this article and then answer the questions.

1 What training schemes are available in your area for the support of the long-term unemployed and unemployed young people? How is the ESF contributing towards these schemes?
2 Give a short talk (no longer than ten minutes) to the rest of your group on the schemes that you have researched.

Long-term unemployed

The UK will receive some 525.7 million ECUs next year from the European Social Fund to support training and employment programmes for the long-term unemployed and help young people get on the job ladder. Announcing the Community Support Framework for 1993 last week in Brussels, Vasso Papandreou said that the Commission was responsive to the need for more resources at a time when unemployment was rising again in the Community.

Source: *The Week in Europe*, 19 November 1992

The Social Charter

As the Single Market approached, the Commission recognised the need to give further assistance to those social groups that would experience difficulties as a result of its operation. The Social Charter was produced by the Commission in 1989, taking into account the views of the European Parliament and the Economic and Social Committee (ESC) – a body representing both sides of industry (employees and management). The Charter was a framework for 'fundamental EC social rights'.

In October 1989, the European ministers for labour and social affairs discussed the final draft of the Charter and it was adopted in December 1989. It sets out the basic social rights of all EC citizens and especially those of workers. Although the Charter does not have a legal status, some of it is being implemented by EC directives which means that these parts will become part of national law in member states.

The content of the Social Charter

There are 12 basic principles making up the Social Charter. The aim of the document is the improvement of working and living conditions of all EC citizens, by guaranteeing them basic rights, backed by law.

1 The right to freedom of movement – this allows all citizens to live and work in any member state on the same terms as nationals of the host country.
2 The right to employment and remuneration – all citizens have a right to employment and to fair reward for that employment. There is an aim here to set a decent basic wage for all workers.
3 The right to improved living and working conditions – this is mainly to do with working time and the bringing into line (where possible) of different labour regulations within the EC.
4 The right to social protection – this aims to guarantee a minimum wage to workers and social assistance for those unable to work.
5 The right to freedom of association and collective bargaining – this recognises the right of all workers to belong to trade unions and to come to agreements with management.
6 The right to vocational training – every worker in the EC has the right to continue vocational training throughout their working life.
7 The right of men and women to equal treatment – this covers equal pay for men and women performing the same work, and equal access to occupations, social benefits, education, vocational training and career opportunities.

8 The right to worker information, consultation and participation – this covers the right of workers to be informed and consulted about changes affecting working conditions and their jobs.
9 The right to health and safety protection in the workplace – every worker has the right to reasonable health and safety conditions in the place of work.
10 The right to protection of children and adolescents – this sets the minimum working age at 16 and gives young people in employment the right to a fair wage.
11 The rights of elderly persons – every person who has reached retirement age is entitled to a pension allowing a decent standard of living. It also includes the right to social and medical assistance for those not entitled to a pension.
12 The rights of disabled persons – all disabled people have the right to improve their position in terms of training, mobility, housing and transport.

ACTIVITY

Read this article and then answer the following questions:

1 Why do you think the Commission wishes social security benefits to be the same in all EC member states?
2 Do you agree that social security benefits should be available to non-EC nationals resident in the Community? Give your reasons.

Commission issues social security guidelines

On Tuesday, the Commission put forward guidelines intended to harmonise and improve social security benefits throughout the EC. Behind this move is the belief that endorsement of the guidelines by member states would show stronger commitment to the Community's social aims than the support given to the Social Charter, adopted in December 1989 with the sole dissent of the UK. The Commission wants a general right to benefits, based on need, to be recognised all over the EC. It also wants such benefits to be without a time limit, to be extended to non-EC nationals resident in the Community, and to be accompanied by access to health care, housing and training.

Source: *The Week in Europe*, 9 May 1991

Implementing the Social Charter

The implementation of the Social Charter depends mainly on the member states and on the two sides of industry in that it is up to them to conclude collective agreements at company, regional or national level.The EC can take action when the aim to be achieved may be more effectively attained at Community level rather than at member state level. This is known as the principle of *subsidiarity*.

However, the Commission cannot exceed the powers granted to it by the Rome Treaty and so it can only cover part of the measures to be taken in order to introduce the Social Charter. Its role is basically to put forward proposals, suggesting ways in which the Charter could be implemented.

Regional development

In terms of gross domestic product per capita, some of the EC's richest regions include parts of France (especially the Paris Basin), Denmark, northern Italy, Germany and parts of southern England. Poorest regions include Greece, Portugal and southern Spain. The richest region in the EC is approximately six times richer than the poorest region. Although there are large differences in prosperity and stages of development in the Community's regions, the EC has made major efforts to bridge the gaps. In many cases, however, this has not been achieved and the setting up of the Single Market simply highlighted further the need to iron out differences. The EC believes that in a single market, regions of vastly differing prosperity should not exist because the richer and stronger regions will be those that are able to secure markets and flourish at the expense of the poorer ones. In these circumstances, capital and labour would be attracted to more prosperous regions. So, the EC has adopted a policy that aims to improve the poorer regions and reduce some of the disparities.

ACTIVITY

1 List the reasons why companies would want to locate in the more prosperous regions of the EC rather than the poorer ones.
2 Under what circumstances might companies be persuaded to locate in the poorer regions of the EC?

What is a region?

The strict definition of a region is an area of land. In the UK, we can suggest many examples – the West Midlands, Northern Ireland or East Anglia. Region is often the label used by governments to describe areas that differ economically from one another – for instance, the affluent south-east of the UK compared with the poorer north-east. Throughout the EC, member states are divided up into regions – the Community targets those areas in most need of assistance.

ACTIVITY

1 In your opinion, which EC member states would have the poorest regions? Give your reasons.
2 Which EC member states would have the richest regions? Give your reasons.

Recognising the need for assistance

The need for an EC regional policy was only officially recognised by the Community in 1972. Before this, the *need* already existed for some sort of policy due to a number of reasons:

- the existence of large income gaps between areas like the rich Paris basin and the poorer southern Italy;
- some of the measures taken by member states to correct inequalities in their regions breached the terms of the Rome Treaty;
- some EC policies worked against the interests of the underdeveloped regions. The Single Market is an example of such a policy.

Until 1975, regional policy was left up to member states to administer. In that year, more recognition was given to the need to take action in the regions of Europe. This resulted in the setting up of the European Regional Development Fund (ERDF) – through this fund, EC regional policy would be directed. The aim of the fund was to offer aid to those EC regions with weak economies and two main types of area in need were identified:

- those that have not undergone industrialisation – for example, much of Ireland;
- those that have undergone industrialisation but which are now in industrial decline – for example, the north of England.

Since the introduction of the Single European Act in 1987, the EC recognised that the completion of the Single Market could result in some regions being further disadvantaged. The membership of Greece, Spain and Portugal added new areas in need of assistance. This meant that more money had to be allocated to the ERDF and, in response to this, the Fund was doubled during 1992.

Areas in need of development

Several areas of the EC are considered to be underdeveloped and therefore are eligible for aid. These are:

Greece
Portugal
Much of Spain
Southern Italy, Sicily, Corsica and Sardinia
Ireland
Northern Ireland.

Other areas have been highlighted by the EC as being areas of industrial decline. There are many of these but the most important are:

Wales
Midlands of England
North and South Scotland
Northern France.

ACTIVITY

Read the article 'Regional convergence imperative' and answer the following questions:

1 Why do you think the success of Economic and Monetary Union partly depends upon ironing out regional disparities?

2 In a class debate, discuss the following statement: 'Regional assistance is vital to the uccess of the European Community'.

Regional convergence imperative

Regional Policy Commissioner Bruce Millan voiced his concern to the European Parliament last week that Economic and Monetary Union would flounder if deep regional economic disparities remained. Economic convergence continued to present a formidable challenge to the Community and Millan warned against any cutbacks in budgetary requirements. The Commission has estimated that 25 billion ECUs (£17.5 billion) will be needed to upgrade infrastructure in poorer regions.

Source: *The Week in Europe*, 2 April 1992

The European Regional Development Fund

The European Regional Development Fund (ERDF) is just one element in the targeting of EC cash to needy areas. It is supported in other areas by:

- the European Social Fund (ESF);
- the guidance section of the European Agricultural Guidance and Guarantee Fund (EAGGF).

The ERDF, set up in 1975, accounted for about 12 per cent of the total EC budget in 1990. In view of the marked regional disparities that still exist, this is a relatively small proportion of the budget (the largest part being allocated to agriculture).

Grants from the ERDF are made to two types of investment projects.

1 **Industry and service investments** these are schemes designed to create new jobs, or to safeguard existing ones. Examples here include construction of factories providing new jobs and the modernisation of manufacturing plants which in the long run would help to safeguard jobs.
2 **Infrastructure investments** schemes that will in some way assist the whole region. Examples include construction of new roads, the improvement of water supplies and the improvement of telecommunication systems.

Generally, the ERDF will provide up to 50 per cent of the cost of a scheme or even 55 per cent in exceptional circumstances.

Problems with the ERDF

A major problem with the ERDF has been that funds allocated by the EC to specific regions have not always been used for the purpose stated. Some national governments receiving aid from the Fund have simply channelled the cash into the national coffers rather than use it to address the problems of the regions. This means that sometimes the region requiring the aid does not actually get it. For the larger states, especially the UK, cash obtained from the Fund has been used to offset payments made to the EC. This is seen as an unacceptable situation as needy regions may not actually receive the assistance they have been promised.

EC member states *expect* some assistance from the ERDF and, unfortunately, the allocation of Fund cash has more to do with looking after the interests of individual member states rather than those of the EC as a whole. Funds such as the ERDF are seen by national governments as one way of being reimbursed for payments that they have made to the EC.

ACTIVITY

Cash flood pours in as UK loses regional aid battle

A battle with the British government to ensure that European Community regional aid goes to designated run-down areas throughout the country instead of being swallowed up by the national exchequer in London has been won by Regional Affairs Commissioner, Bruce Millan.

Britain announced under pressure from Brussels this week that it would introduce a new system in 1993.

This would channel EC funds directly to recipients, who are selected by the European Commission.

The decision paves the way for Mr Millan to release EC aid worth $217 million to Britain's depressed coalmining regions.

The money, destined for more than 50 redevelopment and training projects in central Scotland, South Wales, the North of England and the English Midlands, had been blocked during the 18-month dispute.

The move also lifts the threat that had hung over a further $1.5 billion of EC aid to Britain which Mr Millan had warned he might hold back if agreement had not been forthcoming. Since becoming Regional Policy Commissioner in 1989, Mr Millan has attached great importance to ensuring EC funds are seen to reach their proper destinations.

Source: *The European*, 20–26 February 1992

Read the article 'Cash flood pours in as UK loses regional aid battle' and then answer the following questions:

1 What problems with the allocation of ERDF cash does the article highlight?

2 In your opinion, should member states be able to spend ERDF cash as they see fit, or should it be used for the projects targeted? Give your reasons.
3 What could the Community do to ensure that money targeted for specific schemes and projects is actually spent on them?
4 Write a letter to the editor of *The European* outlining your views on this matter.

ACTIVITY

Aid to UK's industrial areas

Regional Development Commissioner Bruce Millan yesterday announced an allocation of £272.5 million from the EC structural funds budget for UK regions seriously affected by industrial decline. The programmes cover areas in the East Midlands which gets £24.3 million, Humberside (£16.7 million), Manchester (£55.5 million), Merseyside (£80 million), Mersey Basin (£64.25 million), mid-Yorkshire (£14 million) in England as well as the Central Region (£8.5 million) and Fife (£9.5 million) in Scotland. Matching funds will be provided by the UK government, local authorities and the private sector. Commenting on the decision, Millan said that the new programmes continue the sustained Community effort undertaken since 1989 to provide a better future for the UK's industrial areas. Monies will go to assist business, in particular small and medium-sized enterprises, improve transport infrastructure, support research and development, and develop tourism.

Source: *The Week in Europe*, 9 July 1992

Read the article 'Aid to UK's industrial areas' and then answer the following questions:

1 Draw a pie chart to illustrate the total allocation of £272.5 million to the various regions noted in the article.
2 What conclusions can you draw from the article about UK regions in need of assistance?
3 How will the funds allocated to the UK be used?

The Single European Market

The Single European Market that formally came into force on 1 January 1993 was one of the central aims of the EC. This particular 'policy' was considered to be so important that it was referred to in the opening lines of the Treaty of Rome. It spoke of:

- creating a common market;
- the approximation (bringing roughly into line) of the economic policies of the member states;
- increasing stability;
- improved standards of living;
- closer relations between the member states.

The Treaty went on to state that the EC should bring about the four freedoms – free movement of goods, capital, services and people within the common market.

The advantages of free movement within the Single Market

Free movement in:	*Advantages*
a) Goods	Goods are no longer delayed at frontiers between member states. Producers of goods now have access to 340 million consumers. The bringing into line of production methods, technical standards and consumer protection should assist in the removal of trade barriers. Individuals and businesses can choose where to locate anywhere in the EC without hindrance. A high level of health and safety for consumers and the public will exist throughout the EC. Research and development will be more cost-effective due to economies of scale. Consumers should have a wider choice of better and cheaper goods.
b) Capital	All EC citizens are able to invest or save in whichever EC state they choose. Both individuals and businesses are able to transfer funds freely in all member states. EC citizens have freedom of choice in services such as banking, insurance, loans, mortgages, savings and leasing.
c) Services	Services can be offered by companies throughout the EC. This means that consumers can choose the service they want at the price they want. Increased competition in air travel should bring down prices. Road transport should benefit from reduced paperwork. Telecommunications will benefit from co-operation in research and harmonisation of technical standards.
d) People	EC citizens and foreign tourists will not be subjected to checks at member state frontiers. Co-operation between member states exists to control crime. Students are free to study in any country and their qualifications will be recognised in all EC member states. Workers can live in any EC state for employment purposes. No discrimination on the grounds of nationality should exist and terms of employment should be the same for all.

ACTIVITY

1 The table above lists the advantages of free movement of goods, capital, services and labour. With a partner, make a list of the possible *disadvantages* that might arise from the operation of the four freedoms.
2 Imagine that having completed your BTEC National Award you wish to study for a degree in Madrid. What considerations would you have to take into account?
3 For what reasons might a UK manufacturing company wish to relocate in another EC member state?

ACTIVITY

Consider the statements below and decide a) which of the four freedoms they refer to and b) whether you think they are an advantage or disadvantage for EC member states.

1 The number of television channels available to EC citizens should increase considerably.
2 The European Community passport will replace the national passports of the individual member states.
3 An individual resident in the UK can have his or her bank account in Lyons, Naples, or any other EC town or city.

4 Companies will have to improve their standards to conform with EC regulations.
5 Companies can take their capital out of the UK to relocate in any of the other EC member states.
6 The Greek equivalent of a BTEC National Award will allow entry into UK universities and colleges of higher education.

The move towards the Single Market

In the early 1980s, the Single Market seemed a long way off and progress had been hampered by the recession of the 1970s which had made member states focus upon national rather than Community interests. To help speed up the process, the Commission produced a White Paper – 'Completing the Internal Market' and this document listed the proposals that the Commission regarded as being essential in the creation of a single market. The White Paper also included a timetable for the adoption of proposals, including 1 January 1993 as the date for the Single Market. Many of the proposals were adopted in the Single European Act (SEA) and this document amended and supplemented the Rome Treaty.

The Single European Act

The Single European Act, signed by all 12 member states, came into force in July 1987. Its contents were designed to speed up the decision-making process. The Act proposed a step-by-step approach to bringing about the Single Market and, because it was more comprehensive than previous legislation, the EC took more decisions in the first half of 1988 than it had done during the ten years from 1974–84.

The Single European Act had three main themes:

- the internal market;
- European political co-operation;
- institutional reform.

The internal market

The major objective of the Single European Act was the achievement of a single market on 1 January 1993. In order to bring this about, it was recognised that laws and regulations would have to be harmonised (adjusting standards to an agreed EC standard). The Commission identified 282 measures with the following being seen as most important:

- removal of physical barriers;
- removal of technical barriers;
- removal of financial barriers.

Removal of physical barriers frontier controls help to underline the disadvantages of a divided market. Businesses are subjected to various costs resulting from the frontier controls that exist. The aim of the Single Market was to remove these frontier controls.

The controls and formalities in place at the borders of countries largely resulted from the differences between member states in the following areas:

- technical standards;
- exchange controls;
- health and safety regulations;
- indirect taxes;

and from a concern to prevent movement of illegal arms, terrorists, drugs and pornography.

ACTIVITY

Rabies law to be reviewed

Cats and dogs could soon be Channel-hopping on holiday with their owners, free of Britain's six-month quarantine restriction, if the EC endorses a recommendation for 'pet passports'.

National veterinary representatives told the Commission that pets should be able to travel freely across EC internal borders provided that they were vaccinated against rabies and passed strict blood tests. But British vets say that quarantine should remain until rabies is eradicated across continental Europe.

Source: *The European*, 5–11 March 1992

Read the article 'Rabies law to be reviewed' and then answer the following questions:

1 Why does the British government want to continue its quarantine regulations?
2 List the advantages and drawbacks of removing the regulations from a) the UK government's point of view and b) the European Community's point of view.

Removal of technical barriers – before the formal opening of the Single Market, different national technical standards existed in a whole host of areas including:

- food, drink, pharmaeuticals, livestock, fruit and vegetables;
- telecommunications and transport;
- electronic data management;
- trade marks;
- company law;
- vocational qualifications and professional services.

The harmonisation of different standards has taken place in many areas and now European standards are being set by bodies like CEN (European Committee for Standardisation) and CENELEC (European Committee for Electro-technical Standardisation). In addition, the Commission intends to replace the 12 different trademark systems with one Community-wide trade mark. This will ensure that goods bearing the trade mark come up to certain EC standards.

Case study: Tonka Toys

Europe no trivial pursuit for Tonka

The toy and game business is big business and certainly no trivial pursuit. Each year, the makers of best sellers such as Trivial Pursuit, Playdoh and scores of other toys turn over around £500 million – establishing the company as the world's third largest toy-maker.

Yet Europe, with its varying technical standards for toy safety, has always presented a special challenge for Tonka. So much so that in the mid-1980s the company spent two man-years producing a detailed report on the various standards prevailing in Europe.

What they found, for example, was that Germany insisted there should be no PVC in small toys because of an accident in the late 1960s involving a small child; that Italy only permitted plastic bag containers with holes; and that in Scandinavia the bags also had to carry a health warning.

Worst-case approach

To adapt to this situation, Tonka had to follow what their Product Integrity Manager, Europe; Lindsay Harris, calls the 'worst-case' approach. 'What we decided to do', he explains, 'was to make sure that our toys were manufactured in such a way that each aspect would meet the toughest of standards wherever possible. For instance, the German standard on paint, the Italian standard on strength and so on.'

'Of course there were still problems, and in the case of Germany for example, we had to maintain special stocks for that country, thereby increasing both product and stock-holding costs.'

Matters have now changed because of the Toy Safety Directive, which member states have already had to implement.

Tonka sees this as a benefit. 'We welcome the creation of the Single Market, because it means that we can now concentrate on the demands of our customers rather than those of the bureaucrats.'

Among the resulting advantages is an end to the idiosyncratic approach to product features and, for soft toys, a new common 'pull-test' to replace the 22 lb Dutch pull-test for detachable parts of toys, the Irish 50 lb test and a 20 lb test in other countries. Now the test has been standardised at 20 lb – just one example of harmonisation of standards across Europe.

Source: *Single Market News*

1 In what ways has the EC affected the operation of Tonka Toys?
2 How did Tonka respond to the changed situation?
3 Tonka sees the EC's Toy Safety Directive as beneficial. Why should this be the case when it may mean that the company has to *improve* standards?
4 What do you think the possible outcomes would be for a company that did not respond in the way that Tonka did?
5 Imagine you were setting up a new company in the Single Market. How would the harmonisation of standards affect/benefit you?

Removal of financial barriers here the aim was to allow banks, building societies and insurance companies from one member state to establish branches and sell services in all of the others – for example, a branch of the Royal Bank of Scotland in Athens. Changes in regulations regarding this form of business included some harmonisation – for example, bringing into line the format of published accounts.

In most member states, purchases made by governments and nationalised industries are very important. Up until the 'opening' of the Single Market, the markets for public construction projects tended to be restricted to domestic suppliers. Now however, large *procurement* contracts have to be published across the EC, meaning that a Belgian contractor could tender for work to be carried out in the UK.

The harmonisation of tax systems is also being pursued, and the differences in VAT and excise duties will be narrowed eventually.

ACTIVITY

> ### Public procurement
>
> A Single Market in public procurement is nearing completion after ministers at last week's Internal Market Council adopted the Public Services Directive. By the end of 1993, all public authorities, spanning local and regional government and other bodies such as railways, will have to buy services on a commercial basis regardless of the nationality of the supplier. The crux of the Directive, which consolidates existing rules on public works contracts, is the political agreement to open up contracts awarded by utilities in water, energy, transport and telecommunications. These industries will have to buy in such diverse services as advertising and maintenance after competitive bidding. Public procurement accounts for about 15% of Community GDP, some 550 billion ECUs (£385 billion).

Source: *The Week in Europe*, 25 June 1992

Read the article 'Public procurement' and then answer the following questions:

1 What is the Public Services Directive about?
2 In your opinion, how will the Directive affect public works contracts in the UK?
3 List the advantages and disadvantages of a Spanish company, for example, being awarded a contract to maintain UK motorways.

ACTIVITY

Assume that you are a group of three or four European Commissioners. In this capacity, complete the following.

(*NB* Remember that Commissioners pledge an allegiance to the EC over and above their own nation state. These tasks should therefore be approached from an EC perspective rather than a national one.)

1 Identify those factors that you would use in justifying the Single Market to a reluctant UK businessperson.
2 Do you agree that the EC should allow foreign companies (from, say, Japan or the USA) to set up bases and manufacturing plants in the Single Market? Why?
3 The UK government has objected to the removal of passport controls on the grounds that drug smugglers and terrorists would be able to move around more freely. How would you counter the fears of the UK government on this issue?

Small and medium enterprises (SMEs)

The danger of creating a large Single Market that had no place for the smaller or medium-sized business was recognised by the European Commissioner, Abel Matutes. The problem stemmed from the fact that from 1993, companies would be encouraged to think on a much bigger basis. With more choice for consumers, competition becomes fiercer which might force smaller enterprises out of business.

To prepare for this, a programme aimed at SMEs commenced in 1983 with the European Small Business Year. Further steps taken included the Action Programme for SMEs and the establishment of the SME Task Force.

The aim of this Task Force is not to create privileges for SMEs, but to create favourable social and economic conditions for all companies, focusing on those companies with limited resources.

Monetary and political union

Monetary union

The European Community is committed to economic and monetary union, and this arises from the fact that the Single Market would be difficult to operate without it. Economic and monetary union implies complete freedom of movement of goods, services, capital and people, fixed exchange rates between the national currencies of the the member states and the introduction of a common currency such as the ECU.

To bring about this level of union, a number of important requirements have to be met. In particular:

- the economic policies of all member states must largely correspond with one another – the idea of **convergence**;
- national financial policies must be generally similar;
- single monetary policy is essential.

Why economic and monetary union?

The completion of the Single Market has brought member state economies closer together. This means they all have less room for major variations in policy. The Commission argues that only with closer economic convergence, will complete freedom of movement come about. It puts forward a number of advantages for economic and monetary union:

- the reduction of currency fluctuations leading to more certainty for investment, growth and profitability;
- an increase in price stability;
- a reduction of the public debt in some member states due to a lowering of interest rates;
- a boost for employment, especially from the regional and structural policies;
- a 'knock-on' effect for all member states from the reduction of inflation;
- benefits resulting from the single currency including the possibility of the ECU becoming as important as the dollar or the yen.

The European Monetary System (EMS)

The first step towards economic and monetary union was the setting up of the European Monetary System in 1979. Being a member of the EC does not oblige member states to join the system, but all 12 are currently part of it.

The EMS is made up of four components:

Exchange Rate Mechanism (ERM)	European Currency Unit (ECU)	European Monetary Co-operation Fund (EMCF)	Short-term Financing Facility

Membership of the EMS entitles member states to take part in discussions on the operation of the system. The purpose of the EMS, however, is much wider for it seeks to:

- create a zone of monetary stability in the EC;
- provide a framework for collective discipline in economic policy;
- contribute to the convergence of EC economic performance.

At the centre of the EMS is the Exchange Rate Mechanism (ERM). This links the currencies of participating member states and sets a limit on how far each currency can fluctuate in relation to other currencies. This is important, for stability in currency exchange rates is vital in bringing about long-term confidence in the market.

In 1989, the proposal of a three-stage move towards economic and monetary union was put forward.

The three stages of movement towards EMU

Stage One	Commenced in July 1990 and included the completion of the EC internal market, economic convergence of member states and a requirement for all states to join the ERM.
Stage Two	This should commence on 1 January 1994 and involves the setting up of a medium-term programme for economic objectives. In practice, this means that there will be even less variation between national currencies' exchange rates within a tighter ERM.
Stage Three	A more complicated stage involving the adoption of 'locked' exchange rates and the adoption of the single currency by 1 January 1999. As a result of strict conditions laid down at Maastricht, *at least 7 of the 12* members must have achieved 4 important conditions by 31 December 1996, before any movement to Stage Three can be made. The conditions are: – **price stability** inflation rates must be no more than 1.5% above the average of the 3 best performing countries – **deficits** national budget deficits must be less than 3% of GDP – **interest rates** these are to be no more than 2% above the 3 best performing countries over the last 12 months – **exchange rates** the national currency must not have been devalued in the last two years and must have been within the narrow bands of the ERM.

ACTIVITY

Attitude of European citizens to a single currency, December 1990

Member state	*In favour (%)*	*Against (%)*
Belgium	61	18
Denmark	35	50
France	62	19
Germany	50	27
Greece	64	10
Ireland	58	17
Italy	72	11
Luxembourg	47	26
Netherlands	61	25
Portugal	55	16
Spain	53	10
UK	38	43
EC 12	55	23

Source: Eurobarometer

1 Draw bar charts to illustrate a) the top six member states in favour of a single currency and b) the top six member states against a single currency.

2 What conclusions can you draw about a) the six member states most in favour of a single currency and b) the six member states most against a single currency?

3 This survey was conducted in December 1990. Since then the Maastricht Summit and other developments have taken place. How would you expect the figures to alter (if at all) if the survey was conducted today? Give your reasons.

4 Conduct a mini survey of staff and students at your college to find out whether they are for or against a single currency. Devise a method of displaying your results.

'Fast and slow lane' Europe

It is important to note that only those member states that meet the set criteria will be able to progress to Stage Three of EMU. It is in this area that much debate has taken place over the so-called 'fast and slow lanes' of Europe – a two-speed Community where some members are approaching Stage Three and others have a long way to go. Many would argue that rather than bring member states closer together, the effect of this two-speed operation may well drive them apart. At the Maastricht Summit, the UK contributed to this debate by negotiating a special protocol providing her with an 'opt-out' clause. Under this agreement, the UK is not obliged to go to Stage Three until a decision has been taken by the UK Parliament to do so. In this, the UK has to inform the Council of Ministers by 31 December 1996 whether she intends to move to Stage Three or not. Despite this opt-out clause, the UK is still permitted to participate in any decisions affecting EMU in the future.

ACTIVITY

1 What do you understand by the term 'two-speed' Europe?
2 What effects do you think a two-speed Europe might have on the European Community as a whole?
3 Should the UK be allowed to participate in decisions concerning EMU, even though she has an opt-out clause? Give your reasons.

The operation of the EMS

Under the EMS, member states keep the exchange rates of their currencies within a margin of fluctuation 2.25 per cent either side of a *central* rate. If the rate on any given day shifts by more than 2.25 per cent from the standard rates, steps have to be taken by the national governments involved.

Example:
Assume that 1 German mark is equivalent to 3 French francs. In this situation, the permitted deviation is 6.75 centimes. If the German mark rises in value to 3.07 French francs then the German Bundesbank must *sell* marks and *buy* francs to lower the mark value. But, if the mark falls to 2.93 French francs, then the Bank of France has to intervene.

ACTIVITY

In the following cases, a) calculate the deviation allowed against the German mark, and b) state the upward and downward limits before action needs to be taken:

1 assume 1 German mark is equivalent to 750 Italian lira;
2 assume 1 German mark is equivalent to 4 Danish krone (denominations within the Danish krone are known as ore);
3 Assume 1 German mark is equivalent to 21 Luxembourg francs.

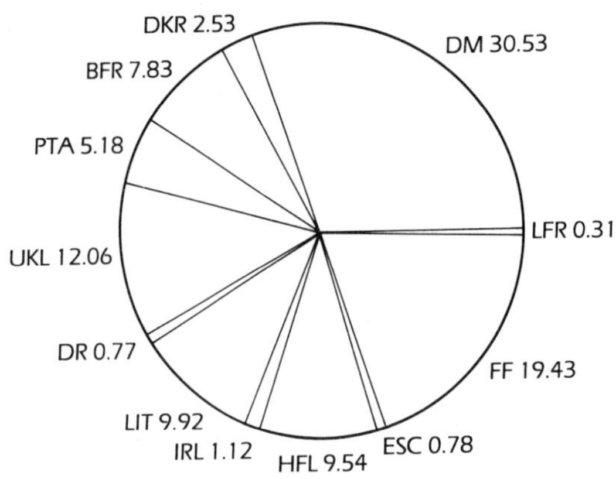

Source: Eurostat

▶ *4.1 Composition of the ECU (1990) % share of each currency*

The ECU is at the core of this system. For the purposes of EMS, it is seen as a basket made up of all the member states' currencies which are weighted according to the economic importance of the member state. The central rate is an ECU rate fixed for each currency.

When national banks are required to intervene, the European Monetary Co-operation Fund (EMCF) provides them with short-term credit for the necessary transactions. The national central banks are then required to settle the accounts within 45 days.

The ECU

The adoption of the ECU as the currency of the European Community was decided by a majority of governmental heads. At the moment, citizens of the EC can use the ECU in a number of ways:

1 by opening a bank account in ECUs;
2 paying with ECU cheques;
3 buying ECU bonds.

However, the ECU still has to achieve a number of features before it becomes an actual currency. These are as follows:

- national governments need to make the ECU legal tender;
- a European central bank which is responsible for the ECU needs to be established;
- ECU banknotes and coins need to be issued.

Some individual member states such as Belgium, France and Spain have minted ECU coins, but these have really been a gesture to indicate their commitment to EMU.

Over the last decade, the ECU has been used increasingly in private markets. In this, it is used as a currency for loans, for lending between banks and to individuals, for settlements between multinational companies and in foreign trade. On the international bond market, the ECU is now one of the top five currencies. The Commission and the European Investment Bank (EIB) have contributed to its legitimacy and increasing role by denominating their loans in ECUs. For example, cash allocated from the European Regional Development Fund is always quoted in ECU values. The ECU also has a central role in the operation of the EMS – the fixing of rates on which possible fluctuations in currency are based.

ECU rates, 19 January 1993

Member state	*1 ECU =*
Belgium/Luxembourg	40.4 francs
Denmark	7.5 krone
France	6.6 francs
Germany	1.9 marks
Greece	262.1 drachma
Ireland	0.7 punt
Italy	1801.0 lira
Netherlands	2.2 guilda
Portugal	176.7 escudos
Spain	139.0 pesetas
UK	0.7 pounds

Source: *The European*

ACTIVITY

1 Visit your college library to find out what the current rates are for each member state.
2 Illustrate the currency rates for January 1993 and for today in a diagram of your choice. What conclusions can you draw from your results?

ACTIVITY

A single currency before the year 2000?

There are many reasons for creating a single European currency. It would eliminate exchange costs, promote trade and generate welfare gains. Not until monetary union has been achieved can the internal market produce its full effects. A single European currency would also make for greater influence and stability in relation to the US dollar and the Japanese yen, which are often subject to wide exchange rate fluctuations. Moreover, a European currency has a symbolic importance in a growing Community which is becoming increasingly attractive to more and more countries. A majority of EC residents are in favour of a single currency. The private sector too has for some time now demonstrated its support for the ECU as the European currency by launching initiatives of its own.

Source: *The ECU*, European Commission

Read the article 'A single currency before the year 2000?' and then answer the following questions:

1 What reasons are put forward by the article for the creation of a single EC currency?
2 Why might a single currency attract new countries to the EC?
3 How do you think the private sector may have demonstrated its support for a single currency?

Political union

With economic and monetary union, political union was identified at the Maastricht Summit as being a major objective of the Community. The treaty on political union restated EC aims for a Community that is now more closely bound and set out a number of steps to be taken to achieve those objectives.

Introduction of Community citizenship
This would establish a 'true' European identity and encourage citizens to think much more in terms of the Community rather than their own individual country. Linked to this is the desire to guarantee the right of the citizen to vote in local and European elections in the EC country where they live. This implies that if an Italian lives in Greece, then he or she has the right to vote there. This underlines the freedom of movement of people contained in the Treaty of Rome.

ACTIVITY Mr and Mrs Euro

The Community is keen to foster a European identity. With this in mind, a local newspaper based in the Midlands compiled a number of facts based on the 'typical' Mr and Mrs Euro. Below is an extract of the newspaper's findings.

- Mr Euro works in the manufacturing industry and takes home £182.25 for a 40.6 hour week, while Mrs Euro earns £67.40 for a 33.3 hour week.
- The Euros are aged 35–45 and have one teenage child (usually a girl).
- All the family speak two languages.
- Mr and Mrs Euro are both overweight but Mrs Euro is on a diet.
- He was 27 and she was 24 when they married, and they lived together for four months before the wedding.
- Before they married he had five sexual partners and she had two.
- Their house is worth £42 750 and was built in the 1950s.
- Mr Euro sees his duties as paying the bills, disciplining the kid, maintaining the house and looking after the car.
- Mr and Mrs Euro have about £200 a week to spend.
- Both are religious but neither goes to church.

Source: *The Sunday Mercury*, 11 October 1992

1 How far do you think this is an accurate description of a 'typical' Euro family? Give your reasons.
2 In your opinion, what would be the main features of a 'European' identity?

Implementation of a common foreign policy
The move towards a Community-wide foreign policy that would be accepted internationally as EC policy rather than just that of a member state. To assist this, decisions taken on the qualified majority basis in the Council would be used. These may then result in joint action being taken – but only on subjects decided unanimously by governmental heads. Joint EC action over the former Yugoslavia is an example.

Implementation of a common security policy
This would represent a Community-wide approach to ensuring the safety of EC member states. The idea is that the common policy would be established by the Western European Union (WEU) and implemented in accordance with obligations arising from the North Atlantic Treaty (signed by NATO members).

ACTIVITY

As a group, discuss the possible drawbacks and benefits of the EC adopting common foreign and security policies.

Strengthening the powers of the European Parliament

This is by means of the 'co-operation' procedure in certain areas (see Chapter 3). The European Parliament now has the additional roles of ratifying treaties and granting approval for the appointment of the members of the Commission.

Widening the EC's jurisdiction

This means extending the areas in which the EC has legislative power. Areas affected would include the environment, social policy, research and development, trans-European networks, telecommunications, health, culture and consumer protection. These are all areas that are traditionally the role of national governments and some would see this as an extension of the 'meddling' nature of the EC.

ACTIVITY

1 Do you think that EC powers should be widened? Why?
2 Choose one of the areas noted and draw up a list of advantages and disadvantages of increased EC power.

Improving co-operation in legal matters and internal affairs

This implies the formulation of common policies in the areas of visas, immigration and right of asylum. An aspect of this is the EC's policy towards terrorism and this has been highlighted in the Schengen Agreement.

ACTIVITY

Read the article 'Anti-Mafia group' and then answer the following questions:

1 Why do you think the 'anti-Mafia group' has been set up by the EC?
2 Why have police experts and magistrates been drafted into the group?
3 What areas of organised crime might the group turn its attention to?

Anti-Mafia group

EC justice and home affairs ministers have decided to create an 'anti-Mafia group' to report on possible strategies to fight organised crime in the Community. EC ministers, whose communiqué strongly condemned the recent murders of two Italian judges, were provided with background dossiers on organised crime by the Italian and French governments. The new group, operating within the European Political Co-operation Framework, will include for the first time police experts and magistrates. A further aim of the group will be to improve the flow of information on crime between member states through the new Customs Information System, the establishment of a European Information System and bilateral training initiatives.

Source: *The Week in Europe*, 24 September 1992

The above are all areas of political concern where the EC intends to take action in order to improve political union. Political union is an inevitable consequence of economic union – as co-operation develops in some areas, it spills over into others. This has been recognised by the EC and explains why political union was a part of the Maastricht Treaty.

ACTIVITY Review your progress: 4

1 Which areas of activity does EC social policy cover?
2 What did the Social Action Programme aim to do?
3 For what sort of schemes is Social Fund cash available?
4 With what is the Social Charter concerned?
5 Explain why there is a need for an EC regional development policy.
6 The European Regional Development Fund offers assistance with two main types of project. What are these?
7 List the four freedoms that the Single Market aimed to bring about.
8 What was the purpose of the Single European Act?
9 Explain what is meant by 'harmonisation'.
10 Explain what is meant by 'economic convergence'.
11 What are the four components of the European Monetary System?
12 For what purposes is the ECU currently used?
13 What do the following stand for: EMU, ECU, ERM, EIB, EPC?
14 What steps have been taken by the EC to further political union?

Summary

- The EC has developed some policies in relation to the operation of the Single Market.
- Some policies offer financial assistance to help iron out disparities between regions or for groups disadvantaged by the operation of the Single Market.
- The Single Market was an important pillar of the Treaty of Rome and this was recognised when the process was speeded up with the introduction of the Single European Act.
- Economic and monetary union is a central policy in the Community. It has a close relationship with the operation of the Single Market and moves to bring about monetary union as quickly as possible have been made.
- The Community recognises the importance of political union and hopes to make further moves in this area.

Assignment 7 European Adviser wanted!

You are applying for the post of European Adviser to local business with the Confederation of British Industry. Prior to your interview you feel that it is important for you to improve your knowledge of European business issues and the European Community in general. The following tasks are designed to help you prepare for the interview, which will culminate in a discussion with other candidates.

Task 1 Prepare a written statement (no more than 500 words) that outlines the background to current EC social policy.

Task 2 Prepare a short formal report (about 1000 words) which deals with the European Social Charter. This is a controversial issue and you are to explain the main features and the opportunities and threats that it presents to UK employers. (*NB*: The above tasks will be submitted to the interview panel.)

Task 3 You have been asked to prepare notes and collect relevant newspaper articles as preparation for a discussion with other candidates on the following question: 'Is the Social Charter good for Britain?' You are generally to side with OR against the Social Charter in the debate.

5 European Community policies: 2

Aims

- To explore the EC's approach to agricultural policy, environmental action, consumer and competition policy
- To develop an awareness of the need for such policies
- To consider the use of Community funding, particularly in the case of agriculture
- To examine the impact of the above policies on the individual, the organisation and member states.

Relevant BTEC Outcome Performance Criteria
3a Main aims and provisions of major EC policies identified
3b Action and support of policies accurately noted and commented on
3c Potential and actual effects of policies identified and assessed

Common Agricultural Policy

Reasons for the Common Agricultural Policy

Before the setting up of the European Community, agriculture had been supported in one form or another by all the member states. Governments often provided managerial and technical advice to farmers, which meant that they already had a major role to play in this sector of their economies. Some form of support within the EC was therefore inevitable.

In addition, the desire to prevent the food shortages which had been a feature of the Second World War was important. Farming was also seen as the means of maintaining the welfare of the rural population, which in turn allowed the development of other services in the urban areas. Agriculture had to be included then, due to its importance as an employer. For these reasons, there was agreement between the original six EC members that agriculture should be a central pillar in the common market. The Rome Treaty was therefore drawn up to include special provision for agriculture and Article 39 details the aims of the Common Agricultural Policy (CAP).

ACTIVITY

With a partner, write down anything that you associate with the Common Agricultural Policy.

What is the Common Agricultural Policy?

Under the terms of the Rome Treaty, the five major objectives of the Common Agricultural Policy are as follows:

- to increase agricultural productivity within the EC;
- to ensure a fair standard of living for Community farmers;
- to stabilise markets for agricultural products;
- to guarantee security of supplies through the Community farm support mechanism (in order to prevent future food shortages);
- to ensure reasonable prices for consumers in the EC.

In order to achieve these objectives, the Community has allowed the CAP to develop in three major ways:

1 a single market for agricultural products with common policies for these products (for example, the guarantee price mechanism);
2 a Common External Tariff (CET) with levies on agricultural goods coming into the EC from outside, making such goods less attractive to consumers;
3 the development of 'common financial responsibility'.

There have also been attempts to restructure European agriculture through the guidance section of the European Agricultural Guarantee and Guidance Fund, with limited success.

ACTIVITY

1 Visit your college library to collect newspaper articles on the Common Agricultural Policy.
2 Set up a display in college which details the CAP.
3 Conduct a mini-survey in college to find out what people think of the CAP. What conclusions can you draw from your survey?

The Guaranteed Price Mechanism

This is by far the most important element of the CAP and is also an area for constant controversy within the policy. This is because the system has promoted over-production in the past. An explanation of the mechanism is therefore required here.

Each year, the prices for EC agricultural products are set by Community agricultural ministers. These prices are based on proposals issued by the Commission. The prices set are known as *target, guide* or *basic* prices, depending on the product concerned. These are the prices that the EC hopes Community farmers will receive on the wholesale market for the coming marketing year.

The price mechanism allows set prices to be maintained by withdrawing the product from the market when market prices fall below a certain level – this price level is known as *intervention, withdrawal* or *buying-in* price (depending on the product) and is set below the target price. It allows the Community to buy the product concerned through the various EC intervention agencies, storing them in warehouses. So, farmers receive intervention prices minus the costs of transport to the intervention centre and handling costs. This is an important mechanism because it guarantees farmers a certain price for certain agricultural products. The whole system is financed from the guarantee section of the European Agricultural Guarantee and Guidance Fund.

Wine lakes and butter mountains

The familiar phrase 'wine lakes and butter mountains' is a direct result of the operation of the guarantee price mechanism, for the system has encouraged over-production. If farmers know they are going to be guaranteed a certain price, rather than be left with goods that they cannot sell, then there is an incentive to produce as much as possible. This happened under the CAP with the result being, in some cases, vast stocks of unwanted agricultural products. Unfortunately, with millions starving in the world, very little of these surpluses are sent to areas of need, because they are the wrong sort of food – for example, oranges and wine. Sometimes, large amounts of stocks have to be destroyed, making a mockery of the system. The guarantee price mechanism has been very expensive and in order to correct this type of situation, limits have been placed on the production of certain goods. The first of these limits was set in 1988 when *production quotas* were applied to milk. Production quotas limit the total amount of litres of milk that a farmer can produce in any given year. Such quotas can be applied to any agricultural goods, not just milk, and are a means of cutting Community production and reducing the surpluses. In the case of milk, quotas managed to reduce the proportion of financial assistance given to them by the EC, by 33 per cent.

A further way of reducing over-production is to encourage farmers to 'set aside' land and not use it for production. This was established in 1988 and ran until 1993, and under the system, farmers received payment from the Community for taking land out of production for at least five years.

ACTIVITY

Level of public stocks in the EC, 1988 (000s tonnes)

Product	*Stock*
Cereals	8312
Olive oil	346
Skimmed milk powder	11
Butter	120
Beef	425
Alcohol	10 556

Source: European Community

As a group, debate the following statement: 'European Community surpluses should be immediately distributed to the starving areas of the world.'

ACTIVITY

Europe's wasted food

It was harvest day in reverse yesterday down on the EC farm. Four million oranges were taken to a field in lorries – and then ploughed into the ground.

More than 900 tonnes of the rotting fruit were buried and tomorrow morning the farmers will start again.

British taxpayers will be helping to foot the bill for the whole operation – a perverse kind of orange aid.

The sickly-smelling pile in a field 200 miles from Athens is just one of Europe's growing food mountains.

Everywhere across the continent lie hidden piles of wasted produce, out of sight of EC taxpayers and out of reach of the world's starving.

The EC beef mountain is higher than ever before. The 414 000 tonnes of beef stored across northern Europe could make 607 million Sunday roasts.

While thousands of pounds are spent keeping the beef in cold storage, 6.6 million people in Albania, Bosnia, Iraq and Afghanistan face a slow death from cold and hunger this winter.

In Africa, nine in ten Somali children are without adequate food. Three million Eritreans and millions more Ethiopians face severe shortages. Only a fraction of the 23 million tonnes of surplus EC grain will go to the starving Third World . . .

Source: *Sunday Express*, 20 December 1992

Read the article 'Europe's wasted food' and then answer the following questions:

1 What is meant by the first paragraph of the article?
2 In your own words, state the main argument of the article.
3 In your opinion, should British taxpayers help in paying the bill for destroying the fruit? Give your reasons.
4 Study the illustration 'The top 20 food mountains' and using the information that it contains and your own views, prepare an article for your local newspaper on the problem of EC food surpluses.

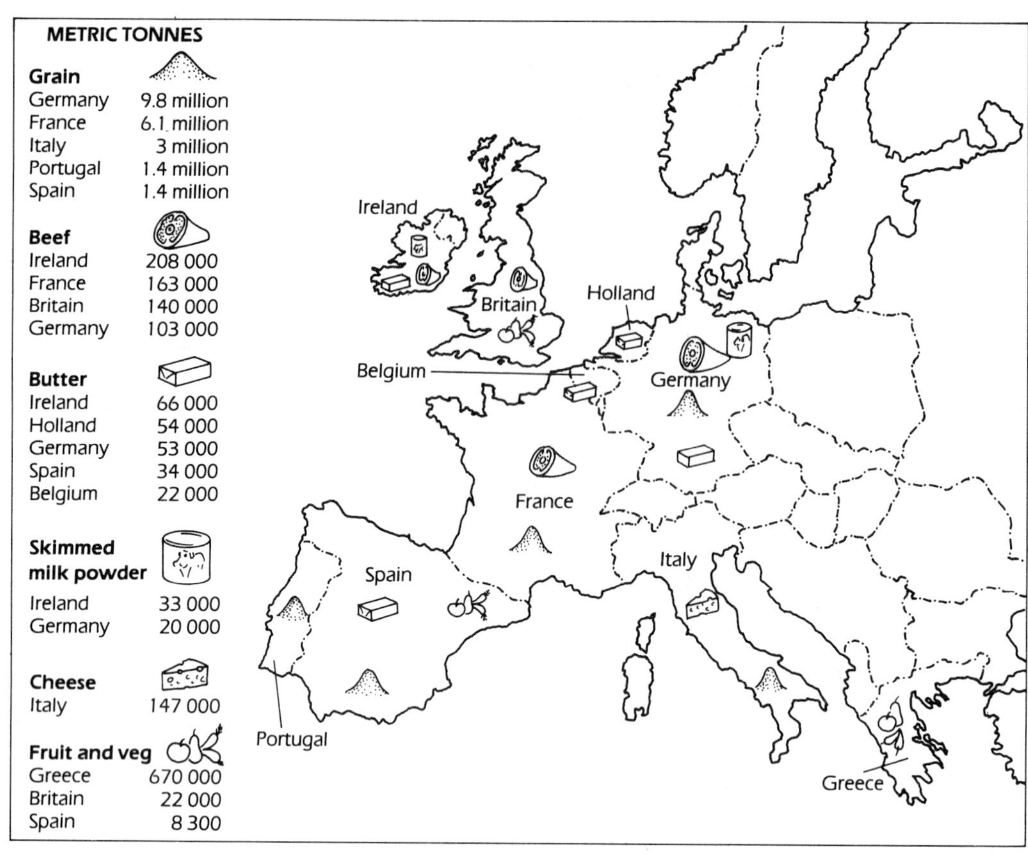

▶ *5.1 The top 20 food mountains*

The Common External Tariff

The purpose of the Common External Tariff (CET) is to allow EC agricultural products to compete on the world market. It guarantees the payment of export subsidies (*restitutions*), so that exporters of Community agricultural products receive a sort of refund. This covers the difference between the lower prices at which they must sell on the world markets and the higher prices within the EC.

For example, if a farmer wants to sell a tonne of wheat at the EC price of say £35, and that farmer has to sell on the world market at £31 a tonne, then he or she receives an export subsidy of £4 from the EC to make up the difference.

The CET also requires levies to be paid on low-cost imports coming into the EC from outside. So, protection is offered to domestic producers from third parties by variable import levies. These are taxes levied on imports at EC frontiers. Levies collected from third party products go into the EC's 'own resources', to help finance the Community budget.

ACTIVITY

1 Do you agree with the system of export subsidies and import levies discussed above? Give your reasons.

2 List the pros and cons of removing import levies in the EC.

Common financial responsibility

This is the idea that the costs of the CAP should be shared jointly. This has given rise to a number of problems. For example, the UK negotiated a number of refunds because the government felt that she only received limited financial assistance under the CAP.

By the early 1980s, it was also clear that some sort of restraint on agricultural expenditure was needed and so, in 1988, it was agreed that agriculture should not exceed 74 per cent of EC GNP. Later, in 1992, the Community agreed a 30 per cent reduction in cereal prices and a 15 per cent reduction in beef prices.

ACTIVITY

Discuss with a partner why the more industrialised member states of the EC should share the financial responsibility for the CAP.

The European Agricultural Guarantee and Guidance Fund

Community expenditure on the CAP comes from the European Agricultural Guarantee and Guidance Fund (EAGGF). This is one of the EC's structural funds, along with the Social Fund and the Regional Development Fund. There are two sections to the fund, with the guarantee sector being by far the largest in terms of the EC budget.

The two sections of EAGGF

Section	*Purpose*
Guarantee	– finances price guarantees to farmers – finances purchases by intervention bodies – pays for storage costs of purchased products – pays for income subsidies – provides subsidies for marketing purchased products – finances export refunds
Guidance	– provides financial help with agricultural development – provides aid for small farmers – offers help for hill farming – assists with infrastructure in difficult areas – assists with retraining and redeployment of farmers retiring from farming

ACTIVITY

EAGGF expenditure

	1985	*1986*	*1987* (million ECU)
Guarantee section	19 744	22 137	22 989
Guidance section	718	720	847

Source: European Community

1. Why do you think a) so much is allocated to the guarantee section and b) so little is allocated to the guidance section?
2. Draw bar charts to illustrate this information.
3. Should the Community try to balance up the two sections of the EAGGF? Give your reasons.

Has the CAP been successful?

The general answer to this question is 'yes'. A number of features point to success:

- greatly improved agricultural production and in more diverse products;
- the achievement of self-sufficiency (in all areas except fruit);
- general prosperity.

Against this it must be stated that apart from being so controversial, the CAP has led to higher prices for the consumer. But it is difficult to estimate the level of prices that consumers would have to pay if the CAP did not exist.

Reform of the CAP

For many reasons, not least of which is the problem of surpluses, the EC has had to shift the focus of the CAP. This means that reform is being considered in the following areas.

- The introduction of a restrictive price policy with gradual reductions in the support prices of those products that are in surplus.
- The introduction of stabilising mechanisms including the system of MGQs (maximum guaranteed quantities). These are used for reducing production levels.
- Development of a policy for encouraging quality at the expense of quantity.
- EC incentives for the use of agricultural products for non-food purposes.
- Providing direct aid to small farmers to encourage retraining.

The CAP in the future

There are many priorities for the CAP in the future, but it is likely that the following areas will concern the Community:

- the need to target the less favoured regions of the EC;
- the depopulation of the more remote areas and the associated problem of ageing populations in these areas;
- the need for strict rules regarding the use of pesticides and fertilisers in agriculture, underlining the EC's commitment to the environment;
- a possible move away from traditional foodstuffs towards more healthy products;
- an increased demand for a greater variety of foodstuffs.

The need to tackle these areas will provide a series of challenges for the CAP of the future.

ACTIVITY

Agriculture Council

EC agriculture ministers took a first look at the Commission's new system to control payments to farmers under the reformed Common Agricultural Policy. The Commission had proposed that 115m ECUs (£82m) of Community finance should be spent over the next three years to develop a rigorous system of control on farmers' land, production and herd sizes. Measures would include the use of aerial photography to ensure accurate monitoring. Member states had mixed views; several doubted that they could implement the system by the scheduled 1 January 1993 and others objected to the obligatory annual declaration of production that farmers would have to submit. Agriculture Commissioner Ray MacSharry, responding to worries voiced about the bureaucracy involved, pointed out that a certain mimimum level of rules was necessary to ensure equal and fair treatment for farmers throughout the Community.

Source: The Week in Europe, 16 July 1992

Read the article 'Agriculture Council' and then answer the following questions:

1 What is the Commission suggesting in the article?
2 Why do you think such measures might be necessary?
3 What objections were raised in response to the Commission's proposed new system?
4 Imagine you are a local farmer who has just heard these proposals. What would your reaction be? Give your reasons.
5 Write a press release (no more than 200 words) for the local farming gazette *Local Farming Community*, outlining the Commission's proposed new system.

Environmental action

The need for EC action on the environment

Europe has a vast array of climates, soil conditions and landscapes – it is home for more than 6000 plant species, approximately 100 000 species of invertebrates and almost 600 varieties of birds. Highly industrialised areas lie adjacent to wild regions where threatened species still survive. For these reasons, the EC has a responsibility towards its environment. Recent disasters, such as those at Chernobyl and Bhopal vividly brought home to the public via their television screens, have helped to raise awareness of the need to look after the environment. Members of the Green Movement within the European Parliament have helped to stimulate action on the part of the EC, and now, environmental policy is a priority in all 12 member states of the Community.

ACTIVITY

1 Produce a list of any environmental issues that you are aware of in your area.
2 As a group, discuss what can be done to deal with these environmental issues.

EC environmental action

Environmental policy was not referred to in the Treaty of Rome and the existence of a policy at all really dates back to 1973. At this time, an Environmental Action Plan was adopted by the Council of Ministers. This was the first recognition of the need for action on the environment although it was realised that responsibility should be shared between the EC and individual national governments. This recognition was later underlined by the inclusion of EC environmental policies under the framework of the Single European Act (SEA). Article 25 of the SEA refers to the EC's duty to preserve, protect and improve the quality of the environment, the protection of human health and ensure a balanced use of resources.

Since 1973, 4 special Action Programmes have been implemented, with over 100 directives and regulations adopted by the EC concerning the environment.

Environmental problems

The EC recognises six broad areas of environmental problems:

Conservation of wildlife	Waste habits	Chemical products	Noise	Water	Atmospheric pollution

ACTIVITY

1. Should the environmental problems recognised by the EC be the responsibility of the UK national government or the EC, or a combination of the two? Give your reasons.
2. Make a list of actions that a) the UK government or b) the EC could take to prevent damage to the environment.
3. What benefits to a) the local community, b) the UK as a whole and c) the EC would be derived from the actions suggested above?

ACTIVITY

Read the article 'Help for the Shetlands' and then answer the following questions:

1. Which ecological disaster does the article refer to?
2. List the effects that a disaster like that caused by the *Braer* might have on a local community.
3. The Commission granted 700 000 ECUs to assist the Shetlands. What other measures do you think the EC could have taken?
4. What do you think is meant by the term 'operational pollution'?

Help for the Shetlands

The European Commission decided on Tuesday to release 700 000 ECUs (about £560 000) from the European Community budget to help clean up the ecological damage in Shetland following the *Braer* disaster. The emergency aid is intended to be spent in helping salmon farmers, fishermen and other islanders who are victims of the oil spillage. In announcing the aid, the Commission said in Brussels that it intended the money as a symbol of the sympathy and solidarity of the Community at large for all those hit by the calamity. The aid will be disbursed by the local authorities in co-operation with the Commission's office in Scotland. The Commission has also called for a speeding up of agreement on its proposals on maritime transport to protect the environment from shipping activities causing oil spills, cargo loss and operational pollution. The Commission sees itself as having an important role in ensuring the application of existing international maritime rules.

Source: *The Week in Europe*, 14 January 1993

ACTIVITY **Case study**

A salty tale

The European Court of Justice sometimes rules on disputes that at first glance seem pretty obscure, but which are of real importance for everyday life. A Dutch horticulturalist suffering from the pollution from a big French factory is just one case in point.

A nurseryman always used water from the Rhine to water his plants, but it became too salty. It started damaging his greenhouse produce and costing him a great deal of money. The people responsible were a French company called Potash Mines of Alsace, who were dumping huge quantities of industrial wastes containing saline residues into the Rhine on a daily basis. When the nurseryman discovered this he was furious and asked the Dutch courts to force the French company to pay for the damage it had caused. An Amsterdam-based foundation concerned with cleaning up Europe's rivers supported his case. Together they took it to the Rotterdam civil court, but the Dutch judges refused to give a ruling. Citing a 1968 European Convention, they said the only court competent to rule on the affair was the one at the place where the salts were being dumped into the Rhine – in Alsace.

The nurseryman still wanted the case tried in The Netherlands and went to the Court of Appeal, arguing that a ruling should be given in the country where the damage was being done. The Court of Appeal referred the case to the European Court of Justice. It ruled that the nurseryman and the foundation could choose whichever court they wanted. They chose the Dutch one, which found against the French company and fined them heavily.

Read the case study 'A salty tale' and then answer the following questions:

1 Which environmental problem does the case study highlight?
2 Why is this case a typical example of those that the EC should become involved in?
3 What is your opinion of the outcome of this case?
4 What measures might the EC take to prevent this type of case from recurring?

The scope of EC environmental action

Three basic principles have underpinned EC environmental policy as it has developed over the years. These are:

- the need to take preventative action;
- the recognition that it is the responsibility of the polluter to pay for the pollution that he has caused – the so-called PPP (polluter pays principle);
- the need for action as early as possible, preferably at the *source* of the problem.

Over a period of time, the EC has gradually widened its scope in terms of the environmental issues that it concerns itself with. The designation of 1987 as 'European Year of the Environment' underlined the Community's commitment to this policy.

ACTIVITY

UK condemned over drinking water

The European Court of Justice ruled on Wednesday that the UK had breached EC rules on the quality of drinking water in 28 areas in England. The ruling followed complaints from Friends of the Earth that the levels of nitrates in water supplied to some 800 000 people exceeded limits set in a 1980 EC Directive. Twenty-one of the zones are in the Anglian Water region, the others are in the Severn-Trent water region, Three Valleys Water area (north of London) and South Staffordshire. The UK claimed to have taken 'all practicable steps' to comply with the standards.

Source: *The Week in Europe*, 26 November 1992

Read the article 'UK condemned over drinking water' and then answer the following questions:

1 For what reasons, do you think, has the UK failed to comply with the standards for drinking water?
2 What sanctions should the EC have at its disposal to ensure that the UK does comply with the standards?

3 Conduct a mini-survey to find out what people in your area think of the quality of their drinking water.
4 Based on the findings of your survey, write a letter to your local radio station either for or against the quality of local drinking water.

ACTIVITY The Corine programme

The European Commission has launched the Corine programme in order to improve the collection of data concerning the EC environment. The Corine programme is a co-ordinated information system on the state of the environment and the natural resources of the Community.

The Corine programme for 1985–90 covered two major areas:

- the compilation of an environmental data base and the setting up of an initial geographical information system on the state of the European environment;
- improving the comparability and accessibility of environmental data.

It is hoped that the Corine programme will assist in the targeting of environmental policies, help in the monitoring of the impact of EC environmental and other policies and assist in the development of models at national level. Information produced by the programme will be used by Eurostat.

1 Why was the Corine programme launched by the EC?
2 What does the programme aim to do?
3 How do you think this type of initiative will help the environment?

EC environmental measures

Details of the Action Programmes

Programme	*Period*	*Area(s) of concern*	*Measures taken*
First Action Programme	1974–7	Fresh water Salt water	Setting up of 'quality standards' in relation to drinking water, swimming, farming and pollutants discharged into water.
Second Action Programme	1978–81	Air pollution	Directives to reduce the level of substances in the atmosphere.
Third Action Programme	1982–6	Preventative measures	Approval for major industrial/infrastructure projects now subject to an assessment of their possible impact on: – human beings, flora and fauna – soil, water, air, climate and landscape – material assets and cultural heritage.
Fourth Action Programme	1987–92	Further preventative measures	Attempts to integrate environmental policy with other EC policies. The setting up of LIFE in 1990 – a special fund to protect endangered species. Ban on CFCs by mid-1997. Reduction of carbon dioxide emissions. New system of eco-labelling to denote environmentally friendly products.

A well-known washing-up liquid carries the following message:

ENVIRONMENTAL INFORMATION

This product is formulated and made with care for the environment. Our detergent materials are broken down into harmless materials by natural processes, i.e. they are biodegradable.

1 List as many products as you can that you consider to be environmentally friendly.
2 How much notice do you think is taken by consumers as to whether or not products are environmentally friendly? What can retailers do to increase customer awareness of such products?

ACTIVITY

Sources of air pollution in the EC, 1988

Sector	*Carbon dioxide*	*Sulphur oxides*	*Nitrogen oxides (% emission)*
Energy	37.5	71.3	28.1
Industry	22.0	4.0	57.7
Transport	16.6	15.4	7.9
Other	21.9	9.3	6.3

Source: Eurostat

1 What is meant by the term 'emission'?
2 Produce a bar chart which compares the three sources of air pollution for the four sectors. What conclusions can you draw from your bar chart?
3 In what ways can industry try to meet its responsibilities with regard to air pollution?

Problems with EC environmental policy

A number of problems relating to EC environmental policy can be identified. These are as follows.

- Difficulty has been experienced in reaching agreement on common or minimum standards. This largely arises as a result of the conflicting expertise that member states have on given environmental issues.
- The costs in preventing pollution or in improving standards in the environment have been a special concern for the less-advanced industrialised member states such as Greece. The Greek government has asked the EC to assist her financially in this. This is because some of the less industrialised states are more concerned about developing their industrialised status than pollution of the environment.
- The Commission was originally in favour of harmonised environmental measures which would apply equally to all member states. This has not been possible due to some of the reasons stated above and so a more flexible approach has been adopted.
- Despite suggestions from the Commission, it is left to the Council of Ministers to decide what action should be taken. This means that member states' governments have a veto on environmental matters.

ACTIVITY

In a group discussion, decide whether the Commission should have more power in insisting on action to be taken by member states' governments.

A better future?

We all want to see a healthier and cleaner environment, and EC initiatives to bring this about should be welcomed by all. Perhaps by offering more scope for legislation to the Community, a better future can become a real possibility.

Consumer and competition policy

Consumer policy

- **According to EC rules, a cauliflower is only a cauliflower if has two green leaves of a certain size!**
- **For EC purposes, goats are classified as sheep!**
- **Hyacinth bulbs are classified as vegetables!**
- **Strict EC rules exist covering chewing gum, silkworms, pistachio nuts, rice paper and prunes!**

ACTIVITY

What is your initial reaction to the above statements? What do the statements suggest about the EC?

You may have found some of the above statements rather ridiculous and perhaps have concluded that the EC is being just a little too silly! But although it is perhaps hard to comprehend, according to EC rules, the above statements are all true. There are many more rules which govern all sorts of goods. The one thing they all have in common is that they aim to *protect the consumer*.

ACTIVITY

If the aim of EC consumer policy is to protect the consumer, why do you think the EC issues the types of rules like those above?

The development of consumer policy

Since 1972, the Community has been developing its consumer policy. Many directives have been approved which aim to bring national legislation into line with regard to consumer health and safety, while at the same time guaranteeing the free movement of goods across the EC. As the Single Market became fully operational, the need for this policy increased because an increasing number of goods became available to consumers. With a much wider choice of products, rules had to be devised to guarantee to the consumer that the consumer was buying what he or she thought.

Consumer protection in the EC has come to refer to three main areas of activity:

- the introduction of EC legislation that is applicable in all member states;
- encouraging consumers to participate in decisions that affect both buyers and users of goods and services;
- allowing consumer organisations (such as the Consumers in the European Community Group – CECG) to exert influence in all aspects of retail practices, both at home and in the Community as a whole.

When is a wine not a wine?
A good example of Community legislation affecting specific products which must be applied in all member states is that of wine.

To be classified as *wine*, the contents of a bottle have to be what the Community has decided they should be. In particular, wine (to be called wine) must have the following characteristics:

- it must be the fermented juice of grapes;
- it must have an alcoholic content not below 8 per cent and not exceeding 18 per cent;
- it can only have those additives that the EC has previously agreed to – for example, sugar in some cases.

To be retailed and sold as 'quality wine', the product must demonstrate even more characteristics:

- it must be produced in a certain place;
- it must be produced from a certain variety of grape;
- it must be generally bottled in the place that it was produced;
- it must not be blended with other wines.

There may also be limitations on the quantity of wine that may be produced from a given acreage of vineyards. There are also strict rules regarding the size of the labels on the wine bottle!

ACTIVITY

1 What is the purpose of the EC insisting that 'quality wine' meets all the above specifications?
2 How do you think the rules affect those wine producers who do not already comply with the specifications?
3 Is the EC being too meddlesome over the question of wine or is this acceptable practice in your opinion? Give your reasons.

Recent consumer protection measures
During the 1980s, before the official opening of the Single Market, a number of measures were adopted by member states in order to protect consumers.

Recent consumer protection measures

EC measure	*Purpose*
Misleading Advertising Directive	This offers protection against advertisements which might mislead the reader or consumer.
Product Liability Directive	This makes manufacturers and importers liable for injury caused by defective products.
Doorstep Selling Directive	This allows for a seven-day 'cooling off' period for certain sales contracts entered into by the consumer.
Consumer Credit Directive	This offers protection to the consumer entering into various credit agreements.
Toy Safety Directive	This attempts to prevent dangerous toys being sold in the Community.
Price Indication Directive	This demands that the selling price of goods be displayed for consumers to see.
Dangerous Imitation Directive	This harmonises national laws regarding food imitation which could cause injury.

Apart from these EC Directives, others are constantly coming into force which deal with all aspects of consumer purchases and protection.

February 1992

Personal protective equipment

April 1992
UK Regulations

Toy safety

UK Regulations
September 1992

Gas appliances

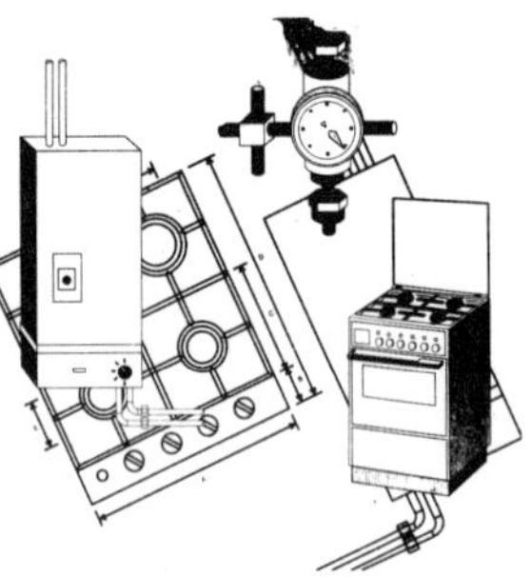

▸ *5.3 Examples of DTI guides on EC directives*

ACTIVITY Consumers in the European Community Group (CECG)

CECG is the umbrella organisation which co-ordinates the representation of the views of its 27 member organisations on EC consumer issues. It was set up in 1978. CECG monitors the way in which EC policies and proposals affect UK consumer interests, commissions research and issues publications. It puts forward its views, as decided by its membership, as widely as possible. CECG is in regular contact with governments, the European Commission, and both UK and European Parliaments.

1 What is the role of the CECG?
2 If EC consumer policy is designed to protect the consumer, why do you think a group like CECG is necessary?
3 List the pros and cons of setting up a local branch of the CECG in your area.

Competition policy

In many ways, competition policy and consumer policy are linked – unhealthy competition may result in consumers being adversely affected by, for example, limiting the choice of goods available.

ACTIVITY

Consider which of the following you think are acceptable under the Single Market:

a) Two rival computer games manufacturers who agree to fix the prices of their products at a similar level.
b) The merging of two ballpoint pen companies in order to expand their market share and increase their overall profitability.
c) An agreement between three rival electrical products companies to divide up the market in video recorders.
d) Agreements between certain wet-shave razor manufacturers which are designed to push other competitors out of the market.
e) An agreement by rival toy manufacturers producing the same toy, to limit the amount of toys allowed on the market in an attempt to drive up prices.

You may have come to the conclusion that with the exception of b), none of the above are acceptable within the Community. In some cases, the Commission could prevent the type of merger that is suggested in b) on the grounds that it would damage the market and limit the choices available to the consumer.

Why competition policy?

As already stated, the EC's Single Market guarantees the four freedoms, one of which is the free movement of goods across the Community. However, even with the free trade that the common market brings, the inclination of many companies and their respective national governments may be to protect their domestic goods. This not only threatens the free movement of goods, but also threatens continued unity, for it calls into question the commitment of offenders to the whole spirit of the European Community.

Competition policy is needed for the following major reasons.

1 Without rules of competition, those businesses that are subject to the fewest regulations (for example, in relation to wages, working conditions, hours, pollution and safety standards) would have considerable advantages over their competitors. For example, if a firm was able to pay wages to its employees which were well below those of its competitors, it may be able to offer its products at a cheaper price to consumers, giving it an advantage.
2 Without rules of competition, firms may be able to conclude agreements to divide up a market in order to sell certain products. For example, a UK manufacturer might set up an agreement to sell products in the UK but not in Italy; or an agreement might be reached where French products entering Luxembourg cannot be sold cheaper than similar goods already on sale there. In both cases, the consumer would not get the full benefits of the common market.

ACTIVITY **Case Study**

Cassis de Dijon and customs officers

Protectionism is a continual threat to European unity. For years countries were able to keep out products that differed slightly from their own because they came from a neighbouring country. Producers complained that they could not export, until the now-famous day when the European Court of Justice removed a major trade barrier dividing Europe's markets.

A German firm called Rewe, based in Cologne, wanted to market a French liqueur called Cassis de Dijon in Germany. But Cassis de Dijon did not comply with German alcohol legislation, which said that liqueurs should be at least 32 per cent proof. As Cassis de Dijon was only 15–20 per cent proof it could not be sold in Germany. Rewe took the case to the Hesse court, claiming that the legislation infringed the Treaty of Rome, by impeding the free movement of goods between Community countries.

The Court referred the case to the European Court of Justice. Germany defended herself by claiming that low-proof alcohols were banned as a health precaution. Cheap, low-proof drinks encouraged consumption and alcoholism, it claimed.

The European judges ruled that Cassis de Dijon was legally marketed in France and could therefore be legally sold in any other EC state. A ban could only be applied if a country could prove that the drink constituted a genuine danger to consumers. The judges felt that in the case of Cassis de Dijon there was no evidence that it constituted a health hazard of any kind. Soon afterwards the German customs let through the first shipment of the drink for sale on the German market.

Source: European Community

Read the case study 'Cassis de Dijon and customs officers' and then answer the following questions:

1 a) What prevented Cassis de Dijon from being sold in Germany?
   b) How did the Germans justify their actions?
2 Why is the case of Cassis de Dijon so important?
3 What are the implications of this case for the consumer?

EC competition legislation

EC competition policy is seen as an important means of promoting economic integration. This is because effective competition is viewed as the main factor in the promotion of innovation and the improvement of productivity, leading to a higher standard of living for the population.

The Community wants to avoid situations where member states are able to grant state aid or exclusive rights to legal monopolies to replace the forms of protection once enjoyed by individual member states, and now removed by the integration of markets.

EC legislation therefore attempts to prevent:

Price fixing	Imposing territorial restrictions which partition the common market	'Ganging up' to discriminate against third parties	Agreements to divide up a market between competitors

The operation of competition policy

An important body of competition law now exists in relation to local and EC-wide trading. The competition rules set by the Community are implemented and interpreted by the Commission and the Court of Justice. Policy is directed at private companies and national governments – so, the Commission has to be sensitive when national governments are experiencing periods of recession.

Basic competition rules are contained in Articles 85 and 86 of the Rome Treaty. They are designed to control agreements that might affect trade between member states and to prevent any enterprise achieving a 'dominant' position in the market. In this, the Commission is able to prevent mergers from taking place which may not be in the Community interest. Linked to this, the Commission has developed a policy which bans:

- price-fixing;
- market sharing;
- production quotas.

In implementing the competition policy, the Commission does not work alone, for all member states already have some form of legislation on restrictive practices – note the existence of the Monopolies and Mergers Commission in the UK for example. This means that in theory at least, offenders can be fined by both the Commission and their national governments.

ACTIVITY

World Cup tickets

The European Commission ruled this week that an agreement between organisers of the 1990 World Cup football held in Italy and an Italian tour operator had restricted competition in sales of package tours to the event. The World Cup organising committee had granted the operator, '90 Tour Italia', exclusive rights to sell entry tickets as part of a package tour, leaving travel agencies unable to 'shop around' for cheaper deals to offer supporters. However, the Commission acknowledged that some selective distribution rights were necessary to guarantee safety at the matches. This is the first time that the Commission has made a decision under competition law on ticket sales at sporting events. Although no fine will be imposed on this occasion, the Commission intends to ensure that distribution systems of major sporting events fully comply with EC competition laws in future.

Source: *The Week in Europe*, 29 October 1992

Competition policy improved

In a speech on Monday to the Centre for European Policy Studies, Competition Commissioner Sir Leon Brittan announced plans to enlist the help of member states and accelerate procedures in the handling of competition policy. Since most complaints referred to the Commission concern almost exclusively member states it was natural, he said, that these should be dealt with by national courts. Sir Leon envisages the Commission taking a proactive role in encouraging and assisting the courts to apply EC law speedily. As for national authorities granting individual exemptions to Treaty rules, the Commissioner said that 'the time was not ripe to take such a step'. There was too great a risk of divergent applications of EC law and of 'forum shopping', companies setting up in the country with the most lenient interpretation of the rules.

Source: *The Week in Europe*, 10 December 1992

Read the article 'World Cup tickets' and then answer the following questions:

1 What aspect of competition policy is being referred to in this article?

2 What problems arose over the distribution of World Cup tickets which prompted action by the Commission? In your opinion, did the Commission act appropriately or not? Give your reasons.

3 What implications does this case have for other sporting events, such as the Olympics or the Wimbledon Tennis Championships for example?

Read the article 'Competition policy improved' and then answer the following questions:

1 For what reasons has Commissioner Sir Leon Brittan announced his plans relating to competition policy?

2 What would be the role of the Commission under these plans?

3 a) Explain what prompted the Commissioner to state that 'the time was not ripe to take such a step'?

b) What is the danger of 'forum shopping'?

ACTIVITY Review your progress: 5

1 Explain briefly why the Common Agricultural Policy was established.
2 What is the purpose of a) the guarantee section and b) the guidance section of the European Agricultural Guarantee and Guidance Fund?
3 What are production quotas?
4 Why does the Common Agricultural Policy continue to take up so much of the Community budget?
5 Large surpluses of many agricultural goods still exist. Explain why you think this is so.
6 Which three areas of activity does EC consumer policy cover?
7 What does the Product Liability Directive aim to do?
8 What are the reasons behind EC competition policy?
9 Why was the case of 'Cassis de Dijon' so important in the development of EC competition policy?
10 Which Articles of the Rome Treaty relate to EC competition policy?

Summary

- Certain EC policies, such as the CAP, are considered to be vital to the interests of the Community and were, therefore, allowed for in the Treaty of Rome.
- Of all EC policies, the CAP is perhaps the most controversial and most expensive.
- The Guarantee and Guidance Fund of the CAP is another example of EC structural funding.
- Other EC policies have developed over time in response to the changing needs of the Community and its population.
- Growing awareness of the environment has made this an important area of action for the Community, in partnership with member states.
- Within the Single Market, the Community recognises that consumers need to be protected from the negative effects of the market.

Assignment 8 The EC Structural Funds

You work for a local business whose managing director is very interested in finding out more about the structural funds that the European Community administers.

Task 1 You have been asked to produce a formal report which covers the following:

- the European Social Fund
- the European Regional Development Fund
- the European Agricultural Guarantee and Guidance Fund.

In particular, you are asked to cover the following:

- the background to the three funds
- how the funds are currently administered
- which group(s) of people may benefit from each of the funds.

Task 2 For a speech your managing director has to give to a group of business associates, prepare a set of structured notes that could be used to deliver the speech. Suggest what visual aids your managing director might make use of.

Task 3 Produce three different visual aids illustrating aspects of the structural funds that could be used during your managing director's speech.

Assignment 9 European Conference for Colleges

A group of colleges in your region have decided to set up a one-day European conference which will help to further awareness of the European Community and, in particular, its policies. The idea is that an MEP and other officials connected with the EC will speak at the conference, but that the main input will come from individual students.

Task 1 Several students have been asked to talk for no more than ten minutes on different EC policies and you have been selected as one of the lucky ones! Prior to the conference, you are asked which of the following policies you wish to talk about:

- European Social Policy
- European Regional Development
- European Monetary Union
- European Political Co-operation
- Common Agricultural Policy
- Environmental Policy
- Consumer/Competition Policy.

Task 2 Prepare a handout (on no more than two sides of A4 paper) which supports your talk on your selected policy that can be distributed to delegates at the conference.

6 The characteristics of Europe: 1

Aims

- To analyse the motives of the 12 member states in the development of the European Community
- To identify and describe the geographical composition of the smaller EC member states
- To develop an awareness of the socioeconomic profiles of the smaller EC member states
- To encourage an awareness of the political systems of the smaller EC member states
- To recognise and consider the cultural characteristics of the smaller EC member states.

Relevant BTEC Outcome Performance Criteria

4a Geographical make-up of member states accurately identified and described
4b Awareness shown of socioeconomic and political profile of member states
4c Cultural diversity of member states recognised and illustrated

The characteristics of the 12 member states of the European Community are quite different and the cultural diversity is a feature of the Community. In this chapter, we shall explore various aspects of each member state including geographical, political and socioeconomic features, as well as cultural differences. A logical starting point is a brief consideration of the historical development of the EC in terms of the reasons why each EC member state pursued Community membership.

The six founder members

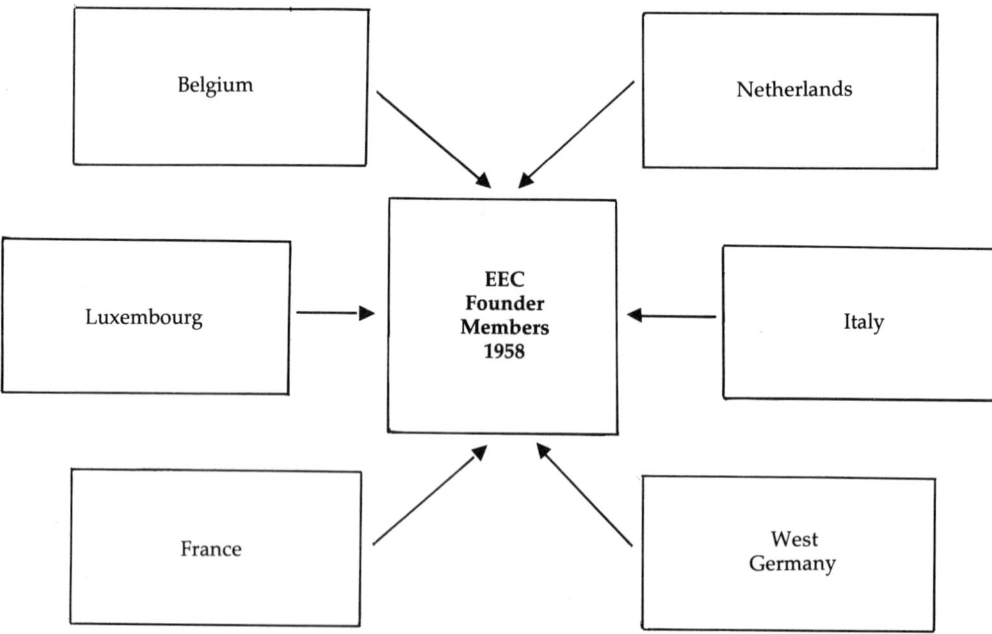

The Benelux states (Belgium, The Netherlands, Luxembourg) the insecure position of the three Benelux countries had been highlighted by the Second World War. Security now seemed to be in some grouping with other states. The position of the Benelux states, in relation to the other powers, was generally weaker (especially in the case of Luxembourg).

These states could only hope therefore to influence developments in Europe (and indeed the world) by being part of a larger and integrated grouping (such as the EC). None of the Benelux states was strong enough economically to be able to ignore any proposals put forward by France and Germany. It was considered desirable then that the Benelux states should have some say in the drawing up of such proposals and membership of the EC would allow this.

France the French government wanted to promote economic growth in the post-war period. The previously established European Coal and Steel Community (ECSC) was beneficial to France, for it gave her access to Germany's raw materials and markets, assisting such growth. A further motivation for the French was the desire to 'contain' Germany – to prevent her from ever being in the position that had led to the Second World War. The ECSC again had helped to promote this aim and membership of the EC (with Germany) would consolidate this position for France.

Germany the German state had lost credibility and respect due to its role in the Second World War. In particular, the German chancellor, Konrad Adenauer, believed the only way that his country would regain her position was through membership of the EC. With the perceived threat of Communism from the East, an economic grouping such as the EC in co-operation with NATO (North Atlantic Treaty Organisation) would offer a significant obstacle to Soviet influence. Germany also hoped that through membership of the ECSC and the EC, she would be able to shake free from Allied restrictions and interferences. Economically, the EC promised open markets in Western Europe and these would offer Germany important opportunities for economic expansion. The German economy became the fastest growing economy in the 1950s, lending weight to this idea.

Italy before the Second World War, Italy had been governed by the right wing, fascist regime of Mussolini. This had suffered defeat at the end of the war and, with it, the country lost respectability. Membership of the EC offered a fresh start for Italy and the promise of credibility. There was also an important political consideration, for Communist activity in Italy appeared to threaten a left-wing revolution. The fact that other Western European governments seemed to be opposed to this type of government in some ways attracted the Italian ministry to membership of the EC with its *democratic* approach. Economically, Italy had particular problems: inflation, unemployment and traditional poverty in the south. Membership of the EC offered new policies and initiatives which might well benefit her. Also promised was the possibility of economic growth.

ACTIVITY

1. Conduct a mini-survey in college to discover if staff and students know who the six founder members of the Community were.
2. Produce a bar chart to illustrate your results.

The post foundation members

The EC has increased from a total of 6 members in 1958 to its current membership of 12. The additional memberships that have occurred are commonly known as 'enlargements'. To date, there have been three enlargements.

EC enlargements

Enlargement	*Date*	*Countries involved*
First	1973	Denmark, Ireland, UK
Second	1981	Greece
Third	1986	Portugal, Spain

United Kingdom in 1958, the associations offered by the ECSC and the EC were the least important of the three relationships that the UK was involved in (the other two being NATO and the 'special relationship' with the USA, and the Commonwealth and Empire). The loss of sovereignty that EC membership implied was an important drawback for the British. However, the UK led the first enlargement of the EC for, by 1961, despite having helped to establish EFTA, she began to see the importance of playing a role in European integration. The threat of isolation, the need for new markets and the increasing disintegration of the Empire encouraged the UK to take this decision. But EC membership was not a formality – the UK's application was initially blocked by the French leader, General de Gaulle, who feared a possible erosion of French influence within the EC. Eventually, the UK was permitted membership in 1973, along with Ireland and Denmark.

Ireland the Irish government had not sought EC membership previously, for the benefits of the ECSC seemed to hold little for the state. Strong ties with the British also hampered earlier entry. However, by 1973, there were several reasons for the Irish application. In particular, Irish trade in agricultural goods had mainly served the British market since independence in 1922. Now this market was considered too small for Ireland to maximise her production capabilities. The prospect of the much wider markets offered by EC membership was therefore very attractive. Linked to this was the search for new markets for industrial goods, after considerable growth resulted from industrialisation in the 1930s. Ireland expected to do well from joining the EC for the competitiveness of her industry had improved and further attractions were the EC Social and Regional Funds, from which she hoped to benefit.

Denmark strong links with other Scandinavian countries and the limited benefits offered by the ECSC meant that EC membership was not an option for the Danes in 1958. Fifteen years later, however, Denmark became an EC member and this was motivated chiefly by the free access to the common market that membership promised. Denmark was capable of producing food that would provide for three times her own population and, thus, the export of goods in favourable conditions was a priority. Coupled with this were apparent new opportunities for the Danish in the area of industrial goods, at least in the longer term.

Greece the Greek economy, with its largely peasant-based approach, had appeared to be unsuitable for ECSC or EC membership in 1958. Yet Greece represented the second enlargement in 1981. This can be explained by the fact that Greece wanted to improve her position and status internationally – EC membership seemed to offer this possibility. There was a hope that the Greek economy would benefit from membership too. The restoration of a democracy in Greece in 1974 helped to accelerate Greek membership of the EC.

Spain Franco's political dictatorship in Spain and the backward nature of the economy in 1958 meant that she was not a serious contender for early EC membership. In fact, it was not until 1986, with the third enlargement of the Community, that Spain achieved membership. The reasons behind the Spanish application included the boost to Spanish agriculture that EC membership would provide (via the Common Agricultural Policy), the promise of funding from the EC regional programmes which would help to raise living standards and an improved base for structural improvements to Spanish industry.

Portugal the political character and backward economy of Portugal meant that she was not considered as an early candidate for EC membership. But, the good prospects for economic recovery and political acceptance, the promise of investment that would come with EC membership and the possibility of financial support for the restructuring of agriculture, in particular, encouraged the Portuguese bid for membership. With Spain, Portugal formed the third enlargement of the Community, formally becoming a member in 1986.

ACTIVITY

1 With a partner, make a list of the possible merits and drawbacks of the UK being a founder member of the European Community. Compare your answers with other members of your group.
2 In a group discussion, consider the validity of the statement below:

'If the UK had insisted on being a founder member of the European Community, instead of being concerned with other matters, then the attitudes that we have towards our European neighbours would be very different from those that we hold today.'

What an enlarged Community means

The three enlargements of the Community have had significant effects upon its operation.

1 The Community is now much larger, with a population of almost 344 million. Members include the more politically important states of Western Europe. The EC is the world's major commercial grouping.
2 Enlargement has made Community decision-making more complicated, especially as more national interests have to be considered.
3 Expansion to 12 members has meant that the 'traditional' strength of France and Germany has been watered down.
4 New members have brought specific problems. There has been a shift away from northern-based agricultural products such as beef, towards Mediterranean-based products such as olive oil. EC policies have to offer assistance to some of the less developed regions of the new members.

Further expansion of the Community is inevitable. Several states have either indicated their intention to join, or are already in negotiations with the EC, including some states previously part of the Soviet Union. Current negotiations for Community membership are taking place with Sweden and Austria. Other EFTA states have also expressed their desire to join, along with Eastern European states such as Hungary and Poland.

ACTIVITY

1 A number of countries have applied for EC membership. Some of these are currently EFTA states and some are Eastern European states. As a group, discuss how you think the membership of these states might alter the Community.
2 Produce an article for a local trade magazine that summarises your views on the possible enlargement of the EC in future. Restrict your article to 300 words.

The smaller EC member states:

Belgium

Key facts about Belgium

Area:	30 519 square km	**Religion**:	Mainly Roman Catholic
Population:	9.9 million	**Government**:	Constitutional monarchy
Employed in:	Agriculture (3%)	**Council votes**:	5
	Industry (29.9%)	**Commissioners**:	1
	Services (67.1%)	**European MPs**:	24
Language:	Dutch, French, German	**Currency**:	Belgian franc
Capital:	Brussels		

Geography

Belgium is a small country, extending 230 km from north to south and 290 km from east to west. However, the geographical location puts Belgium at the centre of the EC. It is situated in one of the most densely populated and commercial regions of the world, and is part of a highly urbanised area stretching from London to Milan. This is underlined by the political role that Brussels plays in everyday EC life.

Belgium is bordered by The Netherlands to the north, Germany and Luxembourg to the east, and by France to the south and west. The country is divided into two major parts – Flanders in the north and Wallonia in the South. The highest point in Belgium is the Signal de Botrange and principal rivers include the Scheldt and the Meuse.

Population

The population of just under 10 million comprises 51.2 per cent women and 48.8 per cent men. Of these, 18.1 per cent are under the age of 15, 67.2 per cent are aged 15–64 and 14.7 per cent are over 65. In terms of density, the average is 323 inhabitants per square km. Of the total Belgian population, 898 000 are foreigners with many coming from EC states, in particular, Italy.

Regional population

Region	*% of total population*	*Official language*
Flanders	57.6	Dutch
Walloon	31.9	French
Eastern Liege	0.7	German
Brussels-Capital	9.8	Dutch/French

Source: INBEL

ACTIVITY

1. Draw a pie chart to illustrate the figures for Belgian regional population as shown above.
2. List the problems that you think might exist in a country where there are three official languages.
3. Does having three official languages make Belgium more or less 'European' in outlook, in your opinion?

Politics and government

Under the Belgian political system, polling day occurs on a Sunday and voting is compulsory for those who are 18 years of age or over. There is also a system of compulsory military service.

Belgium is divided into nine provinces – Antwerp, Brabant, Hainaut, Limburg, Liege, Luxembourg, Namur, East Flanders and West Flanders. The Belgian political system is a hereditary monarchy and parliamentary democracy with the current head of state being King Baudouin I, to whom ministers are ultimately responsible. Constitutional powers in Belgium divide into three separate branches. Government operates at three levels in Belgium, and this results from the need to represent the different languages and regions.

Regional level the three main regions (Flanders, Wallonia and Brussels-Capital) each have authority over regional aspects of areas such as the environment, housing, water, energy, employment, public works, transport and administrative supervision of the provinces and communities.

Community level the three Belgian communities (Dutch, French and German) are self-governing with regard to cultural affairs, the use of language, matters related to individuals, and in domestic and international cultural collaboration. Each community or region has a council consisting of a parliamentary assembly and an executive – in other words, its own government.

National level the national institutions in Belgium comprise three separate branches – the legislature, the executive and the judicial. The legislative arm makes laws and comprises the Chamber of Representatives, consisting of 212 members elected by proportional representation, and the Senate (178 members). These are all elected for four years. The king has the right to convene and dissolve the Chambers, and it is his responsibility to appoint and dismiss ministers after consultation with party leaderships. The executive ensures that laws agreed upon are put into practice. The judicial arm settles disputes arising from the administration of the law via the courts and tribunals.

Political life in Belgium is dominated by three political groups – Christian Social Democrats, Socialists and Liberals. All have Dutch-speaking and French-speaking sections. The Christian Social Democrat Party (CVP) and the Socialist Party (CPS) have been the leading groups in Flanders and Wallonia, respectively, for some time. Two ecological parties have emerged – ECOCO in Wallonia and AGALEV in Flanders. Other regional parties also exist.

Economy and industry

Belgium encourages trade with Europe and the rest of the world, which arises partly from the country's geographical position. Foreign investors are attracted to Belgium by the favourable conditions for setting up business.

Industry Belgian industry has a long tradition which has allowed innovation and modernisation, particularly in the steel and textile industries where technological advances have brought improvements. The leading industrial sector is metal-working, with chemicals, iron and steel, textiles, food, glass, non-ferrous metals and diamonds supporting this. Technology has made a significant impact in telecommunications, computer software, pharmaceuticals, micro-electronics and biotechnology.

Agriculture the combination of climate and fertile soil has encouraged a high output despite the fact that only a small proportion of Belgians are employed in this sector. The Belgian government estimates that each farmer produces enough to feed 80 of his or her countrypeople. The Belgians are famous for horticultural expertise too – especially in the area of ornamental and indoor plants such as azaleas and begonias, and cut flowers like carnations and roses.

Vegetables such as mushrooms, asparagus and chicory are available all year round as a result of new production techniques. In addition, Belgium produces much fruit. In the stock-breeding field, Belgian blue and white cattle breeds are well known for their exceptional yields. Poultry and pig farming are also very productive areas.

Services over two-thirds of Belgians are employed in the service sector. This rapidly expanding sector of the economy includes bankers, insurers, hoteliers, clerical workers, lawyers and paramedical staff. Within the sector, the largest proportion of Belgians are employed in commerce, catering and the hotel business.

The structure of the Belgian service sector (employment) 1990

Area	*% Employed*
Commerce, catering and hotel business	28.7
Other services	17.3
Government and national defence	16.5
Education and research	14.1
Transport and communications	12.7
Financial institutions, insurance, business services	10.7

Source: INS

ACTIVITY

1 What conclusions can you draw from the figures for the Belgian service sector?
2 What reasons might there be for commerce, catering and hotel business being at the top of the list for service sector employment?

Exports over 50 per cent of Belgian national production is exported. Much of this (about three-quarters) goes to the EC states, among which the chief customers are France, The Netherlands and Germany. Belgium has joined forces with Luxembourg in the Belgium – Luxembourg Economic Union (BLEU) and together constitute the world's tenth largest trading nation (accounting for 2.75 per cent of world trade). Major exports include motor vehicles, finished metalware, chemicals, glassware and textiles. Some products within the food industry have a good reputation abroad, Belgian beer being a very good example.

Culture

Belgians celebrate many folklore festivals during the year, and different religions and towns have their own traditions and events. Examples include the celebrated 'Ommegang', an historical pageant which takes place in the illuminated square of Brussels, and the 'Procession of the Holy Blood' which takes place in Bruges. A particularly special feature of Belgian folklore are the many giants which take different forms in different places.

Belgium has spawned notable individuals throughout history including the Flemish painters who specialised in miniatures, Mercator, a geographer who produced the first cylindrical projection of the world to enable navigation, and Herges, the creator of the comic strip cartoon, *Tin Tin*.

Music plays a large part in Belgian culture with many military marches. The annual music festivals in both Flanders and Wallonia attract the best-known conductors and orchestras from within Belgium and from other parts of the world. An international contest, the 'Queen Elisabeth Competition', attracts pianists, singers, violinists and composers.

Belgians tend to enjoy eating and their restaurants have a high reputation. Belgian dishes are often rich and soups (especially *Chervil*) are popular all over Belgium. The Ardennes region is well known for its pâté, smoked ham and many varieties of game. Chips and waffles are widely available as fast-food items throughout Belgium. Wine is usually consumed at special events but beer (the lager-type) is really the national drink with more beer being consumed in Belgium than in the UK. The popularity of beer is underlined by the fact that it is often used in cooking.

A popular pastime in Belgium is pigeon-fancying and many regular publications are available on the hobby. Brass bands are also very popular and this reflects the Belgian preoccupation with music. In the sporting arena, Belgians are keen on cycling, and football is a popular spectator sport.

ACTIVITY

Prepare an oral presentation (no more than ten minutes) on a famous Belgian of your choice.

Denmark

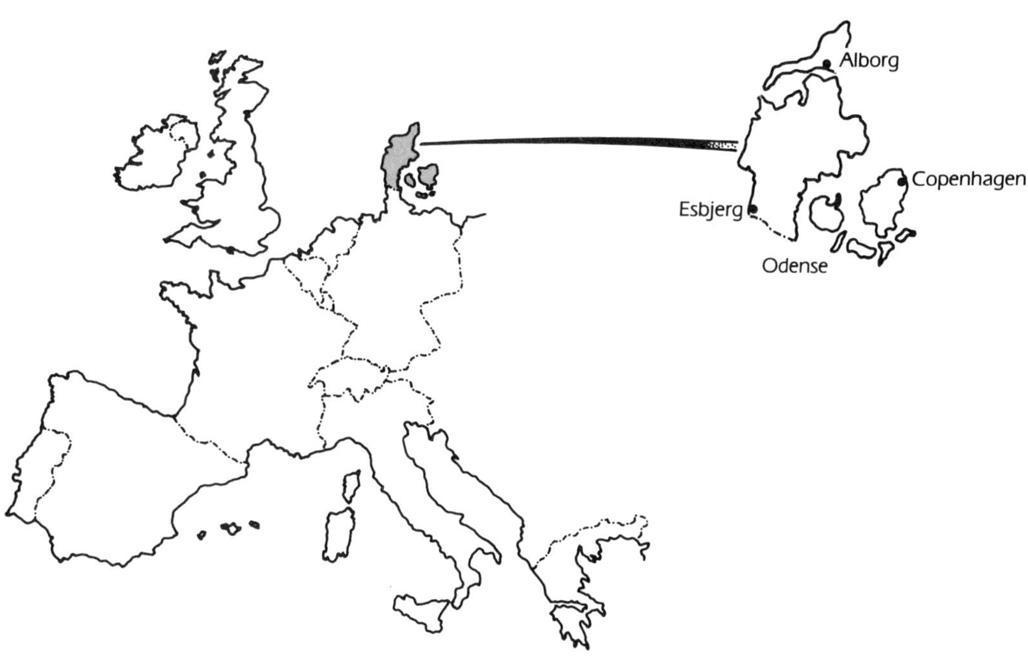

Key facts about Denmark

Area:	43 080 square km	**Religion**:	Evangelical (Lutheran church)
Population:	5.1 million		
Employed in:	Agriculture (7.1%) Industry (26.8%) Services (66.0%)	**Government**:	Monarchy with parliament
		Council votes:	3
Language:	Danish	**Commissioners**:	2
Capital:	Copenhagen	**European MPs**:	16
Currency:	Krone		

Geography

Denmark consists of the Jutland Peninsula which has a 67 km long frontier with North Germany at its base and 483 islands, with about 100 inhabited. The seaboard along the North Sea, Skagerrak, Kattegat and the Baltic Sea runs for some 7300 km. The country is very flat with the highest point rising to just 173 m.

The longest river is the Gudena (160 km), rising in central Jutland and eventually flowing into Randers fjord. The capital Copenhagen is the largest city in Scandinavia and it lies on the island of Sjaelland (Zealand) and the nearby island of Amager.

The Kingdom of Denmark also includes Greenland, the world's largest island, and the Faroe Islands, both located in the North Atlantic.

Population

Of the total population of 5.1 million, 18.8 per cent are aged under 15, 66.3 per cent are aged between 15 and 65, and 14.9 per cent are 65 or over. The average population density is 119 per square km.

The population of the capital, Copenhagen, is 1.2 million. Denmark has approximately 39 000 migrant workers, one-third of which come from EC countries, mainly the UK and Germany.

Politics and government

The Danish electoral system allows for polling to occur on a Tuesday and the vote is available to Danes at the age of 18. A system of military service is compulsory.

Denmark is divided into 14 counties along with the metropolitan region of Copenhagen with Frederiksberg. The country is divided into single-seat constituencies with party strengths in the Folketing being 'topped up' to ensure a proportional result. To gain representation in the Folketing, a party must win a single-seat constituency or obtain 2 per cent of the votes cast nationally, or the average vote required to win a single-seat constituency in one of the three divisions into which the country is split.

The Faroes have had home rule since 1918 with their own assembly and are not part of the EC (as Denmark is). Greenland has belonged to Denmark since 1721 and it obtained home rule in 1979, withdrawing from the EC in 1985.

The Kingdom of Denmark is a constitutional monarchy and a parliamentary democracy. Legislative power lies jointly with the sovereign (Queen Margrethe) and the single chamber parliament (Folketing). This has 179 members directly elected by a system of proportional representation for 4 years, with the Faroes and Greenland electing 2 members each.

The queen appoints the prime minister after consultation with party leaders and the prime minister may call new elections if the government loses its majority. The queen also appoints the ministers with each of them being responsible to the Folketing individually. Ministers can be removed from office by a vote of no confidence.

The Council of State (the queen and the ministers) considers all bills and important government measures. Those bills passed by the Folketing, with the exception of money bills and some others, must be put to a referendum if one-third of the Folketing members request it.

The largest political party, the Social Democrats, has been in government longest. Since 1982, the Conservative party leader has headed non-socialist minority coalition governments.

ACTIVITY

Danes struggle to sell the new deal

Denmark is facing an uphill battle to sell its new Treaty package to the rest of Europe. The Danish parliament will today formally agree the complex deal designed to allow a new referendum to overturn last June's shock 'No vote'.

And Foreign Minister Uffe Ellemann-Jensen will then tour each of the other 11 nations in a bid to persuade them to accept it.

John Major is also looking for support for the deal to cool the opposition to Maastricht from his backbench rebels.

The aim will be to get it ratified at the Edinburgh summit in December, which marks the end of Britain's EC presidency.

A second Danish referendum could then be held later next year.

But the plan, which demands opt-outs from a single currency and common defence policy plus safeguards of Danish citizenship and sovereignty in key areas, is likely to meet fierce resistance from other EC countries.

And EC President Jacques Delors warned Denmark last night that there could be no question of renegotiating the Treaty.

He warned the Danes that 'no one can have such a large right of veto that it prevents others from progressing'.

Source: *Daily Express*, 30 October 1992

Danes vote Yes

The Danes voted on Tuesday to accept the Maastricht Treaty by 56.8% to 43.2% in their second referendum on European union in a year. The result was welcomed immediately by leaders across the European Community. Commission President Jacques Delors said the vote gives the stimulus needed to pull the Community out of a period of gloom and inaction. Denmark would continue to make its contribution to a united Europe, one built on the diversity of its peoples, traditions and culture. In a speech to the Confederation of British Industry (CBI), Prime Minister John Major said Britain, like Denmark, had won crucial concessions over Maastricht, shaping the treaty to create an open wider Europe and 'emphatically not a federal Europe'. Major said Britain should put parliamentary wrangling behind it and get on with doing business for Britain in Europe.

Source: *The Week in Europe*, 20 May 1993

Read the article 'Danes struggle to sell the new deal' and 'Danes vote yes' and then answer the following questions:

1 For what reasons do you think the Danes rejected the Maastricht Treaty in the first place? What may have persuaded a majority of them to vote 'yes' in the second referendum?

2 What objections might the other 11 EC states have to the Danes' new treaty package? Which countries would object the most? Why?

3 The second article seems to suggest that Britain was happy about the Danes' acceptance of the treaty. Why do you think this might be so? Why is the success of the Danish package so important to the British government?

4 Jacques Delors said that the result of the second Danish referendum gave the stimulus needed 'to pull the Community out of a period of gloom and inaction'. What do you think he meant by this?

Economy and industry

In Denmark there is a shortage of minerals which has made industrial development quite difficult, although the output of agriculture has helped the growth of many industries.

Industry there is no coal, iron or hydro-electricity in Denmark although some oil is now obtained from the North Sea. Some other mineral resources such as chalk (used for cement) and granite do exist, however. Kadin, obtained from the Bornholm granite has led to the development of a famous porcelain industry in Copenhagen – the Royal

Copenhagen Porcelain Company was established in 1775 and exports its products all over the world.

With the use of imported raw materials, engineering and electronic industries have been developed in Denmark. There are also large textile industries. Food processing, meat and dairy products, pig products and pharmaceuticals are major Danish industries.

Agriculture that land area which is laid aside for agricultural purposes is used mainly for crops and for pasture. Many crops are grown for animal fodder and include barley, wheat, potatoes, peas, beans, green fodder and rye. Farmers have concentrated on dairy produce, and as such are among the most successful and efficient in the world. Most farms are quite small, so often co-operative methods are used. These produce butter, cream and cheese, and skimmed milk and whey is sent back to farms to provide feed for pigs. There are some 2.2 million cattle, over 9 million pigs and 15 million poultry.

Denmark's many islands have encouraged the development of extensive fishing activities and a busy processing industry. Indeed, Denmark is Europe's second largest fishing nation, after Norway, with a total catch of around 1.6 million tonnes.

Services public service is an important employer in Denmark. So too is tourism, with a large proportion of Danes being employed in the hotel and catering business, and other associated tourist areas.

Exports in 1990, the importance of the various productive sectors, measured by their share of exports was industry (75 per cent), agriculture (15 per cent), electricity and natural gas (6 per cent) and other products (4 per cent). Major exports include foodstuffs, finished goods, machinery and transport equipment and chemicals.

Denmark's main customers are the EC (53.2 per cent), Sweden (11.4 per cent), USA (8.6 per cent) and Norway (7.7 per cent).

Culture

In terms of Danish architecture, visitors to the country can experience Romanesque churches and cathedrals (especially at Ribe and Viborg), as well as castles and palaces from the Renaissance and baroque periods.

Over the centuries, many Danes have made important contributions to science and culture – Tycho Brahe discovered a new star in the constellation Cassiopeia for example, allowing Kepler to discover the laws of planetary motion and later, Newton's gravity laws. The children's storyteller, Hans Christian Andersen, was a famous Dane. In addition, the composer Carl Nielsen continues to grow in stature as a composer.

In the field of art, Danish schools of painting have attracted interest among collectors and museums.

The Royal Danish ballet is considered to be one of the world's leading groups and this has contributed much to Danish culture.

The Danes have an unfamiliar approach to the main meal of the day (*Middag*) which can be consumed at any part of the day, but usually in the afternoon. Danes probably last out until late afternoon due to the hearty breakfasts that are often consumed – these may consist of fruit, muesli, cornflakes, eggs, different cheeses, salami and cold meat, raw herrings, hot meatballs, bread and Danish pastries. The *smorrebrod* simply means buttered bread but this is much more than a simple sandwich – in fact, it can consist of crab, lobster, salmon, turkey, pork, cheese, eggs or any combination of these.

In terms of beverages, Danes enjoy beer like people of many other EC states. Many people are familiar with the Carlsberg advertisements which promote Danish lager-type beer.

Football is the national sport in Denmark and considerable success has been achieved here recently with the Danes winning the European Championship in Sweden in 1992. In addition, swimming, sailing, cycling and cross-country running are very popular sports. An increasing number of people keep fit by jogging too.

The average family spends about 20 per cent of their income on food, beverages and tobacco, some 5.6 per cent on clothing and footwear, and 8.5 per cent on leisure-time entertainment and education.

Greece

Key facts about Greece

Area:	131 990 square km	**Religion**:	Mainly Greek Orthodox
Population:	9.9 million	**Government**:	Parliamentary democracy
Employed in:	Agriculture (28.9%)	**Council votes**:	5
	Industry (27.4%)	**Commissioners**:	1
	Services (43.7%)	**European MPs**:	24
Language:	Greek	**Currency**:	drachma
Capital:	Athens		

ACTIVITY

1 Compare the proportion of people employed in agriculture, industry and services in Belgium and Greece, and draw a bar chart which illustrates these figures. What conclusions can you draw from your bar chart?
2 Why do you think Greece is such a large agricultural employer compared with Belgium?

Geography

Greece covers over 130 000 square km of which about 20 per cent comprises the Greek islands. There are 2000 of these islands with only 134 inhabited, stretching from Kastel-lorizo in the east to Crete in the south, and to Corfu in the west. The islands are widely scattered over the Ionian and Aegean Seas.

Northern Greece borders Bulgaria, Turkey, Albania and the former Yugoslavia. This border extends for 1212 km. The mainland is cut off from the southern part (known as the Peloponnese) by the Corinth Canal which was completed in 1893. The Greek coastline is 15 021 km long.

No major rivers exist in Greece which means that inland waterway networks do not exist either. Those rivers that are present tend to be short, the longest Greek river being the Aliakmon at 297 km. Few people would actually be able to name Greek rivers as they would in other parts of the Community.

Population

Unlike other EC countries where there are significant numbers of immigrants, most of the population are Greeks. The average density of population is 75 inhabitants per square km. Activity tends to gravitate around the capital with over one-third of the total Greek population residing in the Greater Athens area. Indeed, the next largest city, Thessaloniki, has a small population by comparison with 706 000 inhabitants. Of the total population of 9.9 million, 50.8 per cent are women and 49.2 per cent are men. In age terms, 21.3 per cent are under the age of 15, 65.4 per cent are between 15 and 64, and 13.3 per cent are over 65.

ACTIVITY

In a group discussion, consider why Greece has very few immigrants compared with other EC states.

Politics and government

The Greek political system demands that voting is compulsory and that all those aged 18 or over should be entitled to vote. As in some other Community countries, a system of compulsory military service exists for all males over the age of 19 while females may complete *voluntary* military service if they wish.

Greece is divided into 52 *prefecture* (governmental districts) and 13 regions – Eastern Macedonia and Thrace, Central Macedonia, Western Macedonia, Epirus, Thessaly, the Ionian Islands, Western Greece, Central Greece, Attica, the Peloponnese, the Northern Aegean, the Southern Aegean and Crete. The Greek system is a parliamentary democracy and has been since the establishment of the 1975 Constitution which followed nearly ten years of martial law. Constitutional powers in Greece divide into the three branches of legislature, executive and judiciary.

Legislative power is vested in the one-chamber parliament – the *Vouli*, and in the president of the republic, who approves and proclaims legislation. The Vouli is elected every four years and consists of 288 MPs who are chosen by the voters under a system of proportional representation. Twelve other MPs or 'state deputies' are put forward by the political parties and these are proportional to the number of votes that each party receives in the election. In common with other systems, the head of the government is the leader of the party with a majority in parliament.

Executive power is exercised by the president and the government. The president is elected for a period of five years and can serve two consecutive terms. It is the president's responsibility to appoint the prime minister and, indirectly, the other government ministers. The president has a veto at his or her disposal which can be used to block legislation, although this can be overridden by a majority of the total membership of parliament.

Judicial authority is exercised via a system of civil, penal and military courts. The Supreme Court looks at appeals from the lower courts and this is supported by a Constitutional Court which determines whether parliamentary measures passed are constitutional or not.

Economy and industry

Until the beginning of the 1970s, Greek manufacturing industry was made up mainly of family businesses. The period since, however, stimulated by the developments in electricity generation, has seen Greek industry make significant advances. Now industrial products account for an increasing proportion of the country's exports. Despite this, Greece is still relatively poor compared with her European Community partners – she is second only to Portugal in the poorest country league table.

Industry in 1970, the contribution of industry to the Greek economy surpassed that of agriculture for the first time ever. By 1986, industrial products accounted for 45 per cent of all exports (with agricultural products totalling 28.7 per cent). Huge regional disparities still exist in Greece although, generally, the standard of living has been lifted by various investment projects in such areas as hydro-electric power, transport networks and land reclamation. The basis for the Greek economy still tends to be private enterprise, although the state has played an increasing part since the 1960s.

Industries in Greece are generally small and so employ few workers. The most significant of these is textiles, and it is supported by steel milling, petrol refining and food processing. A growth sector has been the construction industry which has expanded in order to cope with the demand for accommodation that increasing population has brought to areas such as Athens and Thessaloniki.

ACTIVITY

1 What do you think the effects on the Greek economy were of having manufacturing industry made up of small family businesses?
2 How does this compare with the economies of the major EC states?

Agriculture the agricultural industry in Greece is still relatively backward with its very labour-intensive approach coupled with poor productivity. In fairness, agriculture is hampered by the Greek climate – rainfall is limited and the quality of soil is generally poor. Furthermore, the nature of the land means that farms are small, patchy and, consequently, uneconomical. Added to this is the lack of technology that has so transformed agricultural sectors in other countries. Thus, production outputs are very low compared with other EC states. Major grain crops harvested in Greece include wheat and barley, and these are supplemented by sugar beet, potatoes, tomatoes, beans and olives, along with cotton and tobacco. Other areas of agricultural or food production such as forestry and fishing remain undeveloped in Greece.

An important feature of the Greek employment pattern is the significant number of inhabitants who emigrate either on a seasonal or permanent basis, to other EC states, particularly the former West Germany.

Shipping the merchant fleet is very important in Greece. Based in Piraeus, this area of activity accounts for 35 per cent of the Community total and provides major support for the Greek economy. Oil tankers form a large part of this merchant fleet, with cruise liners being significant too. Greece is the world's fifth largest ocean passenger-carrying country.

Services centre largely on tourism. Greece has over 20 per cent of the air package holiday market in Europe, with over three-quarters of these coming from Europe. Package holidays, chartered flights and the development of airstrips in all but the remotest of places have made a major contribution to the development of the Aegean islands, such as Rhodes and Crete, as major tourist destinations. The service sector in Greece is still not as significant as it appears in other EC member states, however.

Exports major Greek exports include textiles, chemicals, ores, and metals and farm products such as tobacco, raisins, cotton, wine, olive oil and citrus fruits.

Culture

Greek culture owes much to the heritage of the past – in particular, that of Ancient Greece. It was during these times that famous Greek individuals were prominent – Archimedes, Homer and Plato for example.

In modern Greece, high attendance at church emphasises the important part that religion has to play in cultural life. This is particularly important in the rural areas.

A feature of modern Greek literature are the folk songs which are known as *klephtic* ballads.

Greece has the highest consumption of mutton, lamb and goat, with fish being a very important element in the diet too. Greeks tend to eat more cheese than other EC states, with bread and pasta figuring strongly. Greek cuisine has many bases – rice, figs, yoghurt, wholemeal bread, shish kebabs and dishes such as stuffed vine leaves. Visitors to Greece may also come across sweets made from filo pastry, chopped nuts and honey, known as *baklava*. A further characteristic of Greece is the drink known as ouzo (similar to Pernod and the Turkish raki).

Many leisure activities have been developed in Greece purely to cater for the needs of tourists – thus, surfing, diving and sailboarding can now be found. Sporting pastimes of the richer Greeks include yachting, skiing and motor racing. However, as in various other countries, many Greeks follow football either on television or in person.

Ireland

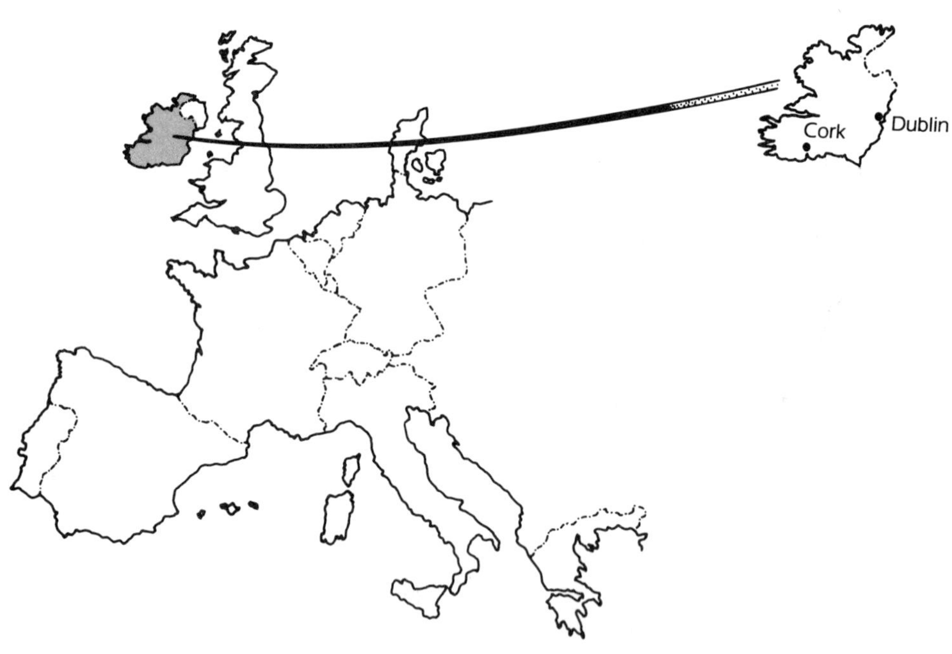

Key facts about Ireland

Area:	68 900 square km	**Religion**:	Mainly Roman Catholic
Population:	3.5 million	**Government**:	Parliamentary democracy
Employed in:	Agriculture (16%)	**Council votes**:	3
	Industry (28.9%)	**Commissioners**:	1
	Services (55.1%)	**European MPs**:	15
Language:	Irish	**Currency**:	punt
	English	**Capital**:	Dublin

Geography
Ireland represents 80 per cent of an island (Northern Ireland accounting for the remaining 20 per cent), which is situated off the western coast of the European 'mainland', and which is in the direct path of the Gulf Stream.

The Irish coastline stretches for a total of 5630 km, and this hosts a number of small and quiet beaches. It is a relatively compact state with the greatest length from north to south being 486 km and the greatest width from west to east being 275 km.

The highest mountain is Carrantuohill, reaching a height of 1040 m. Ireland's many rivers include the famous Shannon (the longest at 370 km) and the Liffey. This is also a land of many lakes.

By English proportions, there are few cities or towns in Ireland – Dublin is the largest as the country's capital with 477 000 inhabitants and is followed by Cork with a total of 127 000 inhabitants.

Population
Ireland's population of just over 3.5 million has been increasing since the early 1960s. Of the total population, women account for 49.8 per cent and men 50.2 per cent. In terms of age, 29.7 per cent are under the age of 15, 59.7 per cent are between 15 and 65, and 10.6 per cent are over the age of 65.

Of the 12 European Community states, Ireland is the least densely populated with an average of 51 inhabitants per square km.

The greater Dublin area has approximately 1 million inhabitants and there are about 88 000 foreign residents in the country, many of whom come from other EC states (about 67 000).

Ireland has two official languages – Irish and English. The Irish language is also known as Gaelic – this is a Celtic language, Ireland's *first* and one of the oldest written languages in Europe. To underline its importance alongside English, all official documents are published in both languages.

Politics and government
The Irish political system allows for all Irish and British citizens aged 18 or over to vote in elections and referendums. There is no compulsory military service in Ireland.

Ireland is divided into four provinces – Connacht, Leinster, Munster and Ulster. Within these there are 32 counties (with 6 counties located within Northern Ireland). Those outside Northern Ireland are Carlow, Cavan, Clare, Cork, Donegal, Dublin, Galway, Kerry, Kildare, Kilkenny, Laois, Leitrim, Limerick, Longford, Louth, Mayo, Meath, Monaghan, Offaly, Roscommon, Sligo, Tipperary, Waterford, West Meath, Wexford and Wicklow.

Ireland is a parliamentary democracy and an independent republic – the basis for this is the Constitution of 1937. Government operates at both local and national level, as in many other EC member states.

Local level elected local authorities administer local services for local communities. Within the structure, there are 115 authorities comprising county councils, county borough councils, borough councils, urban district councils and town commissioners.

National level as in many other EC states, national government consists of three distinct arms. **Legislative** power resides in the *Oireachtas* (the national parliament). This consists of the president of Ireland and two chambers – the *Ďail Éireann* (the House of Representatives) and the *Seanad Éireann* (the Senate). In the Ďail, 166 members are elected by a system of proportional representation for a maximum period of 5 years. In the Seanad, 60 members are elected for the same period – of these, 11 are nominated by the *Taoiseach* (prime minister), 43 are elected by members of the Ďail, of the previous Senate and from local authority representatives, and 6 are elected by the country's university graduates.

Financial bills can only be introduced into the Ďail while any other legislation may be introduced into either chamber. Such legislation only becomes part of Irish law when it has been signed by the president. As with the English House of Lords, the Irish Senate can have a delaying effect on proposals for legislation. A feature of the Irish system is that any bills that would alter the basic constitution of the country are subject to endorsement by the electorate, via a referendum – for example, ratification of the Maastricht Treaty.

The **executive** arm of the Irish system is represented by the president, who is elected for a period of seven years and appoints the Taoiseach upon nomination from the Ďail and the other ministers upon the advice of the Taoiseach. The president can refer bills to the Supreme Court on questions of constitutionality. The House of Representatives is summoned and dissolved by the president on the advice of the Taoiseach.

The **judiciary** deals with any disputes that arise from the administration of Irish law via the system of courts. The Supreme Court can rule on questions of constitutionality.

Irish political life was dominated for a long time by two conservative parties – Fianna Fail and Fine Gael. These parties are two factions of the same organisation – Sinn Fein. A third party, Labour, is now present on the scene – although smaller than the other two, it sometimes is in the advantageous position of holding the balance of power in the Irish parliament.

ACTIVITY

Irish referendum

The Republic of Ireland voted 69% to 31% in favour of ratifying the Maastricht Treaty last week. Welcoming the Irish vote, the European Commission President Jacques Delors said that the country had chosen full participation in the construction of Europe, instead of isolation. The ratification process gave every citizen a unique opportunity to play a role in the future of Europe. Earlier Denmark narrowly voted against ratification.

Source: *The Week in Europe*, 25 June 1992

Read the article 'Irish referendum' and then answer the following questions:

1 Why do you think the Irish voted so conclusively in favour of ratifying the Maastricht Treaty?

2 What do you think Jacques Delors meant when he stated that Ireland '. . . had chosen full participation in the *construction* of Europe, instead of isolation . . .'?

3 What is the value of a referendum on issues such as the Maastricht Treaty and the future of the European Community?

Economy and industry

Industry in the early 1920s, few industries existed in Ireland. Those that were in evidence included Guinness brewing, Irish whiskey distillation and among smaller manufacturers, the traditional areas of textiles and food, producing mainly for the domestic market.

In 1958, the Irish Development Authority (IDA) was established with the aim of encouraging foreign companies to start up new industries in Ireland, by means of tax incentives, grants and other inducements. Today, the Irish government remains committed to rapid economic development in any sectors of the economy that promise growth. The IDA continues to encourage external investment, especially in new technology, and also promotes small businesses. Current exploration work in the drilling for oil and gas suggest that Ireland may be a very promising territory within Europe.

Membership of the EC from 1973 has had a significant effect upon Irish industry – by 1983, Ireland had achieved a growth rate of 15 per cent, far outstripping the growth rate of the EC as a whole. This should be qualified by the fact that Ireland started from a much lower position than its European neighbours.

Today Ireland is a base-metal producer and the Wexford Plain in the south-east region has a substantial manufacturing base, being involved in steel working, vehicle assembly, food processing, rubber and clothing, and footwear. Furthermore, Dublin accounts for about 50 per cent of national industrial output, employing over 40 per cent of the total industrial force. Here, industries include meat canning, bacon processing, brewing, distilling, biscuit and jam production, tobacco and fertilisers.

Sources of overseas investment in Ireland, 1990

Country of origin	*No. of companies*	*Employment*
USA	357	43 800
UK	225	16 900
Germany	151	11 500
Canada	25	2 800
Netherlands	50	2 400
Sweden	28	2 100
Japan	14	1 900
Others	136	9 300
Total	986	90 700

Source: Department of Industry and Commerce

ACTIVITY

1 Produce a bar chart to illustrate the figures shown in the above table.

2 For what reasons do you think the USA is the largest overseas provider of employment in Ireland?

3 Why might overseas companies wish to invest in Ireland? What features does it have that would make overseas investment attractive?

Agriculture for centuries, agriculture was the only industry in Ireland. It currently accounts for 16 per cent of the Irish labour force. In many parts of Ireland, subsistence farming is the norm. In these areas, potatoes, hay and sometimes oats are the only crops possible. There are generally more sheep than cattle and wool is used as the basis for homespun cloth, knitwear and Donegal tweeds. Subsistence is characteristic of the western region too – here the population employed in agriculture rises to about 40 per cent. Poor soils and uneconomical farms, coupled with a relatively old workforce (most farmers are over the age of 50), make change a major problem. However, in the south-eastern region, much of the agricultural land is improved, and it is here that dairy farming and market gardening takes place in order to support the Dublin labour market. Furthermore, the Wexford Plain has fertile soils and is thus able to support crops such as oats, barley, potatoes, wheat and sugar beet.

The important role of agriculture in the Irish economy has been underlined by the impact of the Common Agricultural Policy (CAP). This has helped Irish agriculture to confront some of its problems – under-investment, low incomes and uneconomic holdings to name but a few.

Services well over half of the Irish population are employed in the service sector of the economy. Many are involved in the various facets of tourism that exist – visitors are attracted to Ireland for many reasons – the scenery, fishing and golf, to name a few. Many Irish people are involved in providing the services that are associated with these attractions.

Exports major Irish exports include machinery and transport equipment, food products (meat and dairy), manufactured goods (textiles) and chemicals. Ireland's main customers are the EC, USA and Canada.

Culture

Celtic folklore and tradition are the bases for some aspects of the Irish culture. Evidence of the Celtic past include the stones of megalithic tombs, Celtic crosses and the early Christian manuscripts such as *The Book of Kells*.

Writers and playwrights from Ireland achieved some degree of fame – Sheridan, Oscar Wilde, George Bernard Shaw, James Joyce and Samuel Beckett are all celebrated Irish names.

Folk music is a feature of the Irish culture, and various jigs and reels may be performed in Irish bars and pubs, and at the musical fairs (*Fleadh*) that occur around the country.

Irish dishes are characterised by the use of potatoes, reflecting the staple diet of the past. Also, *disheens* (white pudding made from the entrails of a pig) and black pudding are popular. *Stirrabout* is a porridge which probably originated from Scotland. Other dishes have similar unusual names – *colcannon* (mashed potatoes with chopped greens and onions) and *boxty* (a sort of potato pie) for example. Such dishes may well be washed down with a glass of Guinness (probably Ireland's most famous beverage) or Irish whiskey.

On the sporting scene, the Irish may be seen participating in hurling, different forms of football, yachting or a curious form of bowls known simply as road bowling – this involves the hurling of small iron balls along lonely country lanes!

Luxembourg

Key facts about Luxembourg

Area:	2586 square km	**Religion**:	Roman Catholic
Population:	366 000	**Government**:	Constitutional monarchy and representative democracy
Employed in:	Agriculture (4.2%) Industry (33.4%) Services (62.4%)		
Language:	'Letzeburgesch' is national language, but French and German are used for administrative purposes	**Council votes**: **Commissioners**: **European MPs**: **Capital**: **Currency**:	2 1 6 Luxembourg City Luxembourg franc

ACTIVITY

Make a list of those things that you associate with Luxembourg. Compare your list with a partner. Are you surprised about how little (or how much) you know about this state? Why might this be so?

Geography

Luxembourg is bounded by France, Germany and Belgium. It is a hilly country, rich in woodland. The country is almost 82 km long and 58 km wide. The total length of the country's boundaries is 356 km. The highest point is in the northern area and is part of the Ardennes (over 1800 m). The main rivers are the Moselle, the Our and the Sure.

Population

Of Luxembourg's total population of 366 000, women make up 58.1 per cent and men 41.9 per cent. In terms of age structure, 17.6 per cent are under the age of 15, 69.1 per cent are aged between 15 and 65, and 13.2 per cent are over 65 years of age.

There are proportionately more foreigners in Luxembourg than in any other EC state – the figure is more than 36 per cent of the total population. The average density of population is 141 inhabitants per square km.

ACTIVITY

Why do you think there is a larger proportion of foreigners in Luxembourg than in any other EC state?

Politics and government

Under Luxembourg's electoral system, polling usually occurs on a Sunday and is compulsory. Luxembourgers are eligible to vote at the age of 18. There is no system of compulsory military service in Luxembourg.

Luxembourg is a representative democracy and constitutional monarchy with executive power vested in the grand duke. This power is actually exercised by the members of the government under the co-ordinating authority of the prime minister.

The parliament is known as the Chamber of Deputies and, as in other states, this represents the people. It can, along with the grand duke, introduce legislation. The Luxembourg MPs or deputies, are elected by the voters. The role of the Chamber is to examine and debate bills laid before it. No final vote may be taken on bills until the Council of State has delivered an opinion. The functions of the Council of State are to consider bills and amendments referred to it, to settle administrative disputes and give opinions on any other matters referred to it by the grand duke.

As far as political parties go in Luxembourg, at the last election, the Christian Social party received most seats, followed by the Socialist Workers Party, the Democratic Liberal Party, the Communists and the Alternative Greens.

Economy and industry

The economic structure and geographical position of Luxembourg have led the country into close co-operation with other EC states, especially Belgium and The Netherlands, with the creation of Benelux.

Industry the discovery of iron ore, in around 1850, marked the turning point for Luxembourg. An important steel industry came into being in the south-western corner of the country, drawing thousands of foreign workers into the ore mines and steel factories, and bringing prosperity to the country as a whole. Since the end of the Second World War, great efforts have been made to bring diversity into industry in Luxembourg. Aluminium, glass, cement, tyres and computer manufacturers have established plants in Luxembourg. In addition, dams have been built in Esch-sur-Sure and Rosport, and Vianden houses Europe's largest pumping station producing hydro-electricity. Many incentives such as tax rebates, assistance in obtaining credit and so on have been introduced to encourage companies to set up in the state of Luxembourg. Yet, despite these efforts, Luxembourg's industrial labour is decreasing in number, coupled with an increase in employment in the services sector.

Agriculture of the land set aside for agricultural purposes, 25 per cent is arable and 20 per cent is used for pasture. The main crops cultivated are barley, wheat, potatoes, oats and grapes for wine. The 'Bon Pays' is the main growing area, and is also most important for rearing dairy and beef cattle. Market gardening is important near the towns of the south. Vines are cultivated in the Moselle Valley with Luxembourg's Riesling, Auxerrois and Gewurztraminers being important quality wines.

Services Luxembourg plays a major role as a prominent international financial centre. Numerous banks and important investment trusts have settled in the capital, with fiscal legislation favouring holding companies.

The growing concentration of EC banking interests is illustrated by the fact that there are over 170 banks represented in the state. This has been underlined by Luxembourg's emphasis on Eurobonds and the ECU. Products can actually be purchased with ECUs in Luxembourg.

Big insurance companies have set up subsidiaries in the capital city and Luxembourg could well become one of the major centres of the future in this important part of the business world.

Number of banking firms by geographical origin in Luxembourg, 1990

Country of origin	*Number of banks*
Germany	38
Luxembourg/Belgium	22
France	20
Scandinavia	20
Switzerland	16
USA	12
Italy	11
Japan	9
Other countries	24

Source: Statec

ACTIVITY

1 Draw a bar chart to illustrate the information shown above.
2 Why do you think so many different banks have set up in Luxembourg?

3 List the possible effects of an increased number of financial institutions from other countries wishing to establish themselves in Luxembourg.

Exports major exports from Luxembourg include steel and other heavy industry products, chemicals and agricultural produce. Luxembourg's main customers are the EC (70 per cent of trade), the USA and Switzerland.

Culture

In the past, Luxembourg was at the crossroads of Europe, which means that its culture has various influences exerted upon it including Celtic, Germanic, Roman and Frank.

The City of Luxembourg offers a multilingual, cultural, theatrical and musical life in winter on a high international level. In the summer months, there is a host of public concerts including folklore performances, sports competitions and so on. In addition, many towns hold wine festivals throughout the year.

Luxembourg has various gastronomic specialities including Ardennes ham, served raw or cooked, and *quenelles* (dumplings made from calves' liver). Luxembourg is also noted for its chocolates and confectionery.

The wine industry is an important aspect of the economy in Luxembourg – it offers a range of white wines, with the Moselle versions being very popular. The more select of these are the Riesling and Pinot selections. The grapes produced in Luxembourg are also used for the production of fresh grape juice.

Brewing is a traditional industry in Luxembourg with beer now produced in modern breweries. Such beers are becoming increasingly popular in the countries to which they are exported.

Luxembourgers seem to enjoy the same sort of sports as the other Benelux states – there are two golf courses in the country and this remains a popular pastime.

ACTIVITY

1 Is Luxembourg an insignificant EC member? Give reasons for your answer.
2 Visit a local store to find out what sort of goods, produced in Luxembourg, are available in the UK.
3 What do you think Luxembourg has gained from EC membership?

The Netherlands

Key facts about The Netherlands

Area:	41 160 square km	**Religion**:	Roman Catholic (36%)
Population:	14.5 million		Protestant (32%)
Employed in:	Agriculture (4.9%)	**Government**	Parliamentary
	Industry (28.1%)		democracy and
	Services (67.0%)		hereditary monarchy
Language:	Dutch, Frisian	**Council votes**:	5
Capital:	Amsterdam	**Commissioners**:	1
Political capital:	The Hague	**European MPs**:	25
Currency:	guilda		

Geography

The Netherlands is a relatively small country in European terms, stretching 300 km from north to south and about 200 km from east to west. The country borders Germany to the east and south-east, and Belgium to the south and west. It has a lengthy North Sea coastline as its northern border. Over 50 per cent of the total land area of The Netherlands is below sea level which has meant that, like Belgium, the land immediately behind the North Sea coast has had to be reclaimed (polders). Many lakes, rivers and canals help to characterise the Dutch landscape with three of Europe's major rivers – the Rhine, Scheldt and Maas (Meuse in France) passing through Dutch territory to reach the North Sea. This helps to underline the importance of Dutch international ports.

Population

The population of 14.5 million has been swelled by an influx of people from the former Dutch colonies of Indonesia and Surinam in the late 1960s and 1970s. The number of foreigners resident in The Netherlands amounts to around 559 000 with 76 000 of these being migrant workers (25 per cent of which come from Belgium).

The average density is 349 inhabitants per square km – making The Netherlands one of the most densely populated countries in the world. The greatest concentration of population is in the three western provinces of North Holland, South Holland and Utrecht. The least populated area is the province of Flevoland.

Of the total population, 20 per cent are under the age of 15, 68.1 per cent are aged between 15 and 65, and 11.9 per cent are over 65. Dutch is the national language, although the Frisian minority in the north-east speak their own language.

Politics and government

Under the Dutch political system, polling day occurs on a Wednesday and all Dutch citizens aged 18 or over are entitled to vote. Compulsory military service exists.

The Netherlands is divided into 12 provinces – Groningen, Flevoland, Friesland, Drenthe, Overijssel, Gelderland, Utrecht, North Holland, South Holland, Zeeland, North Brabant and Limburg. The Dutch political system is a parliamentary democracy and a hereditary monarchy, with the sovereign (the queen) and the cabinet together constituting the government. It is the role of the queen to appoint ministers on the recommendation of the prime minister, and to appoint the cabinet with the prime minister. As with other European states, government operates at two levels in The Netherlands – at regional (or provincial) level and at national level.

Provincial level each of the 12 provinces noted above has a Provincial Council and a Provisional Executive (responsible for day-to-day business). Both of these are chaired by a queen's commissioner, appointed by the government.

National level the Dutch parliament (States-General) consists of two chambers. The *First Chamber* comprises 75 members elected indirectly by the Provincial Councils, while the *Second Chamber* has 150 members who are directly elected by a system of proportional representation for a period of four years. It is only the government or members of the Second Chamber that can introduce bills. The First Chamber has no right of amendment. A Council of State (the highest advisory body in the land) advises on proposals for legislation.

An independent *judiciary* exists in The Netherlands. Within this, all courts are presided over by judges who are appointed for life. There is no trial by jury, although a considerable right of appeal exists.

In the Dutch elections of 1986, nine political parties were represented in the Second Chamber. A feature of the Dutch system is that parties are largely organised on a religious basis. This does not usually make for stable government, although an efficient civil service and the presence of the queen in the system means that disastrous consequences are avoided.

ACTIVITY

Many people view the Dutch as being a very liberally-minded people. To support this view, the example of allowing euthanasia in certain cases is often cited. This cannot be carried out without the expert approval of two doctors but nevertheless it still exists.

As a class, discuss whether you think euthanasia is a good idea or not. How would you feel if the EC ruled that it must be allowed in all member states?

Economy and industry

Despite the very efficient agricultural sector of the Dutch economy, the country is also important as an industrial producer. The general government approach is anti-protectionist.

Industry the rebuilding of Rotterdam after the Second World War meant that the port could respond to modern trade trends – such trade in areas like bulk cargoes (especially petroleum and metallic ores) allowed Rotterdam to become the main European petrochemical port, with the Dutch chemical industry located in Limburg. Today, Rotterdam is considered as one of the main gateways to Europe and beyond.

Dutch industry is dominated by four multinational companies – Philips, Unilever, Royal Dutch Shell and Akzo. Philips now employs 345 000 people worldwide in the electrical appliances sector – an industry started up in Eindhoven with the establishment of the first electric light bulb by the Philips brothers in 1891.

The Dutch make extensive use of natural gas – about 95 per cent of domestic households are connected to the supply. Much electricity is also produced using natural gas with a large proportion being exported to European Community partners.

An important feature of Dutch industrial life is the number of people who live in the *Randstad* – an urban arc consisting of Amsterdam, Utrecht, Rotterdam, The Hague and other towns to the west. Over half of the total population lives in this area.

Agriculture although 54 per cent of Dutch land is used for agricultural purposes, less than 5 per cent of the working population is involved in the sector. This is explained by the highly intensive nature of Dutch agriculture with most farms being highly mechanised and many specialising in artifical insemination, selective breeding and computerised feed systems. One result of this 'high-tech' farming has been milk volumes so large that the EC has been obliged to impose quotas to limit production.

The Netherlands has been the principal supplier of goods such as early tomatoes, cucumbers and lettuce for some time, much of which is cultivated in glasshouses. In addition, tulip bulbs are cultivated by the Dutch for sale worldwide and the famous bulbfield trips are merely an off-shoot of this. The Dutch are also the world's largest exporters of dairy products such as milk, butter and cheese (Edam and Gouda cheese, with their distinctively coloured skins, are familiar to most people in the UK for example).

Services The Netherlands is a destination for many tourists. This sector employs many people, especially in the hotel, catering and transport services.

The port of Rotterdam also offers services and is a large employer in areas such as cargo transportation. The capital Amsterdam hosts an international airport at Schipol, which itself has employment opportunities in the service sector and this is supported by the public transport systems required by a modern European capital.

Exports more than 50 per cent of Dutch agricultural products are exported. In fact, the Dutch dominate the world export markets in cut flowers and potted plants. Other major exports include minerals, finished goods (textiles), food, beverages and tobacco, vehicles, electrical appliances and chemical products. Chief customers include the European Community, USA, Sweden and Switzerland.

Culture

A glance at any Dutch travel brochure will reveal a host of events celebrated by the population. In 1992, jazz festivals, a Rembrandt festival, an exhibition of European fine arts and a regatta at Tjalk all took place alongside the usual flower exhibitions – notably, the *Floriade, Keukenhof* and the *Flower Corsos*. These floral exhibitions reflect the horticultural skills that have given the Dutch such a famous reputation across the world.

The Netherlands has spawned a number of famous artists – Rembrandt, Frans Hals and later Van Gogh, to name but a few.

Dutch cuisine is sometimes described as plain or basic – a typical breakfast might consist of a variety of cheeses, ham and salami with bread rolls and jam. There are, however, some Dutch specialities including *Hutspot* (a Dutch hotpot) and fish-based delicacies often involving herrings, smoked eel, mackerel and mussels.

Traditional beverages include *Jenever* (a strong gin), *Advocaat* and *Curacao*. However, Dutch people do like to drink beer too – this is usually the German style.

Many Dutch people are involved in sporting activities – the recent success of the national football team has brought it to the forefront. However, hockey is a major sport in The Netherlands too. The Dutch are also famous for water-based sports including swimming, rowing and sailing. Lesser known Dutch sports include a version of mixed basketball called *Korfball* and a game known as *Kolf*. In addition, a long-distance skating race – the *Elfstedentocht* – is staged between 11 towns in the Friesland province. Any visitor to The Netherlands will probably be amazed at the number of bicycles on the roads – this form of transport seems to be the national mode. This may reflect a Dutch concern for the environment, which in turn may mean that The Netherlands argues strongly on environmental issues within the EC.

ACTIVITY

Consider the Benelux states and then answer the following questions:

1 How important do you think the membership of the Benelux countries in the European Community is?
2 How do you view the three members of Benelux?
3 To what extent are the Benelux states likely to be 'European' minded?
4 Why do you think Belgium has come to assume a central role in the EC?
5 What has The Netherlands gained from EC membership?
6 What is the possible effect on Luxembourg of her being the home of some of the EC institutions?

Portugal

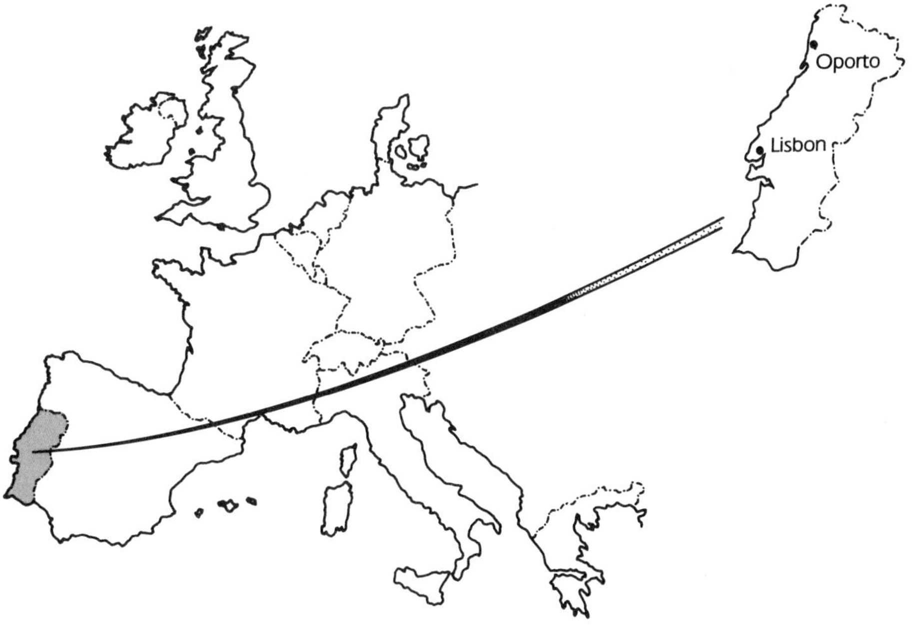

Key facts about Portugal

Area:	92 082 square km	**Religion**:	Roman Catholic
Population:	9.8 million	**Government**:	Parliamentary republic
Employed in:	Agriculture (23.9%)	**Council votes**:	5
	Industry (33.9%)	**Commissioners**:	1
	Services (42.2%)	**European MPs**:	24
Language:	Portuguese	**Currency**:	escudo
Capital:	Lisbon		

Geography

Situated at the extreme south-west of Europe and part of the Iberian peninsula, mainland Portugal is classed as a Mediterranean state. Portugal is a rectangle extending 560 km from north to south, and 220 km from east to west. Its frontier with Spain is 1215 km long. The archipelagoes of the Azores and Madeira form an important part of Portuguese territory, and are autonomous regions with their own political and administrative systems.

The main rivers are the Tagus (910 km), the Douro (800 km) and the Sado. The country's most important trading ports are Lisbon, Oporto and Setubal.

The Azores consists of nine islands in the mid-Atlantic, 1500 km from the Portuguese coast. The two islands of the Madeira group are off the African coast, 1000 km south-west of Lisbon.

Population

Of the total Portuguese population, 24 per cent are under the age of 15, 64.2 per cent are aged between 15 and 65, and 11.8 per cent are over the age of 65. The population has an average density of 110 inhabitants per square km and divides into some 9.3 million living on the mainland, with the remainder resident on the Atlantic islands. The capital, Lisbon, has a population of some 808 000.

Since 1960, about two million workers have left Portugal with about 25 per cent making for other EC countries.

Politics and government

The Portuguese electoral system allows for polling on a Sunday or a public holiday. All citizens reaching the age of 18 are entitled to vote. A system of compulsory military service exists in Portugal.

Portugal is divided up into 18 districts – Aveiro, Beja, Braga, Braganca, Castelo Branco, Coimbra, Evora, Faro, Guarda, Leiria, Lisboa, Portalegre, Porto, Santarem, Setubal, Viana do Castelo, Vila Real and Viseu. Each district has a civil governor, appointed by the government.

The Constitution of the Portuguese Republic was drawn up in 1976, and revised in 1982 and 1989. It is a semi-presidential regime based on a representational democracy.

There are four major bodies exercising power – the president, the Assembly, the Government and the Courts of Law.

The president is elected by universal and direct secret ballot for a period of five years. Subject to limitations imposed by the constitution, the president can dissolve parliament, appoint the prime minister and dismiss the government.

The Assembly represents all Portuguese citizens and exercises legislative power. It is also responsible for ensuring that constitutional laws are adhered to. Made up of 230 members, elected by 20 constituencies by direct and universal suffrage, the Assembly serves for a period of 4 years.

The Government is responsible for running the general policy of the state and the Portuguese civil service. The prime minister is appointed by the president by taking into account the results of the legislative elections. Government programmes have to be approved by the Assembly.

The Courts of Law are responsible for the administration of justice when breaches of constitutional law or government legislation occur.

Current Portuguese political parties include the Social Democrats (the largest party represented in government), the Socialists, the Portuguese Communists, the Social Democratic Centre and the National Solidarity Party.

Economy and industry

The progress and modernisation of the economy is the biggest challenge facing the Portuguese government today. In deciding to join the European Community, the country believed it strengthened its international prestige and worldwide dimension.

Industry Portugal is only moderately industrialised, although rapid developments have been made. Many of the older industries are based on agriculture, forestry and fishing – for example, cork production, paper, wine, olive oil and sardine canning.

Textiles, however, have been important for many years in Porto, Braga and Lisbon. This industry has made use of imported raw materials. Today, metal-working, engineering and consumer goods are among the newer industries set up in recent years. Both Lisbon and Porto have steel-making, engineering and chemical industries, while some of these are also to be found in Setubal, Barriero and Estarreja. In addition, Lisbon and Azambuja are involved in motor vehicle manufacture. As a result of tourist interest, footwear and souvenir manufacture have recently become more prominent.

Small deposits of coal are mined near Porto but most fuel requirements are imported. Deposits of pyrites, kodin and gold are also found in small deposits. Around 47 per cent of power is produced by hydro-electricity.

ACTIVITY

List the problems that you think the Portuguese government would encounter in attempting to modernise their economy. How could the EC help in this objective?

Agriculture Portugal is the world's leading supplier of cork oak with an annual output of around 110 000 tonnes. The pine forests of the north produce timber, paper pulp, turpentine and resin.

Portugal is not yet self-sufficient in food production – the farms in the north are small, often less than 2 hectares in area and grow several different crops such as maize, rye, beans and potatoes. On the other hand, the farms of the Alentejo plain are very large with many producing just wheat. Where ample water is available, rice is also grown.

Typical Mediterranean crops such as olives, figs, vines, almonds and citrus fruit are grown in the Algarve and Baixo Alentejo. Olives are used for olive oil, some of which is important in the process of canning sardines. Livestock is reared on many farms – mostly cattle, although sheep and goats are reared in the south.

Many small ports are involved in local fishing and a few of the major ports use the distant waters of the Atlantic. The main catch is sardines at over 100 000 tonnes per annum. Tunny fishing is also important, especially from the south coast.

Services the pleasant summer climate makes Portugal a major attraction for tourists and it is a major source of income, especially in the Algarve and the area to the west of Lisbon. Some 13 million visitors visit Portugal each year, underlining the importance of this sector.

Exports major Portuguese exports include textiles and clothing, electrical machinery and equipment, food and beverages, pulp and paper, and wood and cork.

Portugal's main customers are the EC with over 70 per cent of exports followed by the EFTA states, the USA and Japan. An important priority for Portugal is to increase the diversity of exports, to increase the technical type of exports and to move away from more traditional products.

Culture

Portugal has a rich cultural heritage. This is illustrated by the Manueline style which reflects a closeness with the sea and the great discoveries of the 15th and 16th centuries. Everywhere, the maritime tradition is celebrated – ropes, knots and anchors adorn many buildings.

Portugal's past is preserved through numerous monuments, such as the Roman Temple of Diana, the Gothic Monastery of Batalha and the Renaissance Convent of Christ in Tomar.

Portuguese folklore is an important cultural aspect and this is celebrated in a wide variety of costumes and singing from all over Portugal. Expert arts such as lace and embroidery working are evident, as is fine pottery work. In many other areas – wrought iron, cork and copper, for example – the skill of the Portuguese can be witnessed. Both jewellery and Arraisolos carpets are also crafted.

The Portuguese tradition remains alive through dancing, singing, habits and customs – rivers are areas around which this culture has emerged. For example, in the Douro area, the tradition of grape harvesting is celebrated annually. Religious interests are expressed in various feasts and pilgrimages which take place from north to south.

The discoveries of lands in the East led to the Portuguese introducing spices such as coriander, pepper, ginger and curry powders into Europe. They were the first to introduce rice and tea, and brought coffee and peanuts from Africa. Portuguese cuisine includes a variety of fish dishes, including grilled sword-fish (*espada grelhado*) and the use of spices is understandably still prominent in cooking. The Portuguese tend to be sweet-toothed and specialities include at least 200 different types of pastry.

Today, the wines of Portugal accompany popular and traditional cuisine – there are over 100 different types apart from the unique Port and Madeira which include the *petillant* or lightly sparkling wines, widely available throughout the EC.

The practice of bull-fighting still exists in Portugal, but has largely been taken over by football as a spectator sport. Here, names like Eusebio and Benfica are world famous. The Portuguese are also keen on marathon running and have achieved success at Olympic level.

ACTIVITY

Imports of the smaller states, 1989 (million ECU)

Importing state	*Total imports*	*EC*	*USA*	*Japan*	*Rest of world*
Belgium/Luxembourg	93 008	64 140	5564	3210	20 094
Denmark	24 723	12 940	1501	760	9522
Greece	14 683	9142	500	969	4072
Ireland	15 687	10 960	2355	723	1649
Netherlands	101 550	61 107	8770	3570	28 103
Portugal	17 145	11 636	764	529	4216

Exports of the smaller states, 1989 (million ECU)

Exporting state	*Total exports*	*EC*	*USA*	*Japan*	*Rest of world*
Belgium/Luxembourg	90 851	66 837	4373	1188	18 453
Denmark	25 942	13 152	1487	1103	10 200
Greece	6883	4486	391	81	1925
Ireland	18 753	13 928	1479	408	2938
Netherlands	105 090	79 575	4521	984	20 010
Portugal	11 498	8196	691	129	2482

Source: Eurostat

Consider the tables above and then answer the following questions:

1 Of the smaller states, which has a) the biggest volume of trade and b) the smallest volume of trade?

2 The Benelux states import a fair proportion of goods from Japan. What sort of goods might these be?

3 What percentage of Ireland's imports are from a) the EC and b) the rest of the world?

4 The Netherlands exports a large proportion to the rest of the world. What products might these be?

5 Why are Greek exports to Japan so few?

6 What do the tables tell you about the importance of the EC to the smaller states?

ACTIVITY

Consider the political systems of the smaller EC states.

1 Draw up a table which compares the features of the different systems. You might include items such as voting age, electoral system, polling day, prominent parties, organisation of parliament, type of system.
2 Which system seems most likely to be effective and which one seems to be least effective in your opinion? Give your reasons.

ACTIVITY Review your progress: 6

1 Which of the seven smaller EC states has a) the largest area and b) the smallest area?
2 List the currencies of the seven smaller EC states.
3 Rank the smaller EC states in order of economic size.
4 What and where are the following:
a) The Ardennes?
b) Jutland?
c) The Corinth Canal?
d) The Ďail?
e) The Scheldt?
f) Polders?
g) The Meuse?
5 How do the political systems of the smaller EC states differ from one another?
6 Match the following agricultural products to the relevant EC state:
a) potatoes, oats and grapes
b) tomatoes, beans, olives and tobacco
c) mushrooms, asparagus and chicory
d) olives, figs and citrus fruits
e) meat and dairy products, pig products
f) cheese, bulbs and salad goods
g) sheep, wool and cattle

Summary

- There is a wide variety of geographical landscapes within the smaller EC states resulting in different products.
- There is a distinction between the Mediterranean-style economies of the southern EC states and those of the north.
- Democratic-style governments are in place in all the smaller EC states, but the forms of government range from republican to parliamentary democracy.
- Each of the smaller EC states has distinctive cultural differences which contribute to a Community of varied tastes and influences.

Assignment 10 The comparative report

Task 1 Select two of the smaller EC states and prepare a comparative report on them dealing with areas such as population, form of government, economy and culture. Draw conclusions from your study.

Task 2 Present your information in an oral presentation (no longer than ten minutes) to your European Studies group. Your presentation should make use of audio-visual aids wherever possible.

Task 3 As part of your oral presentation, prepare a handout which can be used to involve your audience.

Task 4 In a written evaluation, assess your performance in the oral presentation, stating how successful you think your handout was in getting your message across to your audience.

Assignment 11 The European quiz

Task 1 As a whole group, organise a European quiz for other students to take part in. Allocate responsibilities to individual members of your group. You will need to consider such things as:

- location, time and date of quiz
- category of questions to be asked
- the compilation of the questions
- the basic rules of the quiz
- whether a prize will be awarded
- who will ask the questions
- use of audio-visual equipment for picture questions
- entry fees.

Task 2 Having run the quiz, evaluate a) the performance of the group as a whole and b) your individual contribution to the event.

7 The characteristics of Europe: 2

Aims

- To identify and describe the geographical composition of the major EC member states
- To develop an awareness of the socioeconomic profiles of the major EC member states
- To encourage an awareness of the political systems of the major EC member states
- To recognise and consider the cultural characteristics of the major EC member states.

Relevant BTEC Outcome Performance Criteria

4a Geographical make-up of member states accurately identified and described
4b Awareness shown of socioeconomic and political profile of member states
4c Cultural diversity of member states recognised and illustrated

The major EC member states

The five major states of the European Community – France, Germany, Italy, Spain and the UK are by far the largest members in terms of gross domestic product (GDP), area and population. For these reasons, they are sometimes collectively referred to as the 'Big Five'. This status is reflected in the EC institutions, where the five have the largest number of Commissioners, European MEPs and votes in the Council of Ministers underlining their political importance. Of the five, Germany is easily the largest – this was the case even before unification, but now joined with the former German Democratic Republic (East Germany), she is the leading economic force within the EC. Her power has already been experienced in the UK with the 'Black Wednesday' financial crisis on Wednesday 16 September 1992, and the subsequent British withdrawal from the European Exchange Rate Mechanism. Many believed this crisis was due to the stance of the German *Bundesbank* caused by the strength of the German mark which was unchecked by the Bundesbank.

ACTIVITY

1 How do you think the smaller EC states view the higher status of the 'Big Five'?
2 What justifications are there for these larger states enjoying a higher profile and status in the Community?

France

Key facts about France

Area:	544 000 square km	**Religion**:	Roman Catholic (90%)
Population:	55.6 million	**Government**:	Republic
Employed in:	Agriculture (7.9%) Industry (33%) Services (59.1%)	**Council votes**:	10
		Commissioners:	2
		European MPs:	81
Language:	French, Breton, Alsatian, Basque, Corsican, Catalan, Languedoc	**Currency**:	French franc
		Capital:	Paris

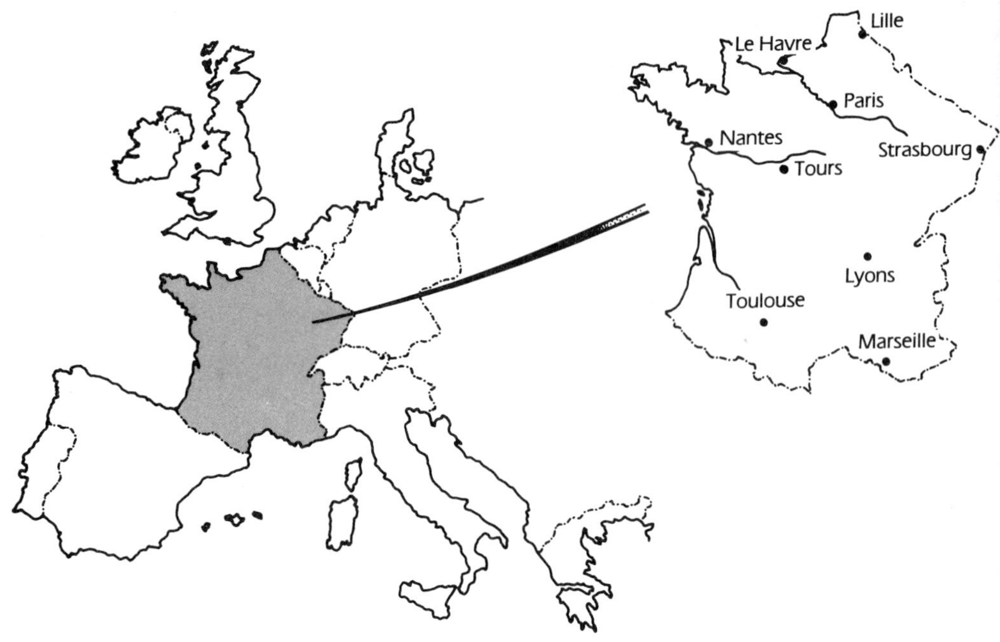

Geography
French coastlines are on the English Channel, the Atlantic and the Mediterranean – they total 3120 km and land frontiers extend for approximately 2170 km. Natural geographical frontiers are provided by the Pyrenees in the south-west (bordering Spain), the western Alps in the south-east (bordering Italy), and the Jura and the Vosges in the east (bordering Switzerland and Germany). France also borders Luxembourg to the east and Belgium to the north-east. The total land area includes the island of Corsica in the Mediterranean, off the west coast of Italy.

France has four main river systems – the Seine (flowing into the English Channel), the Loire and Garone (flowing into the Atlantic) and the Rhône (flowing into the Mediterranean).

French mountain ranges include the Alps, the Alpes Maritimes, the Vosges, the Jura, the Cevennes, the Pyrenees and the Massif Central. The highest mountain in Europe, Mont Blanc (4805 m) lies partly in French territory.

Population
Large urban populations are a feature of France – over 75 per cent of French people live in urban areas, many of whom inhabit the three conurbations of Paris, Lyons and Marseilles (each having over one million inhabitants). The average population density is 101 inhabitants per square km. The total population houses some 4.4 million foreigners – mainly Algerians, Tunisians and Moroccans, but also a sizeable proportion from EC states (850 000 Portuguese, 380 000 Italians and 350 000 Spaniards).

Of the total population of 55.6 million, 21.1 per cent are aged under 15, 65.9 per cent are aged between 15 and 65, and 13 per cent are over the age of 65.

Although the official language is French, it is not unusual to hear many of the dialects that exist.

Government and politics
In France, military service is compulsory for all males. The electoral system allows for polling day to occur on a Sunday, with French people being entitled to vote from the age of 18.

France is divided into 22 regions – Nord-Pas-de-Calais, Ile-de-France, Centre, Picardy, Lower Normandy, Upper Normandy, Brittany, Loire Valley, Poitou-Charentes, Limousin, Aquitaine, Midi-Pyrénées, Champagne-Ardenne, Alsace, Lorraine, Burgundy, Auvergne, Franche-Comte, Rhône-Alpes, Languedoc-Roussillon, Provence-Alpes-Côtes d'Azur and Corsica. There are four overseas departments, four overseas territories and two *collectivites territoriales*.

Under the French Constitution, power is divided between the president, the government and parliament.

The president is directly elected for seven years, is head of the executive and in this capacity appoints the prime minister. The president is also able to appoint and dismiss other ministers on the recommendation of the prime minister, and presides over the Council of Ministers. The president has the power to dissolve the National Assembly (lower chamber of the parliament) and submit major bills to a referendum – for example, the French ratification of the Maastricht Treaty bill.

The government is headed by the prime minister who may be from a different political party than the president. For example, President Mitterand (a Socialist) has worked alongside the right-wing Prime Minister Jacques Chirac. The chief role of the government ministers, under the prime minister, is to determine and direct the policy of the French nation. The government is responsible to parliament.

Parliament has two chambers known as the National Assembly (lower) and the Senate (upper). There are 577 members (*deputies*) in the National Assembly. In addition, there are 317 senators elected indirectly for 9 years by an electoral college made up of the deputies, departmental councillors, the mayors and municipal councillors. One-third of the Senate is renewed every three years.

Bills have to pass through both chambers to become law – if there is disagreement, a committee is formed to seek agreement. If it fails to do so, the National Assembly has the final say. A Constitutional Council consisting of nine members elected for nine years has the task of ensuring that laws passed by the National Assembly are constitutional.

The French judicial system is separate and independent from parliament, illustrating the Western democratic trend of separation of powers. It operates through a network of courts. The death penalty, administered by means of a portable guillotine, was the ultimate sentence until 1981 when it was abolished.

ACTIVITY

1 List the similarities and differences between the French and British systems of government.
2 In a class discussion, consider how successful a republican system of government might be in the UK.

Economy and industry

During the period 1986–90, the French economy experienced something of a recovery which was largely due to falling oil prices, and the beneficial effects of government policy regarding wages and inflation in particular.

Industry France has natural resources in the form of iron ore deposits in Lorraine, natural gas in the south-west, potash in Alsace, bauxite in Provence and some oil in Aquitaine. To these should be added coal deposits in the north, east and in the Massif Central.

France is an important industrial power and among the leading world producers of steel, cars and other manufactured goods. The main industrial centres lie near Paris, the north-east and around Lyons.

The French car industry is the fourth largest in the world (after Japan, the USA and Germany). The industry employs 300 000 workers who produce almost four million vehicles per year. The two main firms are Renault (a nationalised company) and the private PSA (Peugeot-Citröen).

In addition, a very healthy building and construction industry exists in France, with the building and public works sector employing nearly 1 million workers, mostly in the building of houses.

The aerospace industry is also significant. Concentrated around Paris and in Toulouse, it employs 120 000 people and lists among its products Concorde, the Mirage jet and Exocet missiles. France is the third biggest exporter of armaments.

The engineering sector has been successful in France and this success has been exported – for example, the Turkwell Dam in Kenya (Africa's highest dam) is being constructed by a French company. Such engineering expertise has been put to use in the construction of the Channel Tunnel too. French firms have also provided rolling stock for underground rail systems in many US cities.

In the area of electrical generators, turbines, transformers and elevators, France is the fourth largest producer and she has been at the forefront of the development of 'green' industries, such as the pursuit of 'clean' engines.

Agriculture French farms are now well equipped, highly mechanised and heavily subsidised by the state. France's status as largest agricultural country in Western Europe is coupled with her position as second biggest producer of wine (after Italy). Vines cover extensive areas, particularly in Languedoc, Burgundy and Bordeaux.

Arable land and pasture means that France is a large producer of milk, dairy products, beef and fruit juice. However, the most important crop for French agriculture is wheat, followed by oats and maize. Fruit and vegetables are grown in all regions, but especially in the south.

Services the contribution of the services sector to the French economy has been growing rapidly. The most impressive growth has been in the retail sector where Europe's largest retailer, Carrefour, and other groups such as Casino, Auchan and Mammouth have flourished.

In the tourism area, a healthy foreign trade surplus has benefited French hotels, especially the largest group, Accor (ranked fourth largest in the world).

As a provider of employment, the services sector, as in other EC states, is very significant.

Exports major French exports include machinery and vehicles, manufactured goods, chemicals and foodstuffs. Within the export market, luxury goods from the textiles, clothing and footwear sector are particularly important. France's major customers are the EC, the USA and Switzerland.

Culture

In the field of art and literature, there have been many famous French people – Monet, Manet, Delacroix, Toulouse-Lautrec, Voltaire, Rousseau and Satre, to name but a few.

In music too, France has spawned the great – Bizet, Debussy and Ravel are examples of famous classical composers. Important French scientists have included Pasteur and Curie.

French cuisine is famous all over the world, and includes the snails and frogs' legs which people in the UK so closely associate with the French. In addition, there are many hundreds of cheese varieties and a lengthy list of sauces employed in the preparation of dishes, ranging from Piquante to Provencale. A feature of French cuisine is the regional variations that exist.

In terms of beverages, aperitifs are important in France and include Pernod or Ricard and range through to Campari and port, depending upon where in France you are eating.

The French have excelled at rugby and they are also famous for the game of *boules* or *pétanque*, which is played passionately. Cycling, and other outdoor sports such as sailing, fishing and camping, are also pastimes that the French enjoy.

ACTIVITY

Many would say that British people associate themselves most closely with the French of all the EC nationalities.

1 Conduct a quick poll in your European Studies group to determine whether this is the case.
2 Why is the French culture considered to be close to that of the British by some people?
3 How do you think the French perceive the British? What examples can you point to which bear this out?

Germany

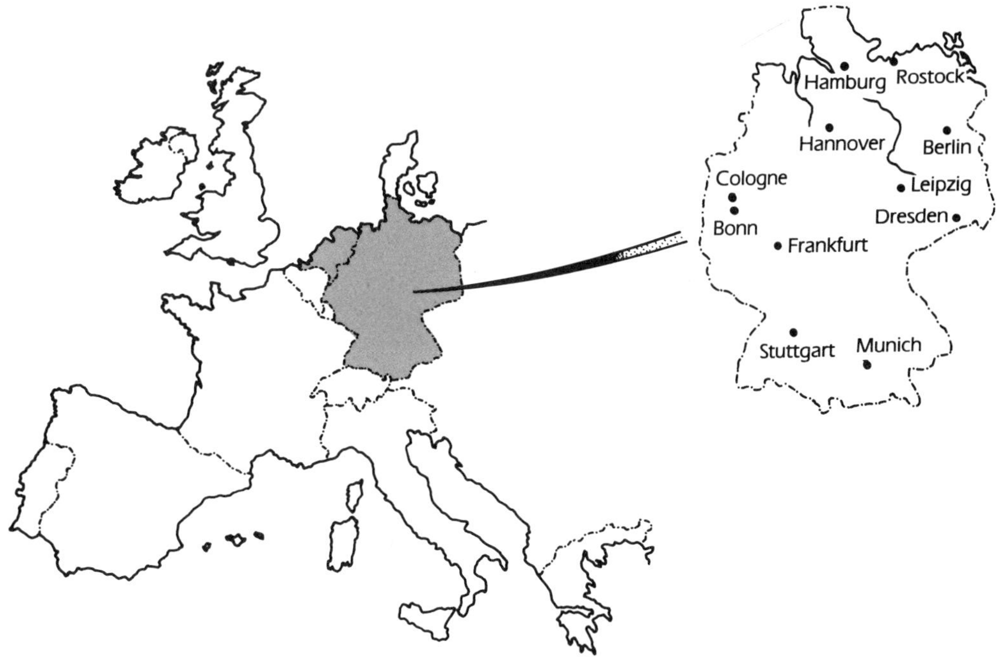

Key facts about Germany

Area:	357 041 square km	**Religion**:	Roman Catholic (43%)
Population:	79 million		Protestant (41%)
Employed in:	*Agriculture (3.7%)	**Government**:	Democratic,
	*Industry (40.9%)		parliamentary
	*Services (37.4%)		state with federal
Language:	German		constitution
Capital:	Bonn**	**Council votes**:	10
Currency:	deutschmark	**Commissioners**:	2
		European MPs:	81

*Figures for the former West Germany only.
**There are plans to reinstate Berlin as Germany's capital.

Geography

The former West Germany covered an area of 248 000 square km which means that unification with East Germany (the former German Democratic Republic) increased the total land area by some 44 per cent. The new Germany borders Denmark to the north, The Netherlands to the north-west, Belgium and Luxembourg to the west, France and Switzerland to the south-west, Austria to the south, and Czechoslovakia and Poland to the east. It could be argued that this places Germany at the very heart of Europe – this is certainly borne out by her political and economic significance within the EC.

The main land area is supplemented by a number of islands – the East and North Frisians, the Schleswig-Holstein islands and those of Mecklenburg and West Pomerania, all situated to the north of Germany. Germany also has one offshore island – that of Heligoland, situated 65 km north of the coast near Denmark.

Natural boundaries include the North and Baltic Seas in the north, part of the Alps, Lake Constance and the River Rhine in the south. The German Alps are located in the Allgau, Bavaria and Berchtesgaden areas.

The main rivers are the Rhine (865 km), the Danube (647 km), the Elbe (700 km), the Weser (440 km) and the Moselle (242 km). Germany's highest mountain is to be found in the Alps – the Zugspitze, at a height of 2,963 m. Lake Constance (known as the *Bodensee* in Germany) covers some 538 square km.

ACTIVITY

1. With a partner, draw up a list of advantages and disadvantages of German unification.
2. What problems do you think the new Germany has encountered by adding significantly to its population?

Population

The greatest population increase in Germany occurred immediately after the Second World War when more than 14 million people fled from the East into the then West Germany. However, the construction of the Berlin Wall put an end to this. After this, the population growth was almost entirely the result of immigrant workers coming to Germany, particularly from Turkey. In fact, there are some five million foreigners in Germany – mostly Turks but also Yugoslavians, Italians and Greeks. Others come from Spain, The Netherlands, the UK, Portugal, France and Belgium. Just less than 1 per cent of the East German population consists of Sorbs (a Slav people) who are native Germans found mainly in the Dresden area. They have their own language which is related to Polish.

The population is unevenly distributed in the way that we have seen in other EC member states – 9 per cent of the old West German population lives in 2 per cent of its former territory around the industrial Ruhr area. Other large conurbations exist too, namely at Frankfurt, Stuttgart, Bremen, Hamburg and Munich in the west; and around Berlin, Dresden and Magdeburg in the east.Since unification (October 1990), the average density of population has become 222 inhabitants per square km. The density is greater in the previous West Germany than it is in the old East Germany.

Of the total population, 16 per cent are under the age of 15, 69 per cent are aged between 15 and 65, and 15 per cent are aged over 65.

Government and politics

Under the German political system, polling day occurs on a Sunday or suitable public holiday. All Germans are entitled to vote from the age of 18. There is also a system of compulsory military service in Germany.

Germany is a federal state and as such it has its own member states which are known as *lander*. There are 16 lander – Baden-Wurttemberg, Bavaria, Berlin, Brandenburg, Bremen, Hamburg, Hesse, Lower Saxony, Mecklenburg-Western Pomerania, North Rhine-Westphalia, Rhineland-Palatinate, Saarland, Saxony, Saxony-Anhalt, Schleswig-Holstein and Thuringia.

Germany is a federal republic – a democratic and social constitutional state based on a parliament. The 'Basic Law' (*Grundgesetz*) of 1949 forms the German constitution. The head of the Federal Republic is the president. The system makes use of a parliament with two chambers and executive power lies with the Federal Government.

The president represents the Federation in national matters and in its international relations. The president is elected for a period of five years by a Federal Convention especially convened for this purpose. The Convention consists of all members of the *Bundestag* (parliamentary chamber elected by voters) and an equal number of members elected by the lander parliaments on the basis of proportional representation.

Parliament is where legislative power is vested. The Bundestag comprises 662 members. The other parliamentary chamber, the *Bundesrat,* consists of members who have been appointed by the separate lander governments. There are 68 members of the Bundesrat divided among the 16 lander. It is through the Bundesrat that the lander are able to participate in legislation and administration of the Federation.

Federal Government here executive power is exercised. The government consists of the Federal chancellor, elected by the Bundestag on the president's proposal, and the Federal ministers who are appointed by the president on the proposal of the chancellor.

The Basic Law allows for judicial authority to be vested in the judges, with the Federal Constitutional Court occupying a special position. It decides on the interpretation of the Basic Law in the event of constitutional disputes between government bodies, on aspects of Federal and lander law, and complaints made by individual citizens regarding constitutional matters. Half of its members are elected by the Bundestag and the other half by the Bundesrat.

After the 1990 elections in Germany, the prominent political parties were the Social Democrats (SPD), the Christian Democrats (CDU), the Christian Social Union (CSU) and the Free Democrats (FDP). Other parties include the Greens and the Party of Democratic Socialism.

ACTIVITY

The powerful German lander

German lander are the most politically powerful of all Europe's regions, with vast budgets allocated by the central government. They pay the teachers, police and other bodies, and sometimes charge their own excise taxes on wine and beer. Income tax is levied by Bonn and then redistributed among the lander – a subject of considerable friction. Central government is responsible for all foreign policy and defence. Lander are jealous of their powers, and have become worried over the years that the EC system – which concentrates on the 12 signatory states of the Treaty – allows the federal government to take decisions which should properly be taken by the landers. That accounts for their desire to be present at the EC's council meetings. Flushed with a new sense of German pride and purpose following unification, the lander show no sign of wanting to take their independence further.

Source: *Sunday Telegraph*, 8 March 1992

Read the article 'The powerful German lander' and then answer the following questions:

1 Why are the German lander so powerful?
2 Why do you think the levying and distribution of income tax is a concern for the lander?
3 Why do the lander have reservations about the EC system of decision-making?

Economy and industry

The economic success of Germany the 'German economic miracle' has been explained by some in terms of the social market economy that was set up after the Second World War. Such a system revolves around maintaining a balance between an effective market and social interests (such as social insurance). In the new Germany, we must draw a distinction between the rapid and successful development of the West and the depressed East.

Industry the industrial revolution came late to Germany but when it did arrive, it took place very rapidly. This was assisted by the presence of mineral resources such as lignite, coal, iron and copper ores and potash. Today, Germany's industrial strength lies in the manufacture of machinery of all types – vehicles, machine tools and industrial plant machinery. But it was not until the late 1960s that manufacturing became the most important sector of the West German economy. The major manufacturing industries are iron and steel, mechanical engineering, vehicle building, electrical engineering, precision instruments, and optical goods and chemicals (with very large companies such as Hoechst, BASF and Bayer being involved in this area). All this means that Germany is one of the world's greatest manufacturing powers – for example, its iron and steel industry is the fourth largest in the world (with steel produced mostly in the Ruhr area) and it is the third largest producer of cars behind Japan and the USA. In addition, the German aerospace industry is significant, employing some 76 000 workers.

The former East Germany was a vital supplier of complete industrial plants, machine tools and precision equipment to other Soviet bloc states. In this, the manufacturing of cars was deliberately restricted in order to favour trains, coaches and freight cars, trucks, farm machinery and ships. It has been suggested that would-be purchasers of Trabant cars had to wait for a period of 15 years before one would become available! East German industry also involved the production of chemicals on a large scale – in particular, plastics and resins which were utilised by the Soviet bloc states.

ACTIVITY

In a class discussion, consider the following statement: 'The German economic miracle is a modern irony. Had Germany not been defeated in the Second World War, this miracle would not have occurred. Of all the Western European powers in 1945, she ultimately gained the most.'

Agriculture family farms are still the norm with about 50 per cent of them worked on the basis that the main family income comes from another source, usually industry. The number of large farms has continued to increase – there were over 5400 farms of over 100 hectares in 1985, for example.

Major products of German agriculture are cereals, potatoes, sugar beet, vegetables, fruit and wine. Pig and poultry farms are also important and are generally run on modern factory principles.

About 43 per cent of the total area of the former East Germany is set aside for agricultural purposes. Here, the produce is basically the same as in the West. The majority of farms fall into the collective category, organised on this basis by the former Soviet bloc authorities.

Throughout Germany the farming of woodland is important – the Western part harvests much timber which meets about 50 per cent of the total domestic demand, while the woodlands of the east have suffered from over-cutting.

Fishing is another facet of German agriculture, although recently total catches in tonnes per year have dropped, forcing the Germans to import a large proportion of fish from other EC countries.

Services as with other EC countries, the service sector of the German economy is the largest. In fact, growth in private services has tended to exceed growth in the manufacturing side of the economy. Although there are certain regulations relating to service employment within Germany, the sector remains very important.

Exports major German exports include road vehicles (Mercedes, BMW), machinery, chemicals, electrical appliances, iron and steel, food, beverages and tobacco. Other successful German exports have been optics, cameras, clocks and watches, radio and television sets, office and data processing equipment. German exports are important to the extent that 25 per cent of jobs depend upon the market. The importance of exports and trade in general is reflected in the inland waterways and harbours that Germany has. The ports of Hamburg, Bremen, Bremerhaven and Lübeck are important examples.

Germany's major customers are the EC, the USA, Switzerland, Austria and Sweden.

Culture

Religion is an important part of cultural life in Germany, with the country roughly dividing up into a Protestant north and a Roman Catholic south. In the southern lander of Bavaria, the religious passion play held every ten years in the village of Oberammergau is an example of the role of religion. A part in the play is sought after by many locals with young women refusing to marry so that they may be considered for the role of the Virgin Mary.

An important part of the German culture is the sense of *heimat* that many Germans feel – this is a sense of belonging to a particular community first and Germany afterwards.

There have been many famous Germans – in the field of science, art, literature and music, names such as Handel, Bach, Beethoven, Goethe, Marx, Brecht and Ernst come to mind. Many Germans have been awarded the Nobel Prize, especially in the physics and chemistry fields.

German architecture spans many different and important periods, and there are examples of buildings from the Carolingian Renaissance, Romanesque, gothic, Renaissance, baroque and rococo. Many chapels, churches and cathedrals exist from these periods, along with the many castles that line the banks of the Rhine. The castle of Neutchwanstein in Bavaria is visited by thousands of people each year.

Sport is a serious business in Germany – with extremely successful professionals in the tennis world (Becker and Graf for example) and on the football pitch, few could blame the Germans for enthusing about sport. Thus, many sports halls and gymnasiums exist throughout the country. Important sports include gymnastics, tennis, shooting, handball, skiing, swimming and angling. Football is the national sport, however, with almost five million Germans belonging to a football club.

Germans have a high preference for meat products, especially pork, and German cuisine includes *sauerkraut* (chopped pickled cabbage), *knodel* (dumplings), many types of *wurst* (sausage) and *kartoffelensalat* (potato salad). Such fare may be washed down with various wines produced in the Moselle or Rhine regions, or one of the many beers that Germany is famous for. In fact, Germans top the list for the consumption of beer and spirits – celebratory festivals such as the *Oktoberfest* held in Bavaria involve much drinking of beer with music provided by brass bands. It is this sort of festival that reinforces the foreign view of Germans as lederhosen-clad individuals.

ACTIVITY

1 Compare the German culture with that of the British. What similarities and differences are there?

2 Why are German people still viewed with suspicion and mistrust by many British people?

ACTIVITY

Race murders shame nation

Violence against foreigners in Germany reached a new pitch on Sunday when neo-Nazis fire-bombed the homes of immigrant workers. They killed two Turkish girls, aged 10 and 14, and a 51-year-old woman.

The attack in the small town of Mölln, between Hamburg and Lübeck, was the worst in more than a year of racist violence, bringing total deaths to 16. Unknown assailants claimed responsibility in a telephone call to police, which they ended with the words '*Heil* Hitler!'

Nine other people were injured, five seriously, when other Turkish occupants of the two fire-bombed buildings were forced to escape from burning upper floors using knotted curtains suspended from the windows. They included a woman of 82 and a young baby.

The brutality of the attack sent shock waves through Germany's political establishment, which has recently attempted to take a firmer stand against racist violence through demonstrations and tougher measures against neo-Nazis.

President Richard von Weizsacker described the attack as 'shattering and disgraceful'. Chancellor Kohl said it was 'a terrible experience and a disgrace for Germany'. There were spontaneous demonstrations against the killings in several cities.

Source: *The European*, 26–9 November 1992

Read the article 'Race murders shame nation' and then answer the following questions:

1 Why do you think these race murders occurred in Germany?
2 Turkish immigrants have been working in Germany for some time. Why should angry Germans decide that now is the time to attack them?
3 'Violence against minority groups is a feature of the German people.' Discuss this statement in your class.
4 How do you think an onlooker from outside Germany would view the German people, based on these killings?

Italy

Key facts about Italy

Area:	301 300 square km	**Religion**:	Roman Catholic
Population:	57.1 million	**Government**:	Parliamentary republic
Employed in:	Agriculture (11.2%)	**Council votes**:	10
	Industry (33.6%)	**Commissioners**:	2
	Services (55.2%)	**European MPs**:	81
Language:	Italian, German, French, Slovene, Latin	**Currency**:	lira
		Capital:	Rome

Geography

Italy borders France to the north-west, Switzerland and Austria to the north, and Yugoslavia to the north-east. The total land area includes the islands of Sicily and Sardinia. Surrounded by Italian territory is the independent republic of San Marino and the Vatican City state.

Italy extends for 1300 km from north to south and has a 7500 km coastline in total. Italy is surrounded by four seas – the Ligurian in the north-west, the Tyrrhenian in the south-west, the Ionian in the south and the Adriatic in the west. To the south of Sicily is the Mediterranean.

About 80 per cent of the total land area consists of hills and mountains with peaks such as a section of Mont Blanc (4807 m), some of the Matterhorn (4477 m) and the Monte Rosa (4634 m). The southern edge of the Alps falls down to the River Po plain, south of which is the 1000 km Apennine Peninsula. The longest river in Italy is the Po at a length of 652 km and it rises in the Cottian Alps and then makes it way down into the Adriatic Sea. Other main rivers include the Arno (rising in the Apennines) which passes through Florence and the Tiber on whose banks the Italian capital, Rome, is built.

Population

At the turn of the 20th century, a population explosion in Italy combined with a general flight from the land into urban areas, led to large-scale emigration, mostly to the USA. However, the number of Italians emigrating has now settled at somewhere in the region of 120 000 per year. Even so, Italy is the most densely populated state in Europe after Germany and the Benelux states with an average density of 189 inhabitants per square km.

About 72 per cent of Italians live in urbanised areas with the population of Rome exceeding 2.8 million, Milan 1.5 million and Naples 1.2 million.

There are many foreigners in Italy with a large proportion originating from European Community countries such as France, Germany and the UK. Recent immigration has tended to be from developing countries.

Of the total population of 57.1 million, 19.9 per cent are under the age of 15, 67.3 per cent are aged between 15 and 65, and 12.8 per cent are aged over 65.

Government and politics

Under the Italian electoral system, polling takes place on Sunday and Monday mornings. All Italians are entitled to vote from the age of 18. The Italian system makes use of compulsory military service.

For administrative purposes, Italy is divided into 20 regions, 5 of which – Valle d'Aosta, Trentino-Alto Adige, Sicily, Sardinia and Friuli-Venezia Giulia – have special constitutions granting them a much wider degree of self-government than the others (Piedmont, Liguria, Lombardy, Veneto, Emilia Romagna, Tuscany, Marche, Umbria, Latium, Abruzzo, Molise, Campania, Apulia, Basilicata and Calabria).

Within the Italian Republic, there is a president and two parliamentary chambers.

The president is elected by parliament and has the power to appoint the president of the Council of Ministers (effectively, the prime minister) and on the PM's recommendations, the other government ministers. The president is also responsible for proclaiming laws and is able to hold up legislation passed by parliament for reconsideration. The president is also commander-in-chief of the armed forces and presides over the High Council of Defence and the High Council of the Magistrature. He is appointed for a period of seven years and can dissolve parliament at any time during his last six months of office.

The parliament is where legislative power resides under the Italian system. Unusually among Western European powers, the two chambers – the Chamber of Deputies and the Senate – have equal powers which means that they can block each other. In the Chamber of Deputies, there are 630 members (deputies) while the Senate has 315 senators. Both chambers are elected for five years by a system of proportional representation. Senators are elected regionally and the president is able to appoint not more than five 'distinguished persons' to the Senate. Another unusual feature of the Italian system is that senators and deputies vote by secret ballot – this means that no one knows whether they have voted for their particular party or not.

About 15 political parties are active within Italian politics, although the Christian Democrats have dominated the coalition governments that are a well-known feature of the Italian Republic for many years.

ACTIVITY

Read the article 'The strength of Campanilismo' and then answer the following questions:

1 Describe in your own words what is meant by 'campanilismo'.
2 For what reasons might the *Leghe* favour a north–south regional split?
3 What might the economic effect on southern Italy be, if this regional split came about?

The strength of 'Campanilismo'

Italy is still dominated by 'campanilismo', the belief that nothing outside the shadow of the local church spire can be worth bothering about. There has been a steadily developing policy of transferring power to the regions. Now, in the prosperous north, the *Leghe* or leagues are favouring a radical north–south regional split, to rid themselves of the fiscal encumbrance of the south.

Source: *Sunday Telegraph*, 8 March 1992

Economy and industry

In the late 1980s, the Italian economy was characterised on the one hand by high unemployment, high interest rates, high public spending and relatively high inflation, while on the other, exports achieved an all-time high, state industries were successfully restructured, Italian firms remained European leaders (Fiat and Olivetti for example), and small and medium-sized businesses like Benetton continued to thrive. In the decades prior to this, Italy had developed from a basically agricultural state to an industrial one. Yet the pace of economic development was not uniform throughout the country and, today, significant differences still exist between the prosperous north and the poorer south.

Industry Italy has few natural minerals with the only important ones being sulphur in Sicily, bauxite and lead ore in the south, and marble quarries in Carrara.

From the turn of the 20th century, modern industrial plants were established in Milan, Turin and Genoa. Among the many industries set up at this time were Fiat (cars), Pirelli (tyres), Olivetti (typewriters and other office machinery), Vespa and Lambretta (scooters), Guzzi (motor-cycles) and Necchi (sewing machines), as well as textiles and chemical industries. State participation in industry commenced with the setting up of IRI, a state-controlled holding company, during the world depression of the 1930s, which soon gained control of most of Italian iron and steel, cement, shipbuilding and machinery industries. It was IRI that founded Alfasud (a branch of Alfa-Romeo, the car manufacturer) and sponsored extension of the Italian motorway system (*autostrada*). In the late 1950s, ENI, another state-sponsored body, started to explore for oil and other energy sources. It took over AGIP (state-owned petrol company) and eventually branched into oil refining and petro-chemical manufacturing. All this meant that by the end of the 1970s, despite the oil crisis of the early part of the decade, Italy (or at least northern Italy) was one of the most advanced industrial regions in Europe.

Today, the major industrial concentration lies within Lombardy, Piedmont and Liguria – this is the centre of Italy's wealth production. Industrial products today include Fiat cars, Feruzzi chemicals, Olivetti office machinery, Buitoni processed food and Benetton clothing. In fact, textile manufacturing is Italy's third biggest business after engineering and construction. Companies such as Buitoni and Benetton started life as small family concerns – now the former exports 30 per cent of its products to the USA (mainly pasta and canned food) and the latter is universally acknowledged as a worldwide name. Another famous Italian export is the hat – the company Barsolino has manufactured headwear for many celebrities across the globe.

Agriculture in the past, Italy's main industry was always agriculture. In the 1930s, the sector employed nearly 50 per cent of the workforce. Between 1954–79, however, about four million agricultural workers left the land, many of them moving into the industrial areas such as Milan and Turin. Now the figure is in the region of 11 per cent, compared with 34 per cent employed in industry. Cereals are the main products of Italian agriculture, particularly wheat, but also corn and rice. Italian farmers produce about 66 per cent of all cereals consumed by the population. Grapes, citrus fruit, olives and almonds are grown extensively. These are supplemented by sugar beet, hemp and flax. Italy is among the world's top producers of olive oil and wine, and produces about 75 per cent of the beef and veal consumed by Italians.

Italian farms, however, tend to be small – some as small as 1 hectare only. The European Community is assisting agriculture with technological training for farmers, co-operative processing and marketing techniques, and soil conservation, among other initiatives.

Although Italy has a very lengthy coastline, the fishing industry is only very small scale and localised, with the total catch being some 50 per cent less than that of France for example.

Exports Italy's major exports are machinery and vehicles, textiles and clothing and food products. Her main customers are the EC, the USA, Switzerland and Libya.

ACTIVITY

Make a list of those items that you would associate with Italy or Italians. Compare your list with a partner. What similarities and differences are there in the two lists?

Culture

Rome is home to temples and museums that are over 2000 years old. It is also the home of St Peter's Basilica, the Castel Sant'Angelo and the Pope. Although 99 per cent of Italians are Roman Catholic, it is probably true to say that the young are no more devout in their religion than young French or Belgians. Many are more anti-church due to the 'closeness' of the Pope. But in the Mezzogiorno, religion is still an important part of life with the parish priest still being an influential figure in the local community.

Italy has spawned many famous people, including Napoleon, Garibaldi, Leonardo da Vinci, Volta, Dante, Donatello, Michelangelo, Botticelli, Raphael, Vivaldi, Rossini, Verdi, Puccini, Mazzini, Cavour and Sophia Loren, and is also famous for the celebration of its saints, e.g. Saint Francis, Saint Thomas Aquinas and Saint Catherine of Siena.

Music and drama festivals occur all year round in Italy and they include ballet and opera in Florence, classical drama in Syracuse and the annual Rossini festival held in Pesaro. A full-blown annual opera season begins each December and runs through until May or June. The principal opera houses are in Rome, Venice, Florence and Naples.

Other traditional Italian festivals are numerous and range from the almond blossom festival of Agrigento in February to the historical regatta of Ventimiglia in August; from the bare-back horse-racing (*palio*) that occurs in many parts of Italy to the annual fair of sweets, toys and presents on Twelfth Night in Rome; and from an exhibition of traditional handicrafts in Aosta in January to the 16th-century football played in medieval costume (*Gioco del Calcio*) in Florence in June.

We tend to associate pizzas and pasta with Italian cuisine, although it is interesting to note that the former were not originally a product of Italy but of Italian immigrants resident in the USA. Italian food is, however, almost universally acceptable – the number of Italian restaurants in many different parts of the world bears this out. The main ingredient, of course, is pasta of which there are many shapes and sizes. A variety of meals making use of this basic food will also contain such ingredients as pine nuts, parmesan, tomatoes, spinach, mushrooms (*funghi*) and ham. Italian delicacies include Parma ham and the special ice-cream that only Italians seem capable of making. Fish, veal, octopus and famous cheeses such as Gorgonzola also contribute to Italian cuisine.

Campari is a distinctly Italian drink and this is supplemented by the many wines that are produced in Italy – white versions such as Soave and Frascati, and red versions such as Valpolicella and Chianti (probably Italy's most famous wine).

In terms of sport, Italians like to cycle and also are passionate football fans. Football is big business in Italy with many talented professionals from other countries being tempted to clubs like AC Milan, Juventus and Latzio, usually for astronomical transfer fees.

ACTIVITY

Lovers fight off racketeers

Young Neapolitan lovers have turned the tables on a gang of racketeers who demanded 'protection money' from them as they canoodled in their cars – by having the men arrested.

Traditionally, courting couples all over Italy have been forced by lack of privacy to make love in parked cars in secluded spots. But the young people of Naples faced an added obstacle in their attempt to find a quiet place – a gang calling themselves 'Security love' had begun charging a 2000 lira admission fee to one of Naples' time-honoured 'lovers' lanes', a disused lay-by at Arzano.

'On Saturday night the park was packed out with over 100 cars ranging from Fiats to Mercedes', says Marshal Salvatore San Filippo, head of the local Carabinieri. 'The gang even sold soft drinks and contraceptives. After 30 years' service I thought I'd seen everything, but this beats the lot. Only Naples could come up with this.' The gang even handed out leaflets offering directions on how to reach their 'sweetheart park'. Most couples thought nothing of paying to enter 'the Park of Love'.

Source: *The European*, 17–20 December 1992

Read the article 'Lovers fight off racketeers' and then answer the following questions:

1 Do you think this type of incident could ever happen in the UK? Give reasons for your answer.

2 What does the article tell you about Italian culture?

3 How do you think British lovers would react to the demand for 'protection money'?

Spain

Key facts about Spain

Area:	504 760 square km	**Religion**:	Roman Catholic
Population:	38.6 million	**Government**:	Constitutional hereditary monarchy/ parliamentary democracy
Employed in:	Agriculture (16.9%) Industry (32.1%) Services (50.9%)		
Language:	Spanish (Castilian) Catalan, Basque Galician	**Council votes**:	8
		Commissioners:	2
Capital:	Madrid	**European MPs**:	60
		Currency:	peseta

Geography

Spain is the third largest country in Europe after the former Soviet Union and France. It has a total of 3904 km of coastline and 1945 km of land frontiers with the countries that it borders; France in the north and Portugal to the west.

With Portugal, Spain forms a considerable part of what is known as the Iberian Peninsula. This is the area of south-western Europe that is separated from the rest of Europe by the Pyrenees mountain range, and from Africa by the narrow Strait of Gibraltar. The east coast of the peninsula is on the Mediterranean Sea and the west coast is on the Atlantic Ocean.

At the centre of the Iberian Peninsula is the Meseta – an arid plateau over which the Rivers Douro and Tagus cross, continuing into Portugal. The Meseta contains several mountain ranges and is drained by five major rivers.

The main mountain ranges, apart from the Pyrenees (separating Spain from France), are the Cordillera Cantabrica and the Cordillera Iberia in the north, and the Sierra Nevada in the south. The major Spanish river networks include the Ebro (910 km), the Guadalquivir (280 km), the Duero (922 km), the Tegus (1082 km) – called the Tajo in Spain and the Tejo in Portugal – and the Guadiana (820 km) which forms part of the Spanish border with Portugal. None of these rivers are navigable for any appreciable distance.

Population

The population in Spain is very unevenly distributed – a current trend is the desertion of the Meseta area for the coastal areas for example. Recent high urbanisation has occurred, leaving two large cities – Madrid and Barcelona. In Madrid, the Spanish capital, there is a population of 3.2 million. Despite this, Spain has one of the lowest population densities in Europe – an average of 76 inhabitants per square km.

Of the total population, 227 000 are foreign residents with over 50 per cent coming from EC states – mostly the UK, Portugal and Germany. Within the total, 23.9 per cent are under the age of 15, 64.3 per cent are aged between 15 and 65, and 11.8 per cent are over the age of 65.

The growth rate in population is low in Spain – about 0.4 per cent, and very similar to that of France and Portugal.

There is little or no immigration into Spain of people from her former colonial territories – this may be due to the lack of jobs available until recently. This means that the population is mostly Spanish, although some disclaim their Spanish nationality with 16 per cent claiming to be Catalan, some 8 per cent Galician and 3 per cent Basque.

ACTIVITY

Why do so many British people find Spain attractive? What does the country offer that people cannot obtain in the UK?

Government and politics

Since 1978 when a new constitution was drawn up, Spain has been a parliamentary monarchy with all power passed from the people through the monarchy to the parliament (*Cortes*), and then on to the elected government. The king, currently Juan Carlos, is commander-in-chief of the armed forces and the head of the state. In this role, he is a symbol of the unity and permanent nature of the state. He represents Spain in her relations with the outside world.

Under the Spanish political system, elections are held every 4 years with all Spaniards aged 18 or over entitled to vote. A system of compulsory military service for men exists.

A feature of the Spanish system is the existence of 17 autonomous communities which have varying degrees of self-government. So far, Catalonia, the Basque Country, Galicia and Andalusia have received the broadest measures of self-rule. The other Spanish communities or provinces are Asturias, Cantabria, La Rioja, Navarne, Aragon, Valencia, Murcia, Castile-La Mancha, Estremadura, Castile-Leon, Madrid, the Balearic Islands and the Canary Islands. The North African cities of Ceuta and Melilla are to be granted special status.

The Spanish parliament (*Cortes Generales*) has two chambers like many of the other EC states. Within the Cortes, the *Congress of Deputies* (lower chamber) consists of 350 members elected by a system of proportional representation in elections in the provinces. The upper chamber – the Senate, consists of 225 senators who are either elected by the provinces or appointed by the legislative bodies of the autonomous communities. Local elections for Spanish councillors in some 8000 municipalities are held at the same time as general elections.

Spanish legislation is normally adopted by both chambers, but the final decision lies with the Congress of Deputies, if agreement cannot be reached. The Chamber of Deputies therefore enjoys a similar status to that of the lower chambers of many EC member states. Like the UK House of Lords, the Spanish Senate has limited powers to delay legislation passed to it by the Chamber of Deputies.

Under the 1978 Constitution, a Spanish judiciary is responsible for maintaining and protecting the basic freedoms and legitimate interests of all citizens.

Spain also has a Constitutional Court (which is separate from the judiciary) to deal with laws that are no longer considered to be constitutionally acceptable, and to settle disputes between the state and the autonomous communities.

Economy and industry

Since 1982, successive socialist governments in Spain have pursued an economic policy involving the containment of inflation, encouragement of more freedom and flexibility in business, and rationalisation and modernisation of heavy industry.

Industry compared with other Western European states, industrialisation came late to Spain and in many ways the modernisation programme created in 1984 was a necessary development. This programme aimed to make cuts in the workforce, to restructure and to introduce modern technology. Spain is now the tenth largest industrial country in the world – the north coast has large coal reserves (producing 16 million tonnes per year) and the Sierra Morena region is a substantial producer of metals such as copper, silver and lead.

In terms of heavy industry, a public holding company – INI (National Institute for Industry) – has dominated for some time. INI is one of the 50 biggest trading companies in the world and accounts for more than 30 per cent of all Spanish production – in iron and steel, coal, electricity, aluminium, shipyards, and air and rail transport. Other industries in Spain are experiencing booms – the construction industry now employs over one million people while in electronics, an agreement in 1986 between ATT and Telefonica, resulted in the construction of Western Europe's biggest microchip factory, near Madrid. Spain is also the fourth largest car producer (after Germany, France and Italy) in the EC, but many feel it has the greatest *potential* in this area. Five multinational car manufacturers have factories in Spain.

Agriculture Spain has always been able to feed its own population which is not something that can be said of all EC states. Spanish agriculture tends to be characterised by the absentee landlord system, with large estates and fragmented farms. Despite the range of products cultivated by Spanish agriculture, not all agricultural areas are wealthy – for instance, Galicia and Andalusia are still classed as underdeveloped, in need of financial assistance from EC funds such as the European Regional Development Fund (ERDF).

The Meseta is an important agricultural area, not only as a producer of crops such as barley, wheat and olives, but also as the centre of the livestock trade. Here, high-quality pork and lamb are produced along with the breeding of fighting bulls in the Salamanca area. Another important agricultural area, and one of the richest, is the Murcia coastland (in south-east Spain). It is here that the *Huertas* (terraced coastal lowlands) produce cereals, tobacco, oranges, tomatoes, artichokes, cereals and rice. Terraced slopes behind the huertas produce vineyards and olive groves. Spain is able to offer an array of agricultural products ranging from grain through to livestock, and from fruit to sunflower oil. Sherry and brandy have been exported from Spain for many years too. Fishing is also a reasonable employer, providing jobs for some 110 000 Spaniards.

Services tourism is a very important part of the Spanish service sector and it accounts for about 8 per cent of GDP. About 1 million Spanish families are involved either directly or indirectly with the tourist trade, making it the largest employer in Spain (providing work for approximately 10 per cent of the population).

In the period 1986–8, a second industrial revolution occurred in Spain and this allowed the service sector to grow quickly, providing employment in such areas as finance and insurance, transport services and other areas. Current government plans to improve the transport infrastructure will mean that the service sector should expand again with new employment opportunities.

Exports the period of Spain's second industrial revolution was really based on the export market for goods such as processed foods, textiles, consumer goods and cars (Seat). Major exports today include cars, iron and steel products, machinery and fruit. Tourism, as we have seen, is also a very important area. Spain's main customers are the EC and the USA.

Culture

The Roman Catholic Church and the feasts of various saints play a large part in the social and cultural life of Spanish communities, particularly in the more rural areas. It is often at these feasts that the traditional yet controversial use of animals such as bulls and chickens can be witnessed.

A host of different cultures have left their mark on Spain – the earliest seems to be the palaeolithic remains in the caves of Altamira and Puerte Viergo, and the rock carvings of the eastern coast. Other cultures present include those of the Romans, Visigoths, Moslems and the Moors who left the Alhambra Palace.

Art and architecture is in abundance in Spain – there are the buildings of the Catalan architect, Gaudi, and a wealth of Romanesque, gothic, Renaissance, baroque and neo-classical art. The baroque period was especially important for Spanish art – this is clearly evident in the fine collection in the Prado Museum in Madrid. Art had a golden age in the 16th and 17th centuries with de Zurbaran, Murillo and Velazquez. These were followed by de Goya and then, in the 20th century, Pablo Picasso and Salvador Dali.

Spanish medieval literature had themes common in Romanesque literature elsewhere – for example, the anonymous *Song of El Cid*. One of the most famous pieces of literature in the world, *Don Quixote* was produced by the Spaniard, Cervantes.

A feature of Spanish cuisine is the serving of *tapas* (appetizers) with aperitifs. Tapas take many forms, hot or cold, and may include smoked ham, cheese, olives and nuts, *chorizo* (spicy pork sausage), tuna and sardines. Without doubt, the most famous Spanish dish is *paella*. This originates from Valencia and may include lobster, prawns, mussels and other small fish. Wine is the national drink and apart from sherry (*jerez*), the most universally available is Rioja. Brandy is also popular as is *sangria*, especially with summer visitors. Sangria consists of red wine, lemon juice, soda, sugar and brandy, and is garnished with sliced oranges. Light beer or *cerveza* is also plentiful in Spain as is cider (*sidra*).

In terms of sport, Spain has successful local football teams such as Real Madrid as well as the national team. It has also produced a few great golfers such as Ballesteros. Then there is bull-fighting. This is perhaps not as popular as it once was, but during the season, many towns host *corrida* (the Spanish name for bull-fights). Some doubt exists as to the future of bull-fighting as it is likely to conflict with certain EC legislation.

ACTIVITY

Madrid, city of culture and dirt

Madrid is the dirtiest capital city in Europe, ranking top of the league for overflowing bins, graffiti, dog mess and street litter.

The city was one of six European capitals to take part in the first international street cleanliness survey.

But the label has angered the city, which ironically is the 1992 European City of Culture. Esperanza Aguirre, councillor for the environment, said: 'We have carried out our own comparisons. They show that London still has the title of the most unkind capital in Europe.'

To compile the survey, the Tidy Britain Group also monitored Berne, Rome, Paris, Brussels and London without warning local authorities. Madrid's streets were at best filthy and at worst disgusting. Many cafes and bars were given a Grade D – the lowest survey rating and monitors saw several people spitting in the street.

At the other end of the scale was the Swiss capital, Berne, seen as a glowing example of cleanliness. Researchers were impressed by recycling bins for glass and cans, and by dog bins with free 'poop-scoop' bags, especially near lamp posts.

Source: *The European*, 20–6 March 1992

Read the article 'Madrid, city of culture and dirt' and then answer the following questions:

1 Do the contents of this article surprise you in any way? Give your reasons.
2 What did the Tidy Britain Group do to ensure an accurate assessment of the cities surveyed?
3 Why do you think the Spanish survey concluded that London was the most 'unkind' European capital?

ACTIVITY

Spanish bulls get the thumbs up

Stung by accusations of cruel and unsporting behaviour, the guardians of Spanish bull-fighting have for the first time granted the bull the chance of a reprieve.

From next week spectators can give a 'thumbs up' sign to save a bull which has shown special bravery and willingness to fight.

Previously, the animal's fate was sealed once it entered the ring, no matter how many matadors it got the better of. Now the pardoned bull will be put out to stud to guarantee the fighting pedigree of the next generation.

The 'thumbs up' rule is the most radical of a series of changes to improve the sport's tarnished image at home and abroad. But opponents of Spain's national sport claim that they are cosmetic and do nothing to make the slaughter of bulls more acceptable.

The first significant rule changes since 1962 were introduced under the auspices of Spain's interior ministry. The new regulations ban 'shaving' a bull's horns to make them less dangerous – a trick which infuriates fans.

The animal will also have to have a full veterinary check before a corrida.

Animal rights' campaigners claim that the changes are designed to please fans rather than to reduce animals' suffering.

Source: *The European*, 5 – 11 March 1992

Read the article 'Spanish bulls get the thumbs up' and then answer the following questions:

1 What is your reaction to this article?
2 How will the 'thumbs up' sign offer a reprieve to Spanish bulls?
3 What does bull-fighting tell us about the culture of the Spanish people? How does this differ from the culture of British people?
4 Write a letter to the editor of *The European* offering your views on the issue of bull-fighting.

United Kingdom

Key facts about the United Kingdom

Area:	244 111 square km	**Religion**:	Mainly Protestant, 35% Catholic in N. Ireland
Population:	56.6 million		
Employed in:	Agriculture (2.6%) Industry (32.4%) Services (65%)	**Government**:	Constitutional, hereditary monarchy
		Council votes:	10
Language:	English, Welsh, Gaelic	**Commissioners**:	2
		European MPs:	81
Capital:	London	**Currency**:	pound sterling

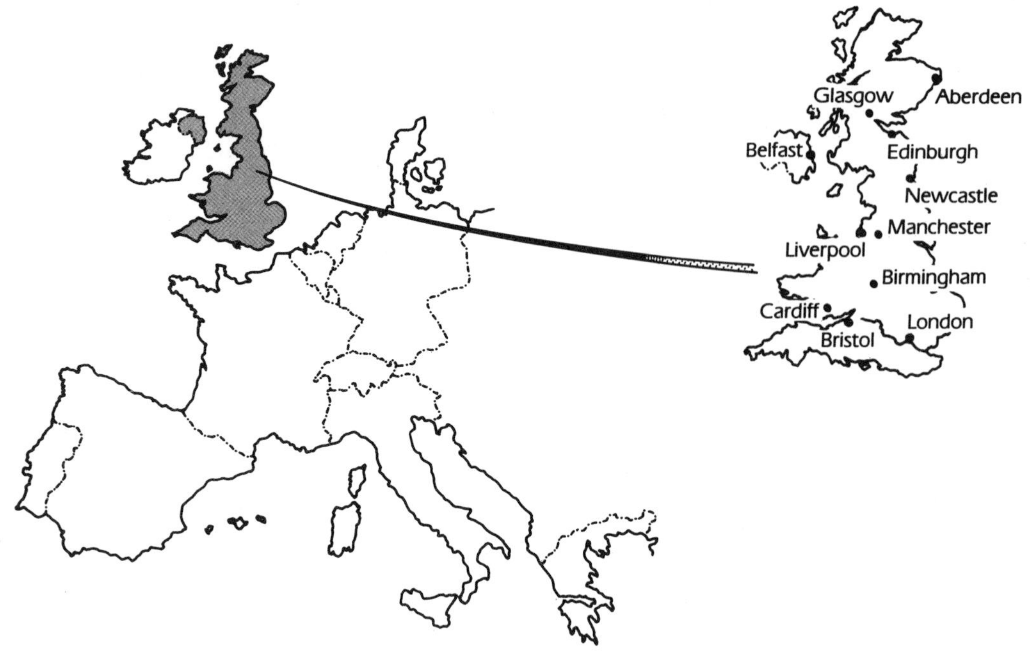

Geography

The United Kingdom consists of one very large island comprising England, Scotland and Wales, plus part of a smaller island to the west (Northern Ireland) which is separated by the Irish Sea. The total area of the UK includes six Northern Ireland counties which are still run by Westminster, and many islands around and off the coast. Two offshore groups exist to the north of Scotland – the Shetlands and the Orkneys – and there are also the Scilly Isles to the south-west of Cornwall and the Isles of Wight and Man.

Within the UK, nowhere is further than 120 km from the sea. In the west, Wales is dominated by the Cambrian Mountains, extending from north to south with Snowdon the highest Welsh peak at 1085m. To the north lies Scotland, another mountainous area with the Grampian Mountains containing the peak of Ben Nevis (1342 m), and lying to the north of the central Forth-Clyde lowlands. The north-west highlands have many sea lochs and are an area of scenic natural beauty.

Important UK rivers include the Thames (338 km) which rises in the Cotswolds and flows into the North Sea. It is tidal as far as Teddington and below London protection from flooding is provided by the Woolwich or Thames Barrier (completed 1984). The River Severn (338 km) rises in North Wales and flows into the Bristol Channel. The River Trent (275 km) is the UK's third longest.

Population

Of the total population of the UK, 80 per cent are English, 9 per cent are Scottish, 5 per cent are Welsh and 3 per cent are Northern Irish. The population also includes two to three million immigrants from countries such as India, Ireland, West Indies, Kenya, Pakistan, Arabia, Greece, Turkey and West Africa. About one-third of these immigrants live in London.

The average density of population in the UK is 231 inhabitants per square km. London has a population of 7 million, Edinburgh 460 000, Belfast 360 000 and Cardiff 280 000.

Of the UK population 19.5 per cent are aged under 15, 65.7 per cent are aged between 15 and 65, and 14.8 per cent are over the age of 65.

The official language is English, but Welsh is spoken as is Gaelic in some areas. The Indian languages of immigrant communities are spoken in bigger areas of immigrant concentration. In addition, Chinese-speaking communities exist in Liverpool, London and Cardiff, to name but a few.

Government and politics

In the UK, unlike many other European Community states, military service is not compulsory. In keeping with the political systems of other member states, people are entitled to vote from the age of 18 onwards. Polling day is on a Thursday, and sometimes both local and general elections and/or European Parliament elections may be held on the same day.

In administrative terms, parliament has supreme power in the UK. However, Scotland and Wales have some degree of autonomy, especially in the area of education and, in Scotland, the legal system. Cabinet members, known as secretaries of state, exist separately for Scotland, Wales and Northern Ireland.

Local government administration (or more particularly the cost of it) is often a cause for concern for central government and the last reform of the system occurred in 1974. As a result, England is divided into 46 counties, Wales into 8 and Scotland into 12. Northern Ireland consists of 26 districts. However, the government has plans to reorganise local government. Part of this reorganisation involves the rationalising of the various police forces.

An unusual feature of the UK political system, contrasting it with other EC states, is the lack of a formal written constitution. This means that as new laws are passed, the constitution constantly changes, for it represents all laws passed and judicial decisions taken. Under the system the separation of powers occurs with a separate legislature, executive and judiciary.

Executive power lies with the leader of the majority party in the lower chamber, the House of Commons, and is conferred on that person by the queen. The majority party leader thus becomes the prime minister. The sovereign can dissolve parliament and call a general election on the advice of the current prime minister.

Legislative power is vested in parliament, a two-chamber body. The lower House of Commons has 650 MPs who are directly elected by simple majority in single-member constituencies. A system of voting by proportional representation has consistently been rejected, particularly by the two major parties – Conservative and Labour – who both have interests in maintaining the current simple majority system. The upper chamber, the House of Lords, has been the focus of much speculation and debate in the past, as many see it as being out of date. It currently consists of about 1000 members – most of which are hereditary peers (lords who have their titles passed to them by family ties), but also including life peers, the two archbishops and the senior bishops of the Church of England. In addition, the senior law lords sit in the House of Lords.

Legislation in the House of Commons can be introduced both by the government and by private members (MPs). Private member's bills are usually referred to a Select Committee of the House of Commons, but are not often successful. The House of Lords has a delaying power which applies to most legislation apart from *budgetary* or financial legislation.

Judicial power is vested in the UK court structure. A system of criminal and civil courts exists with the magistrates' courts at the bottom of the structure and the House of Lords, as the highest court of appeal, at the top.

Since 1945, British governments have alternated between Labour and Conservative parties. A third group, the Liberal Democrats, are the third largest political party and it is this group that most wants to see electoral reform in the UK.

Economy and industry

Before the Thatcher administration commenced in 1979, a high degree of consensus existed between the two main political parties in the UK, in relation to the economy. The 1980s saw a move away from this and towards a high degree of centralisation, allowing sweeping changes to be made to the economy. Thus, a shift towards emphasising the markets and rejecting the idea that government should be a prime mover in the economy came about.

Industry Britain was the world's first industrialised nation. The traditional industries such as coal, iron, steel, textiles and ship-building have all declined in recent times, partly as a result of changing patterns in world trade. Part of this decline was experienced by the mass car market too – by the 1980s, only Rover remained a British manufacturer and this is partly owned by the Japanese Honda. The once-famous UK motorcycle industry had virtually disappeared and the civil aircraft industry was reduced to supplying parts for the European airbus.

On the other hand, the UK is self-sufficient in oil and a new technology has developed in the extraction of oil from North Sea fields. This has had a positive effect on the balance of payments. Coupled to this has been the huge development and expansion, during the 1980s, of high-technology industries and services. These include satellite communications, robotics and information processing.

In some industries, the UK still competes well – the chemical industry is the third largest in Western Europe, with over 50 per cent of output exported. Here, ICI is responsible for half of the industry's production. The UK is the ninth largest steel producer in terms of volume and British Steel is the third largest steel company in the world, accounting for about 75 per cent of crude steel production. Furthermore, the UK aerospace industry is the third largest in the world. In the field of electrical and electronic engineering, output has risen steadily since 1982.

Agriculture within the UK, about 60 per cent of full-time farms are devoted to dairy, beef or sheep farming. With cattle rearing, the Friesian breed is the most popular while in the sheep farming sector, more than 400 breeds are reared in the UK. For sheep farmers, lamb production is the main source of income, although wool is also important. Another important sector in UK agriculture is pig and poultry production, and this is especially the case in eastern and northern England.

Of the crops produced in the UK, the most important are wheat, barley, oats, potatoes, oilseed rape and sugar beet. Agricultural products also include meat, eggs, milk, cheese and butter. In addition, horticulture has an important role with glasshouses used for the cultivation of tomatoes, cucumbers, sweet peppers, lettuces, flowers, pot plants and nursery stock. Agricultural exports include fresh salmon, Scotch whisky, biscuits, jam and conserves, beef and lamb carcasses, and cheese.

Services with the contraction of the manufacturing industries has come the growth of the service industries in the UK. In 1960, these accounted for about 45 per cent of GDP, while in 1987, the figure had risen to 60 per cent, with some 68 per cent of people employed in the service industries.

In terms of the number of people employed, the fastest growing services have been the leisure/personal services, finance, distribution, and hotels and catering. It has been estimated that by 1995, services will account for over 70 per cent of employment.

A major service area is tourism which is increasingly important, particularly as an employer. In 1987, an estimated 1.4 million people were employed directly or indirectly in tourism. Retail trades are also important with a turnover of some £100 billion in 1987. The largest multiple retailers are in the grocery trade and include Sainsbury, Tesco and Asda. These are joined by giants from other sectors such as Marks and Spencer, Woolworths and Boots.

The expansion of services in the UK is partly explained by the growth in real incomes, which have increased since 1948 at an annual rate of 2.8 per cent.

Exports major UK exports include machinery and transport equipment, manufactured goods, mineral fuels and chemicals. These are supported by food/live animals, beverages and tobacco, animal/vegetable oils, fats and waxes, and miscellaneous manufactured articles.

The UK's main customers are the EC, the USA, Australia, New Zealand and Canada – the last three underlining the importance of the UK relationship with Commonwealth states.

Culture

Few Anglo-Saxon churches exist in the UK, as English architecture really starts with the Norman Romanesque style and is followed by Early English, Reformation, Tudor and Elizabethan, Jacobean, Georgian and Regency and Victorian.

In literature, the UK has spawned the likes of Shakespeare, Bacon, the Brontës, Austen, Dickens, Hardy, Milton, Keats, Shelley and Wordsworth. Great artists include Reynolds, Turner, Constable, Gainsborough and Hogarth, while music has been provided by Elgar, Vaughan Williams, Walton and Britten. British scientists have also contributed significantly – namely Watt, Newton, Darwin and Whittle to name but a few.

As far as food is concerned, traditional foods perhaps help to caricature the British – bacon and eggs, which incidentally originated from Denmark, and the traditional Sunday roasts. These are added to by regional variations such as Lancashire hot pot, faggots and peas, and Cumberland sausage. However, perhaps due to the exposure to different cultures and foods brought about by membership of the EC, many more 'continental' type foods and meals are now consumed in the UK.

British beer is distinctive because of the many different styles that exist which are generally not available in other EC states – mild, bitter and stout, as well as the more common lager. Not surprisingly, only Belgians and Germans drink more beer than the British. Wine has become very fashionable since the UK's entry to the EC and this is highlighted by the opening of many 'trendy' wine bars in many parts of the UK. Other important UK beverages are sherry, whisky and other spirits. Yet tea remains an essential part of British life – the British actually drink more tea than any other nationality in the EC. Consumption of milk and dairy products is also high.

In the sporting arena, games like football, cricket and rugby are watched and played extensively by UK citizens. However, more curious sporting traditions such as fox-hunting and croquet are still enjoyed, along with angling and game shooting. Snooker and darts have become immensely popular as indoor spectator sports and are often televised. However, the greatest 'sport' for many people is the television itself – probably the biggest indoor leisure activity in the UK.

Recent successful British sportspersons have included Nick Faldo, Sally Gunnell, Linford Christie and Nigel Mansell, although in some sporting areas, particularly tennis, success seems still to be evading UK sportsmen and women.

The UK has the highest level of ownership of leisure electrical equipment in the EC and is ranked third in the number of cars purchased. There is some awareness of environmentally friendly products in the UK, but this has not yet reached the level that currently exists in Germany.

Military service for all British youngsters!

A headline such as the above would be sure to cause a stir in the UK, but as we have seen, in many EC states, military service is compulsory.

1 Do you think compulsory military service is a good idea? Give your reasons.
2 How would you feel if you were asked to complete three years' compulsory military service?
3 Conduct a mini-survey of students in your college to discover whether or not they agree with compulsory military service. Discuss your results with your European Studies tutor.

ACTIVITY

Consider France, Germany, Italy and Spain.

1 Which of the four do you think the British public identifies with most? Why?
2 Why do France and Germany enjoy such a strong position within the EC?
3 In what ways do you think Italy has benefited from EC membership?
4 What can Spain contribute to the EC?

ACTIVITY

Italian men laziest around the home

Continental women who want a husband prepared to do something approaching his fair share of the housework had better cross the English Channel.

According to a new survey, Englishmen are the most house-trained in Europe, while Italians conform to the Mediterranean stereotype and hardly lift a finger around the home.

The Latin reputation is slightly redeemed by the Spaniard, however, who does more housework than the Frenchman or German and is Europe's best food-shopper. Sadly though, he is also the laziest gardener.

Seven thousand people in The Netherlands, Germany, France, Spain, Italy and the UK were questioned for a consumer report on the European Community. And while 60% of men agreed that they should share more of the everyday household chores, the reality falls far short.

Source: *The European*, 26–9 November 1992

Read the article 'Italian men laziest around the home' and then answer the following questions:

1 Do the results of the survey surprise you? Give reasons for your answer.
2 What features make up the 'Mediterranean stereotype' do you think?
3 What qualities does an Englishman have that might make him more attractive to a continental woman?

ACTIVITY

Write a short article (between 200 and 300 words) for a marketing magazine, *Your Market*, that compares population statistics for the five major EC states. Illustrate your article with at least two graphs or charts.

ACTIVITY

Produce a leaflet which gives 20 useful phrases for businesspeople in the languages of the five major EC states.

ACTIVITY

Imports by major EC states, 1989 (million ECU)

Importing country	*Total imports*	*EC*	*USA*	*Japan*	*Rest of world*
France	182 681	118 882	12 941	5488	45 550
West Germany	244 679	130 559	17 099	14 389	82 632
Italy	138 963	78 827	7581	3206	49 349
Spain	61 599	34 981	5610	2748	18 260
UK	178 654	91 316	20 974	10 745	55 619

Exports by major EC states, 1989 (million ECU)

Exporting country	*Total exports*	*EC*	*USA*	*Japan*	*Rest of world*
France	167 994	103 474	10 670	3159	50 691
West Germany	308 682	169 155	22 533	7384	109 610
Italy	127 799	72 040	11 010	2925	41 824
Spain	42 265	26 106	2947	391	12 821
UK	137 532	68 772	17 919	3378	47 463

Source: Eurostat

Consider the tables above and then answer the following questions:

1 Compare the imports and exports for the five major EC states and present the information as a series of graphs.
2 What conclusions can be drawn from the graphs about the nature of trade in the five major EC states?

ACTIVITY Review your progress: 7

1 Which of the five major EC states has a) the largest area and b) the smallest area?
2 List the currencies of the five major EC states.
3 State the total population of each of the five major EC states.
4 What and where are the following:
   a) Massif Central?
   b) Woolwich Barrier?
   c) The Meseta?
   d) The Bodensee?
   e) The Mezzogiorno?
5 How do the political systems of the major EC states differ from one another?
6 List the main a) industrial and b) agricultural products of the five major EC states.
7 List the main exports and customers of the major EC states.
8 List three cultural characteristics of the five major EC states.

Summary

- The geographical compositions of the five major EC states are varied and lend themselves to different forms of land use.

- There are similarities between the socioeconomic characteristics of the major states, yet these states are distinctly individual.
- All of the major states have democratic style governments, although political systems differ in detail.
- Clear cultural differences exist between the major EC states.

Assignment 12 European Business Week

The local chamber of commerce is staging a 'European Business Week' and the chairperson has contacted your college to see whether a group of students would be prepared to contribute to the exhibition. She has particularly asked that, if possible, a section on the characteristics of the five major EC states be produced.

In groups of three or four, complete the following.

Task 1 Produce a written report which details the characteristics of the five major EC states. The report could include the following:

- basic statistics about the member states
- maps showing geographical features
- comparisons between political systems, economies and culture.

Task 2 Produce a display for use during the European Business Week which illustrates the results of your research.

Task 3 In a group discussion, evaluate each group's display.

8 The infrastructures of the EC member states: 1

Aims

- To identify the communication and media systems of all EC member states with specific reference to the larger five states
- To note and consider the different transport systems in place in the EC member states with specific reference to the larger five states
- To encourage the comparison and contrast of aspects of the infrastructures of the EC member states.

Relevant BTEC Outcome Performance Criteria
5a Communication systems identified and contrasted
5b Transport systems identified and contrasted

Communication systems

In this chapter, we shall consider the various communication and media systems in place within the EC member states. The focus will be on the press, radio and television, and telecommunications.

The press

Freedom of the press
In many of the EC states, freedom of the press is guaranteed and is often part of the country's constitution. Freedom of the press means that a newspaper can publish its opinions and views freely even if they do not comply with the views of the government. In the UK, much concern has been raised about the reporting of the royal family's activities – for example, the so-called 'Dianagate' tapes. Here the press has argued that it has a right to report findings to the public. This freedom is an important element of any democracy and the EC likes to see a democratic form of government in place in a state before sanctioning its membership of the Community.

Freedom of the press arrived relatively late in some EC states, notably Spain, where freedom of thought and expression were only officially recognised in the 1978 constitution (upon the death of Franco). In Greece, the freedom of the press has only been guaranteed since 1925. The French press operates under a law dating back to 1881 which established liberal conditions for journalism. In the UK, there is no law specifying the operation of the press, but certain pieces of legislation affect the activities of newspapers – for example, the Defamation Act and the Official Secrets Act. In Germany, many of the lander (local government units) have introduced laws that define clearly the democratic role of the press and allow certain journalists access to some sources of government information. In Ireland, the Roman Catholic Church exercises some influence over opinions and views expressed in the press.

ACTIVITY

In groups of three or four, consider the following questions:

1 Do you think the UK press should be able to report freely on the activities of the royal family? Does the public have a right to know? Give your reasons.
2 Why do you think freedom of the press is an important element of a democratic state?
3 Why does the EC consider it important for states applying for membership to have some form of democratic government in place?

Be prepared to share your answers in a group discussion with the rest of the class.

The circulation of daily newspapers in the EC states in 1984

United Kingdom	23 206 000
Germany	21 362 000
France	11 598 000
Italy	5 477 000
Netherlands	4 474 000
Spain	3 053 000
Belgium	2 209 000
Denmark	1 837 000
Greece	981 000
Ireland	663 000
Portugal	495 000
Luxembourg	130 000 (1979 figure)

Source: Eurostat

The smaller states

A number of general points can be made about the press in the smaller EC states.

- The number of daily newspapers varies from six in Luxembourg (published in French, German and Luxembourgeoise), the most popular being *La Voix du Luxembourg* to 47 dailies in Denmark, where most papers are privately owned and one of the most popular is *Ekstra Bladet*.
- Despite high levels of readership, no newspapers are available in The Netherlands on Sundays, while in Greece many papers are not available on Mondays.
- Most Portugese papers are based in the capital Lisbon and in Oporto.
- In Belgium, papers are printed in French, Dutch and German.
- The most popular newspapers in Ireland include *The Irish Independent*, *The Evening Herald* and *The Evening Press*.

ACTIVITY

Consider the table showing the circulation of daily newspapers in the EC and compare this with the population of each member state.

1 Using the table that shows the circulation of daily newspapers in the EC, draw a pie chart to illustrate this information.
2 What do the two sets of figures tell you about the relative importance of newspapers in the EC states?
3 In your opinion, why does the UK have the highest circulation of newspapers when it has a considerably smaller population than that of Germany?
4 For what reasons might Portugal have the second lowest circulation of daily newspapers?

Operation of the press in the major states

National newspapers

In *France* daily newspapers are divided into those based in Paris and those based in the provinces. As a result, there are virtually no *national* daily newspapers. The biggest-selling

French daily is *Ouest-France*, a regional newspaper produced in Rennes which covers the entire north-west of the state.

The lack of a truly national newspaper is also a characteristic of the *Italian* and *Spanish* press. In Italy, a few major dailies have considerable circulations outside their regions of origin – notably *La Stampa*, *La Repubblica* and *Corriere della Sera*. Unlike the UK, there are no popular tabloids in existence in Italy.

In *Spain*, publications such as *ABC* and *El Pais* are basically regional papers which may be obtainable outside the region of origin.

In *Germany*, newspapers are published in various locations ranging from Hamburg (*Bild*) to Munich (*Suddeutsche Zeitung*) and from Cologne (*Express*) to Frankfurt (*Frankfurter Allgemeine*). In a sense, these are not national newspapers either due to their regional publication, but the large circulation figures for many newspapers would seem to suggest otherwise – for example, *Bild* has a circulation of over 4.5 million.

In the *United Kingdom*, a clear distinction between national and regional newspapers exists. The *Sun*, the *Daily Mirror*, *The Times* and the *Daily Telegraph* are quite clearly national publications. This status may result from the small physical size of the UK in relation to its four major EC counterparts. Many regional newspapers also exist. An important feature of the composition of the UK press, which contrasts sharply with the other EC states, is the fact that two clear categories of newspaper exist:

- the *tabloid press* (or 'popular press') including publications such as the *Sun* and the *Daily Mail*;
- the *quality press* consisting of publications such as *The Times* and the *Daily Telegraph*.

Number of daily newspapers in the major EC states

France	91 (1984)
Germany	358 (1989)
Italy	108 (1985)
Spain	120 (1990)
UK	98 (1990)

▶ *8.1 Popular newspapers in the major EC states*

France French newspapers have tended to perform poorly (in terms of sales) compared with their German and UK counterparts. Despite this, *le Monde* is still considered by many to be one of the best newspapers in the world. This reputation is perhaps based on the moderate political nature of the publication, coupled with a very stern format with no photographs. In addition, coverage of news items is dealt with extremely seriously. As a result, the educational élite in France consider it to be essential reading. Despite the nature of the newspaper, its circulation is relatively high (over 362 000 in 1991). A lively new challenge to *le Monde* is now offered by *Liberation*, a publication generally critical of the French establishment and generally well written. The flagship of the press empire of the tycoon Robert Hersant is *le Figaro*. This has a very high circulation (almost 450 000 in 1991) and is a major rival for *le Monde* and other daily newspapers.

Germany popular German newspapers include daily, Sunday and weekly publications. Of the top five newspapers in terms of circulation, three are published in Hamburg, and the other two in Essen and Hanover. This underlines the regional nature of the German press. In addition to the dailies, five Sunday newspapers exist, of which *Welt am Sonntag* is an example. There are also 37 weekly newspapers. *Bild* topped the German press circulation table in 1987 with a considerably larger circulation then the next daily rival, *Westdeutsche Allgemeine*. The federal lander system of government perhaps helps to perpetuate a system of many regional newspapers.

Italy the Italian newspapers *La Stampa, La Repubblica* and *Corriere della Sera* all contain a large proportion of meaty, analytical articles dealing with various issues including those associated with the business environment. Of the other general daily newspapers, coverage of business affairs tends to be limited. All Italian dailies are in some way linked to big industrial names – for example, *La Stampa* and *Corriere della Sera* belong to the successful Agnelli Group. Daily newspapers are supported by over 600 weeklies and over 2700 monthly periodicals.

Spain several of the Spanish daily newspapers also appear on Sundays and these include *El Pais, ABC* and *La Vanguardia*.

UK the unique position of the UK with its dual system of daily newspapers (tabloid and quality) is underlined by the popularity of the former over the latter. The *Sun* is the most popular daily, offering an often light-hearted, easy-to-read approach. The political allegiance of the publication is fairly clear and it often does little to disguise this fact. Other tabloids, though perhaps less popular in terms of sales, offer a similar format – examples include the *Daily Mirror*, the *Daily Express* and *Today*. By contrast, the 'quality' newspapers, such as the *Guardian* and the *Daily Telegraph*, generally offer a more serious approach and adopt different print layouts. Both offer analytical articles dealing with topical subjects, including the business environment, as do other competitors.

Business information The press in the major EC states is an important information source for European business and commerce, as follows.

- Hersant's *Le Figaro* is an important source of company and business news in France. This tends to be reported fully and fairly in the pink economic pages of the publication (rather like the *Financial Times* in the UK). In addition, business periodicals have their place in the French press network. Publications include the fortnightly *l'Expansion* and the weekly *le Nouvel Economiste*. The former of these has a circulation of 180 000 plus, while the latter reaches over 99 000 readers.
- Although a daily newspaper, *Frankfurter Allgemeine* leads the way for German business. A serious general publication with a distribution across Germany, it devotes a whole section every day to the business environment. Furthermore, editorial columns are heavily weighted towards the business world. The leading specialist business paper (and equivalent to the UK's *Financial Times*) is *Handelsblatt*, a financial daily with a circulation of 131 000. It should also be pointed out that many economic and business news agencies exist in Germany, and these are important information sources.

- Italian business people read *Il Sole 24 Ore* and *Italia Oggi*. Until recently it had the largest circulation of any European business paper. However, it has now been overtaken by the UK's *Financial Times* (itself very widely read in Italy). *Il Sole 24 Ore* is also printed on pink paper like the *Financial Times* and the economic section of *le Figaro*. A number of business periodicals also exist. Of these, the most significant is *Il Mondo* (published by the Rizzoli Group). Two other, strictly financial, weekly publications are *Lettera Finanziasia* and *Milano Finanza*. The latter of these has a circulation of 50 000.
- From a UK business viewpoint, many newspapers cover business affairs with the quality press offering the most analysis. The *Financial Times* is widely read by anyone in business and carries analytical features which predict economic trends, and act as a pointer to company growth or decline. Other publications include *The Economist*, which has a circulation of 262 000, and deals with economics, finance and current affairs.

Characteristics of the press in the major EC states

Ownership In terms of ownership of the press in the major EC states, the following observations can be made.

- The problem of concentration of ownership of the press has been recognised in all the major states, although in France, the trend is less advanced. Legislation to prevent this has been introduced in these states. In Italy, this has taken the form of 'Opzione Zero' (Zero Option) – a series of regulations designed to restrict ownership of the press. In the UK, the problem has been highlighted by the Labour party, an organisation that perhaps stands to gain from dilution of press ownership.
- In all major states ownership of the press tends to be in the hands of a small number of groups or associations. In Italy, the huge car group, Fiat, owns/publishes *La Stampa* and *Stampa Sera*.
- With the exception of the UK, newspapers in all major states have close associations with political parties. The UK differs in that no newspaper is directly owned by a political party.
- Uniquely, Spain has an official government news agency – Agencia EFE. Despite the high degree of government control of the agency, and the tendency to associate offical agencies with the old Communist bloc states, the Spanish state does not monopolise the distribution of Spanish news abroad.
- At least two of the major states, Germany and the UK, have national press councils. These lay down guidelines for press activity and investigate complaints brought against the press. The German version, established in 1956, comprises publishers and journalists, while the UK council is now known as the Press Complaints Commission.

ACTIVITY

1. Why do many of the EC states wish to prevent too much concentration of newspaper ownership in the hands of a small number of people?
2. 'We should look to the Italian example and allow major political parties in all EC member states to own a daily or weekly newspaper – this would help to educate people about policies.' What are the possible implications of this proposal for a) the EC in general and b) the UK?
3. With a partner, draw up a list of the possible advantages and drawbacks of all EC member states having official state news agencies such as Agencia EFE in Spain.

Advertising All newspapers in the major EC states carry advertisements and these represent a healthy source of income for the press. Revenue is substantial, with Spain deriving almost 58 per cent of its total advertising income from newspaper adverts; the UK over 50 per cent, and Italy and Germany each deriving 44 per cent. The vast circulation of many newspapers means that advertisements are seen by many readers and this is an important channel of communication for businesses throughout Europe (and indeed the world). Successful companies have mastered effective advertising and will be aware of the more successful publications. The huge potential readership of the advertisements that appear in national daily and weekly papers is reflected in very high advertising costs, as shown in the table below.

Aspects of daily newspapers in major EC states

	Newspaper	*Est.*	*Price*	*Circ.*	*Cost of advert**
France	*le Figaro*	1826	FFr7.00	443 006	FFr431 000
	le Monde	1944	FFr6.00	362 443	FFr340 000
Germany	*Frankfurter Allgemeine Zeitung*	1949	DM1.60	363 856	DM43 432
	Die Welt	1946	DM1.60	222 116	DM34 214
Italy	*Corriere della Sera*	1876	1200L	684 879	950 000L
Spain	*ABC*	1905	Pta200	280 356	Pta2 328 000
UK	*Sun*	1969	£0.25	3 687 455	£26 000
	Daily Mirror	1903	£0.25	2 897 008	£29 800
	Daily Telegraph	1855	£0.40	1 059 546	£33 500
	Guardian	1821	£0.40	411 324	£15 500

* Advertisement rates are for a full page mono

ACTIVITY

1 a) Find out the current rates of exchange (against the UK£) for France, Germany, Italy and Spain. Use these exchange rates to convert the price of each newspaper in the table to UK£.
b) Draw a suitable graph or chart to illustrate this information. What conclusions can be drawn from your graph or chart?

2 a) Which newspaper has the highest circulation and which newspaper has the lowest circulation?
b) Produce a league table showing the circulation of the daily newspapers illustrated.

3 a) Using the current rates of exchange, convert the costs of adverts for each of the newspapers listed into UK£.
b) Write a short formal report for Mr R. Doyle, Manager of Business Furnishings PLC which presents the findings from 3 a). Make your recommendations as to which newspaper it would be useful for him to advertise in.

Recent trends As far as the press in the major EC states is concerned, a number of trends have been identified in recent years. These include the following.

- A general decline in the number of daily newspapers published within the major EC states over recent years.
- A general increase in household expenditure on items such as newspapers, periodicals and books. This is probably linked to the point below.
- A general increase in the readership of periodicals, particularly radio and television-based magazines. This is especially so in France where 40 per cent of households receive such magazines. This emphasises the increase in leisure time that people across Western Europe have experienced. A conclusion to be drawn here is that television and radio are increasingly important channels of communication for the population of the European Community, and indeed for the world of business.
- In Spain, a recent trend has been a marked decline in readership of the local press, coupled with an increase in the significance of the regional press. This may well reflect

the fact that some Spanish regions have become autonomous (self-governing), leading to the increased importance of more regionally-based interests. This contrasts with the UK where, although provincial newspapers exist (for example, the *Birmingham Post*), national newspapers would appear to be more widely read.

ACTIVITY

1 Obtain copies of newspapers from two or three different EC states – for example, the UK, France and Germany. Compare the newspapers in terms of layout, type of information communicated, mix of photographs and text, advertisements, business news and other features. Draw up a table to illustrate this information.
2 Select a news item that appears in all the newspapers considered (preferably to do with the EC). Try to decide how the reports differ by considering the different perspectives of the member states involved and which item is most successful in putting across its message. (You will need to make use of language skills here.)

Radio and television broadcasting

Ownership and organisation of the broadcasting of radio and television in the EC member states varies from country to country. In some member states, supervision of broadcasting is carried out by the national government, whereas in others, responsibility for broadcasting is left to a public organisation. All 12 member states broadcast radio programmes and television programmes, although there is some variation between the number of stations/ programmes offered. Within the EC in general both radio and television are considered important channels of communication.

ACTIVITY

Compare the number of TV sets in use in the EC with the population figures for each member state. Complete the following.

1 Draw a pie chart to illustrate the number of TV sets in use in each of the EC states.
2 For what reasons might Denmark have the highest number of TV sets per 1000 inhabitants, despite the fact that she has the third smallest population of all the EC states?
3 What do the figures for the number of TV sets in the EC suggest about the importance of television as a communication channel in the major EC states?

Number of television sets in use in the EC, 1987 (per 1000 inhabitants)

Denmark	386
Germany	385
Spain	368
United Kingdom	347
France	333
Netherlands	325
Belgium	320
Greece	272 (figure for 1985)
Italy	257
Luxembourg	249
Ireland	228
Portugal	159

Source: Eurostat

Broadcasting in the smaller states

Several points can be made with regard to broadcasting in the smaller states.

- In The Netherlands, eight main associations, supported by several smaller ones, are responsible for the broadcasting of radio and television programmes. The Dutch enjoy 5 national, 10 regional and 150 local radio stations, plus 3 television channels.
- In Ireland, there are just two radio stations (Radio 1 and Radio 2), plus an Irish language station and two television channels, all the responsibility of the RTE (a state organisation).

- Belgian broadcasting is in French and Dutch, with five radio programmes and two television channels being offered in both languages.
- Danmarks Radio (a public corporation) provides radio broadcasts for the Danes with one national television channel and several local ones.
- Portugal has four national radio stations and two television channels.
- In Luxembourg, a private company, RTL, offers five radio stations and three television channels.
- Greek broadcasting is carried out by a government-supervised organisation. ERT 4 broadcasts radio programmes, supporting this with two television channels – ERT 1 and ERT 2.
- Advertising on radio and television is generally accepted in the smaller states, although it is limited in terms of time allocated. Exceptionally, Denmark does not allow advertising through either of these media.
- Many of the smaller states enjoy cable and satellite television. For example, over 75 per cent of Dutch households received cable TV in 1986. The exceptions are Greece and Portugal which have yet to experience this media on any sort of scale.

The major states

Ownership and organisation of broadcasting All major EC states have public organisations set up to organise broadcasting within the national state. These are as follows:

France	Conseil del'Audiovisuel
Germany	Association of Public Broadcasting Organisation (ARD)
Italy	Radiotelevisione Italiania (RAI)
Spain	Radiotelevision Espanola (RTVE)
UK	British Broadcasting Corporation (BBC).

Broadcasting in these states has certain characteristics as follows.

- Most of the major EC states organise broadcasting nationally. The sole exception is Germany where the federal structure of government is reflected in broadcasting. There are several German public broadcasting organisations which all belong to the ARD. Each member broadcasts three or four channels. A further point should be made regarding the Spanish autonomous regional governments which have responsibility for broadcasting in their particular area.
- The national broadcasting organisations tend to be supported in each of the major states by private broadcasting companies. In the UK, the ITC (Independent Television Commission) operates alongside the BBC. Its role is to licence and regulate regional companies for independent television. Not a producer of programmes like the BBC, the ITC awards franchises to independent companies (such as Central TV).
- The issue of broadcasting advertisements is regarded differently in the major EC states. In France, the state-run TV channels are allowed to take advertisements, as are the private ones. TF1, a former state channel, now privatised, is largely funded by advertisements. By contrast, the Italian state-owned RTI channels are allowed very few commercial breaks during shows. Private channels can take adverts in Italy and the blossoming of these has led to a huge increase in TV adverts. Private channels can use up to 18 minutes per hour for advertisements (13 minutes at peak times). In Germany, TV adverts are severely hampered by government codes – the two state-owned TV networks are allowed only four, strictly-timed, blocks of commercials per day (and these have to appear at specified times). The industry watchdog, WERBERAT, closely monitors adverts to ensure they are moral. In Spain too, strict time limits are applied to TV advertisements. The UK tends to have a combination of the possibilities – the BBC is not allowed to advertise at all while the ITC franchised channels make full use of their advertising opportunities. Commercials on radio stations tend to operate in a similar way – in the UK, adverts are not allowed on BBC-led radio programmes, but independent radio derives extensive revenue from them. Adverts on private radio stations have been permitted in France since 1984.

- Broadcasting in the major EC states is also funded from sources such as licence fees and sponsorship. Many Italian TV programmes are sponsored – both on state-run and private channels. The Standa supermarket chain for example, presents variety shows in Italy.

Radio

In all of the major EC states, radio is extensively used as an important communication channel. As well as the radio stations provided by the various government organisations, commercial radio networks also exist in the major EC states. In general, radio stations offer a wide range of programme content, ranging from entertainment and information to education, and from music and news to the arts and culture. Some states, such as Italy and Spain, offer a foreign and overseas service for listeners – for instance, Radio Roma broadcasts in 27 languages.

Television

France TF1, the former state channel, is rivalled mainly by A2. These two channels have the best viewing figures with 40.9 per cent and 22.8 per cent respectively, followed by La5 and FR3. A2 is received by over 96 per cent of the French population. Early morning TV programmes were established in France in 1984.

Germany Members of the ARD combine to produce the First Channel (Erstes Programm), while the Second Channel (ZDF) is controlled by a public corporation of all lander. Within the ARD members, the largest viewing share is held by WDR (Nordrhein Westfalen lander) with 25 per cent, followed by Norddeustcher Rundfunk (Schleswig-Holstein, Hamburg lander) with 19 per cent and BR (Bayern lander) with 17 per cent. Private TV was introduced in 1981.

Italy There are more than 1000 privately-owned TV stations in Italy with as many as 30 in major cities. The state-owned RAI networks each have a distinct political identity – Christian Democrat (Uno), Socialist (Due) and Communist (Tre). These three networks share 52 per cent of total viewing (with Uno being most popular), while major commercial networks account for 36.3 per cent. In 1989, a Roman Catholic network was established.

Spain The one-time monopoly of TVE in Spanish broadcasting was broken recently with the establishment of privately operated commercial channels. Overwhelmingly, the most popular channels in Spain are TVE1 and TVE2 – these share over 70 per cent of viewing between them. Regional channels, of which there are nine in Spain, account for about 16 per cent of viewing with private channels attracting about 11 per cent.

UK The most popular TV network in the UK is ITV (Channel 3) accounting for 42.5 per cent of viewing. It is closely followed by BBC1 with 39.2 per cent. BBC2 is marginally more popular than Channel 4. A new Channel 5 is due to come on line at the end of 1994.

Satellite and cable

Satellite and cable TV are generally available in three of the major EC states – namely France, Germany and the UK. As yet, Italy has no provision for either medium, but recent Spanish legislation has given the go-ahead for consideration of cable development. Collaboration between France and Germany resulted in a broadcasting satellite, TV-Sat. Satellite services are offered by BSB in the UK.

Cable TV appears to be relatively successful in France with 78 000 subscribers in 1989. Germany has recognised the potential of this medium and has invested heavily in a cable network. By contrast, cable TV has developed slowly in the UK. Cable operations are regulated by the ITC which is also responsible for the licensing and regulation of satellite television in the UK.

ACTIVITY

1 a) Many of the EC member states strictly limit the amount of advertising that takes place on television. List the pros and cons of increasing advertising time on television stations.
   b) The BBC is not allowed to broadcast commercials. Why is this so?

2 In groups of three or four, imagine that you represent a group of UK businesspeople. Prepare a convincing oral presentation (maximum of five minutes) which attempts to convince your Danish counterparts that television advertising is desirable.

3 'There is a strong case for a European Community radio and television network, offered in several languages. This could be used as a mouthpiece for the EC and its citizens.' What are the implications of this proposal?

ACTIVITY

Read the article, 'Television Without Frontiers Directive' and then answer the following questions:

1 What is the purpose of the EC Directive on television within the EC?

2 What do you think is meant by the phrase 'global audio-visual strategy'?

3 What sort of topics might 'European' programmes deal with?

Television Without Frontiers Directive

The 'Television without Frontiers' Directive came into force on 3 October bringing into being a global audio-visual strategy for the EC. One of the Directive's main features is to bring in the free circulation of TV programmes throughout the European Community. Another is to promote 'European' programmes, notably from independent producers.

Source: *The Week in Europe*, 10 October 1991

Telecommunications

Number of telephones in use in EC, 1989

Germany	28 412 000
France	25 454 000
United Kingdom	24 400 000
Italy	20 091 000
Spain	10 972 000
Netherlands	6 466 000
Greece	3 618 000
Belgium	3 525 000
Denmark	2 792 000
Portugal	1 849 000
Ireland	834 000
Luxembourg	167 000

Source: Eurostat

Telecommunication systems in the EC are largely operated by the national governments of the member states. This would seem to be logical, especially when one considers the national approach demanded by a postal system for example. Many EC members have made use of the great advances in technology that have characterised the past few decades. An illustration of this is the number of member states that now make use of mobile telephone systems.

Generally, telecommunication services are administered by a state agency or department within EC member states. Services usually include postal services, telephones, telex, fax and other data services. In Greece, a total of 11 different telephone systems exist! A feature recently has been the move towards increased mobility of communication systems.

The major states

Telecommunications services in the major EC states are offered by specific organisations. These are as follows:

France	France Telecom
Germany	Deutsche Bundespost
Italy	Ministry of Post and Telecommunications
Spain	Telefonica de Espana SA
UK	British Telecom and Royal Mail

Postal services

France the postal service is run by the state-controlled PTT. In general, the postal service is unimpressive with letters taking several days to arrive within France. Letters often take well over a week to reach the UK. The fastest way to send letters and parcels in France is via the CHRONOPOST system – this guarantees a maximum delivery time of 72 hours.

Germany each working day, Bundespost forwards some 44 million letters and 800 000 parcels. Bundespost is Europe's largest service enterprise and is probably the most expensive in the world! The German post office is a federal agency – sole authority for it lies with the Bonn government.

Italy postal services in Italy are notoriously inefficient. For example, mail can take up to two weeks from city to city! This means an increasing number of businesses make use of fax facilities and private carriers. An internal carrier service does exist – CAI-post – and this is available at main city post offices. Delivery to EC states should be within 48 hours, but this is not always so!

Spain although it is claimed letters to the UK from Spain normally arrive within five days, the Spanish government has invested in the postal system in order to improve it. In this respect, a Spanish Airline Postal Service known as LACE, has been established.

UK the postal service in the UK probably ranks as one of the best among the five major EC states. Two classes of mail exist – first class is more expensive and faster, with the Royal Mail claiming that it will deliver 90 per cent of first-class mail on the first working day after posting. Second class should be delivered within three days. Services offered are quite extensive and include 'recorded delivery', 'special delivery', a 'registered letter service', 'Swiftair' (express airmail letter service to all countries), 'Datapost' (an express letter and package service) and 'Red Star' (operated by British Rail).

ACTIVITY

Green Paper on postal services

At their weekly meeting on Wednesday, the Commissioners adopted the Green Paper on postal services which seeks to stimulate debate among users, operators, governments and employees on the development of the services in the Single Market. The Paper, drawn up by the EC directorates for competition and telecommunications, envisages two definite branches of the postal services; a universal service fulfilling an EC-wide public obligation to provide a good postal service for business and individuals; and services, such as bulk direct mailing and express deliveries, which may be opened to free market competition for greater efficiency.

Source: *The Week in Europe*, 14 May 1992

Read the article 'Green Paper on postal services' and then complete the following tasks:

1 Write down what you think the Commissioners wish to establish from the debate on postal services.
2 As the manager of a UK-based business that makes extensive use of the current postal service, consider what you would want from a universal EC-wide postal service. Draw up a list of points that could contribute to the debate and include these in a formal letter to the Competition Commissioner.

Other telecommunication services

The characteristics of the telecommunications systems in the major EC states are:

France large-scale government investment has led to a modern telecommunications infrastructure, offering a wide range of services. Of these, the MINITEL service is the most visible success. MINITEL can be linked to any telephone and is free of charge in many areas. The service provides users with a nationwide telephone directory coupled with over 6000 other services. The modern telephone system with more than 50 per cent of lines linked to a fully electronic exchange is virtually exclusively controlled by France Telecom. Private companies have been operating in France for some time. Another aspect of the telecommunications network is the provision of telex and fax, the latter being on the increase in France.

Germany although the market for modems, teletext and faxes has been opened to private companies in Germany, Telekom (part of Bundespost) retains the monopoly over the national telecommunications network and, indeed, over the supply and maintenance of the first telephone to be installed. Telex and fax services are widely available in Germany. A recent trend is the increase in the number of mobile telephones which are very popular.

Italy telex and telegraph services are provided by the Ministry of Post and Telecommunications. Such services, including fax, are available at major post offices. The main telephone service is provided by SIP (Societa Italiania per l'esercizio telefonica SpA), which also handles data networks and radio paging. ASST also provides Italy with an international telephone service and administers pay telephones.

Spain a long-distance telecommunications network has been provided by optical-fibre lines between Barcelona and Madrid. The Spanish post office provides telegraph, telex and a public fax system known as BUROFAX. As in other EC states, mobile telephone systems are in place and are popular.

UK in the telecommunications area, British Telecom plays a major role. BT offers a national telephone system, telex, a national data service and PRESTEL. The monopoly over telephones was recently broken when Mercury Communications Ltd was granted a licence to operate a telephone service, creating a duopoly in this area. Complaints about telecommunications services are dealt with by the regulatory body, OFTEL.

Comparison of costs of various telecommunication services to the UK in France and Germany, 1991

	Post	*Telegrams*	*Telex*	*Telephone*
France	FFr2.30 under 20g	FFr81.00 + FFr27.00 for each add. 5 words	FFr3.00 per minute + FFr35.00 tax	FFr11.00 per min. (peak) FFr3.65 (off-peak)
Germany	DM1.00 under 20g	DM0.80 per word + base fee of DM5.00 (minimum: fee DM5.60)	DM3.00 for first 3 mins + DM0.90 for each add. min.	DM0.30 for 12 secs (peak) 42 secs (off-peak)

ACTIVITY

A report consisting of four sheets of A4 paper has to be sent to the Manchester head office of a computer software company from the two EC branches – Düsseldorf and Lyons. Use the table on page 160 to decide the following.

1 a) How much will it cost to send the report by post to the UK from the EC branches?
b) How much will it cost to fax the report to the UK from the EC branches?

2 Convert the costs from 1a) and b) to UK£ using current exchange rates. How do the costs of sending the report by post and by fax compare in France and Germany?
A summary of the reports has to be forwarded to the EC branches by the Head Office in Manchester.

3 a) Find out how much it would cost to post the summary (six A4 pages) to the EC branches
b) Find out how much it would cost to fax the summary to the EC branches. (Your college may have a fax machine.)

4 Convert the costs in 3a) and b) to the relevant national currencies for France and Germany. How do the UK costs for posting and faxing the summary compare with costs in the two EC states?

Transport systems

Under the terms of the Rome Treaty, transport was supposed to be a common policy area (like the CAP). As yet, however, little has emerged by way of common solutions to EC transport problems. Largely, transport systems including those such as road freight, railways and inland waterways rely heavily on the old national government structures. This approach is in fact, supported by member states who for varying reasons wish to pursue their own transport policy. However, enlargements of the EC have meant that transport questions need to be addressed on an EC-wide basis, underlining the need for an integrated European transport network. Indeed, the growing complexity of European transport systems has been highlighted by the development of a European system of motorways, the development of container and cargo distribution (like the Europort in Rotterdam) and by projects like the Channel Tunnel. Let us now consider the various transport systems in place in the member states of the EC.

The smaller states

Comparison of railway, motorway, main road and inland waterway usage in the smaller EC states, 1989

	Length of railway used (km)	*Length of motorway used (km)*	*Length of main road used (km)*	*Length of inland waterway used (km)*
Belgium	3513	1631	12 855	1951
Denmark	2344	601	3968	–
Greece	2749	91	9526	–
Ireland	1944	8	5255	–
Luxembourg	272	75	941	37
Netherlands	2828	2045	2030	4831
Portugal	3061	243	na	–

Source: Eurostat

ACTIVITY

1 Draw a bar chart that illustrates the length of railway operated in the smaller EC states. What observations can you make from your bar chart?

2 In your opinion, for what reasons is there such a large difference between the length of motorway in The Netherlands and Belgium, compared with the other smaller states?

3 What conclusions about use of inland waterways in the smaller EC states can be drawn from the table?

Railways

The following observations can be made about railways in the smaller EC states:

- Luxembourg has one of the densest rail systems in Europe – run by a state-owned company, this operation is heavily subsidised;
- in Portugal, the transport infrastructure is generally not as advanced as it is in other EC states;
- in general, heavy-duty rail systems are supplemented by light rail services in many major cities and towns – for example, the Belgian SNCV and the Irish DART system;
- in The Netherlands, long-distance commuting to Amsterdam, and indeed to neighbouring EC states, has been positively encouraged by state subsidies, making rail transport more attractive to commuters.

Road networks

- Of the smaller EC members, the Netherlands has the highest amount of roadway (totalling almost 112 000 km in 1985), compared with just over 5000 km of roads in Luxembourg.
- In Luxembourg, the proportion of motorway is just 1 per cent of the total length of her roadways.
- In Greece, Ireland and Luxembourg, very little motorway exists at all.
- Portugal probably has the least densely populated roadways.

Air transport

The smaller EC states all have major international airports which deal with the busy flights from other EC states. Principal airports are as follows:

Belgium	Brussels	Luxembourg	Findel, Luxembourg
Denmark	Kastrup, Copenhagen	Netherlands	Schipol, Amsterdam
Greece	Athens	Portugal	Portela, Lisbon.
Ireland	Dublin		

Inland waterways

In three of the smaller EC states – Belgium, Luxembourg and The Netherlands, inland waterways provide an important form of transport.

- Luxembourg's 37 km of the Moselle River are navigable and provide direct and important access for Rhine shipping.
- In The Netherlands, there is an extensive network of navigable inland waterways, with various canals and rivers providing important direct links with neighbouring EC states.
- In the other EC states, although stretches of water are navigable, few are used for commercial purposes.
- The exception is Denmark where no internal waterway system exists at all.

Passenger ferries

Many of the smaller EC states operate car and passenger ferry services, and these are important elements in the overall EC transport system. They are nationally important too – for instance, in Denmark, the various bridges and ferries that exist are essential for links between the various islands and, therefore, they have to be efficient.

ACTIVITY

For what reasons would EC member states wish to retain their national transport systems rather than adopt Community-wide measures?

ACTIVITY

Select a town in one of the seven smaller EC states (Belgium, Denmark, Greece, Ireland, Luxembourg, The Netherlands, Portugal). Find out as much as you can about the transport systems in place in the town of your choice. (The list of national tourist agencies in Appendix 2 of this book may be useful.) Compare the transport system of your selected European town with your own town in the UK. Present this comparison orally to the rest of your class.

The major states

Railways

Despite the fact that the railway systems of the EC states have developed at different times and at different rates, it is possible to travel by train from London to the south of France, and indeed beyond this. A major contrast between the UK and the rest of Europe is that the UK tends to make more use of cheaper, road freight haulage, while the latter tend to favour rail freight haulage. This is explained by the fact that longer distances between stations in Europe have encouraged the development of high-speed trains such as the French TGV and German ICE. Thus, goods that have to be transported long distance within the Single Market are more likely to travel by rail. Indeed, in some of the major EC states, notably Germany, state subsidies and the advent of new technology, have encouraged and stimulated freight services within the rail network. In fact, most of the revenue that Deutsche Bundesbahn receives is from freight traffic.

Comparison of aspects of railway networks in major EC states, 1989

	Length of railway used (km)	*Passenger km travelled (millions)*	*Rail freight traffic (million tons per km)*
France	34 469	64 492	48 414
Germany	27 315	41 144	54 755
Italy	16 030	44 443	18 442
Spain	12 565	14 715	8273
UK	16 932	33 323	17 050

Source: Eurostat

ACTIVITY

1 Calculate the proportion of *total* railway length used by each of the five major EC states.
2 For what reasons do you think France has the highest length of railway used?
3 Compare the Italian figures for length of railway used with passenger km travelled. What do these suggest to you about Italian railways in relation to the other major states?

Key features of rail networks Each of the major EC states has specific organisations responsible for their respective national rail networks:

France	SNCF
Germany	Deutsche Bundesbahn
Italy	FS (Ferrovie dello Stato)
Spain	RENFE (Red Nacional de los Ferrocarriles Espanoles)
UK	British Rail

Of the major EC states, the efficiency of the French rail system, operated by SNCF, perhaps most sharply contrasts with many people's perceptions of British Rail. The French TGV train is the fastest in the world, capable of 400 km per hour, and European train services tend to run to schedule and more efficiently, which perhaps highlights a major difference between the UK and the rest of Europe. Reliability is a feature of the German rail system too, although this has not necessarily promoted the service provided by Deustche Bundesbahn for it is the most underused of the major EC state railways (in terms of km travelled per inhabitant). This is all despite the fact that Germany boasts the largest rail station in Europe, at Frankfurt. The modern German system makes use of high-speed, inter-city trains (ICE) and up-to-date technology for booking. Efficiency appears to be the keyword for Italian state railways too – particularly the electrified link that runs down both sides of the country. It also provides a high-speed, first-class rail service linking major Italian cities.

Spanish railways are currently undergoing a 13-year modernisation programme, which aims to improve and renovate existing track, and to introduce faster sections on inter-city routes.

In many respects, the UK network appears to be the poor relation of the major EC states. One reason may be that the system was the first to be developed in the 19th century. However, British Rail has pledged to introduce a faster service for the UK by introducing high-speed trains, more efficient timetabling and track electrification. BR is also in the process of attempting to improve its image by retraining staff in customer care skills and by having a critical look at its catering facilities.

Many major EC towns and cities play host to the Trans Europe Express (TEE), which provides an important European link.

All of the major EC states operate extensive metropolitan transport systems with use of trams, trolleybuses or underground railways. The Paris Metro, for instance, carries over eight million passengers a day. West Berlin has a total of 106 km of metropolitan railway, virtually all underground. Many German towns make use of trams too. Trolleybuses operate in some Spanish cities, supported by trams and light railways. In the UK, London Regional Transport operates the most extensive underground railway in the world and in 1989/90 carried 760 million passengers.

In terms of rail systems, the major EC states seem to be generally well equipped to deal with the demands of a growing European community.

The Channel Tunnel British Rail has collaborated with the French SNCF in the exciting Channel Tunnel project, which will eventually provide a direct rail service of road vehicle ferry trains, and passenger and freight trains, from London through to the European continent. This controversial project results from a treaty signed between the UK and France in 1987. When completed, the tunnel will have a total length of almost 50 km, of which 37 km will be actually under the sea-bed.

The construction of the Channel Tunnel has combined both French and British engineering expertise in order to link the main European continent with the British Isles. It remains a controversial issue, largely due to the increasing costs of the project.

ACTIVITY

THE EUROTUNNEL SYSTEM

Eurotunnel will connect the road and rail networks of Europe. Trains and shuttles will whisk passengers across in comfort and safety. There will be three tunnels side by side in the impermeable chalk beneath the bed of the Channel. Two single track tunnels will carry the traffic. The third, a service tunnel, will lie between them – providing ventilation, access for maintenance and for evacuation in an emergency.

The services provided

Four types of train will operate:

- Passenger shuttles for cars and coaches.
- Freight shuttles for lorries. The shuttles will operate between terminals at Folkestone and Calais.
- Euro-city passenger trains capable of high speed operations.
- Through freight trains serving the expanding European markets.

Taking vehicles across

Cars and coaches will go straight to the terminals at Folkestone or Calais.
There, vehicles will be driven through the frontier controls of both countries, if still required, and onto a waiting shuttle. Within minutes, the shuttle will be on its way.

The trip will last just 35 minutes, and passengers will stay with their vehicles in the well-lit, air conditioned shuttles. At the other end passengers will drive off and join the motorway.

Going by passenger train

Comfortable high speed trains, jointly operated by British, French and Belgian railways, will operate from city centre to city centre. London to Paris will take just over three hours, and Brussels to London three hours ten minutes (two hours 40 minutes after 1995). Some trains will stop at Ashford, Calais or Lille.

Moving the goods

Eurotunnel will speed freight in two ways:

- In through freight trains, running between centres in Britain and continental Europe.
- In lorries carried on special shuttles, connecting British and continental motorways.

The tunnel has the capacity to take 400 train paths per day in each direction at opening. This could ultimately be increased to 600.

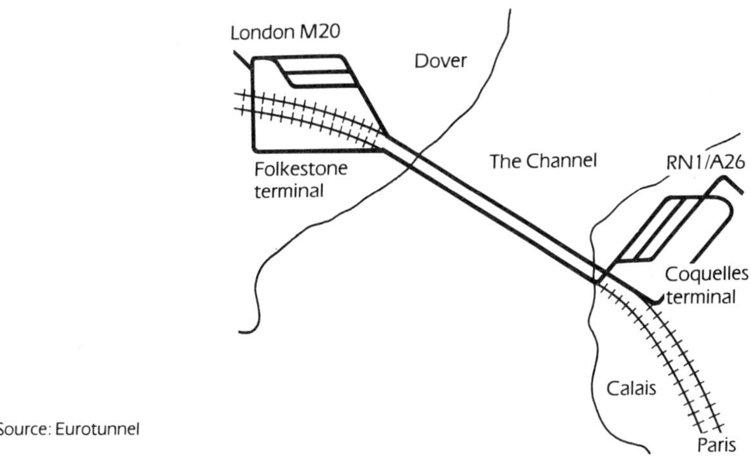

Source: Eurotunnel

1 With a partner, draw up a list of the advantages and disadvantages of the development of the Channel Tunnel. Try to consider the implications that such a development has for UK business.
2 In a group discussion led by your tutor, share your thoughts and opinions on the Channel Tunnel with the rest of the class.
3 At your work experience placement (or workplace) conduct a survey, using a short questionnaire that seeks to discover the views of managers and employees, on the development of the Channel Tunnel and its possible effects. Present your findings as a selection of graphs, drawing conclusions from them.

Other features
France:

- the rail network is divided into 23 regions, all under the general direction of Paris;
- the Paris transport system, comprising metro, rail and bus networks, is controlled by RATP (Regie Autonome des Transports Parisiens). RATP is heavily subsidised by the French government in order to offer low fares for users;
- three provincial French cities also have underground systems – Marseilles, Lyons and Lille;
- tram services became popular in France in the 1980s, with networks being introduced in Nantes and Grenoble, with plans for systems in other towns and cities;
- a small number of independent railways are in existence.

Germany:

- reunification brought the problem of two separate rail systems. The treaty signed between West and East Germany envisaged the eventual incorporation of the East German Deutsche Reichsbahn into Deutsche Bundesbahn. Until this occurs, the two rail networks will continue to operate separately;
- there are plans for a new high-speed inter-city train which would travel at around 250 km per hour;
- some non-federal railway networks exist in Germany;
- metropolitan rail systems exist in Frankfurt, Munich, Nuremburg, Hanover, Cologne, Ludwigschafen, Mulheim and Stuttgart. Trams operate in many other towns and cities.

Italy:

- an important geographical feature of the Italian rail system is the network of rail tunnels that cut through the Alps, and link Italy with Austria and France;
- some Italian routes use a high-speed, tilting train service;
- many small private or local rail companies exist alongside those offered by FS;
- commuter rail and tram networks are popular in Italian cities, and many are either already in place or planned for the near future. In particular, trams exist in Milan, Naples, Rome, Turin and Trieste. Trolleybuses also operate in some areas.

Spain:

- RENFE controls 85 per cent of Spanish state railways, with the remainder run by FEVE. This organisation also looks after most of the narrow-gauge track that exists in Spain;
- underground light rail systems exist in Madrid and Barcelona, with metros planned for other towns and cities. Tram and trolleybus services operate in some areas.

UK:

- in London, LRT, like RATP in Paris, operates both the underground rail system and bus services;
- metropolitan rail systems also exist in Birmingham, Glasgow, Liverpool and Newcastle with light rail systems planned for other areas;
- some regions and areas are considering the reintroduction of trams as a more efficient transport system. Trolleybuses are not as common in the UK as in some EC states.

Road networks
Key features of motorways All of the major EC states have well-developed and generally efficient road networks. In particular, the motorway systems of these states (and

indeed others) allows travel from one end of the EC to the other, relatively efficiently. This is assisted by by-pass systems in many cities, although these may not always be as effective as intended – anyone who has witnessed the UK M25 or the Paris 'Peripherique' at peak times would agree with this. On the whole, though, European motorway systems allow generally smooth changeovers between different motorway routes. In some of the alpine regions of the EC, feats of engineering have allowed impressive motorway tunnels to be cut out of the rock, thus making access much easier. In general, road surfaces on the continent are good and are at least comparable with those of the UK.

A clear contrast between UK and other European motorways is the question of motorway tolls. Paying for the 'luxury' of driving on a motorway is something that we in the UK have yet to witness, although tolls have long been a feature of the motorway systems of some other states. In fact, in France, Italy and Spain, the majority of motorways are toll-paying. In general, the motorist collects a ticket on joining the motorway and the toll is calculated on leaving the motorway, based upon the distance travelled on that particular stretch. For drivers travelling long distances, these tolls can add considerably to costs and are an important factor when considering transport alternatives. Of the major EC states, only the UK and Germany do not impose tolls on their motorways. This apparent lack of income does not appear to have harmed the German network (although many have argued that tolls would benefit the state of repair of UK motorways!), for an excellent system exists which is very fast and relatively uncongested. The number of repairs under way contrasts sharply with the UK, where very often, these seem to be taking place at the most illogical of times!

Another feature of the European motorway, compared with its UK counterpart, is the abundance of motorway services and rest places. Alarmingly, many long stretches of UK motorways are without these. However, the trend in Europe is the opposite. Again, the German system is particularly noteworthy with numerous, spacious parking and rest places for motorists. These are complemented by generally good motorway service areas, many of which offer facilities such as showers for long-distance travellers, encouraging overnight stops by freight drivers and businesspeople alike.

Apart from the obvious difference of driving on the right which most British motorists find a little daunting at first, there are many similarities between driving in the UK and in Europe. Road signs have been standardised to a very large extent and, despite a few exceptions, are universally understandable. Some variations occur with local signposting – German local direction signs are yellow for instance, whereas the French and UK equivalents are white. However, warning or hazard signs are usually red, advice signs blue and places of interest brown in all member states of the EC, and this aids understanding. National motorway speed limits do vary, however, but mostly fall into the 70–87 mph band. Some stretches of motorway also stipulate *minimum* speed limits in certain lanes.

A further difference between the UK and Europe is the obligation to carry spare bulbs and a warning triangle (for use in case of breakdown) in many of the UK's European neighbours.

Major road networks in the EC form part of a larger European Community system with key routes being allocated common reference numbers – for example, E20.

Comparison of length of various grade roadways in the major EC states 1989, km

	Motorway	*Main road*	*Secondary road*	*Other roads*	*Total*
France	6206	28 395	352 000	421 000	807 601
Germany	8822	31 063	133 976	325 000	498 861
Italy	6091	45 779	109 027	141 666	302 563
Spain	2286	18 671	70 812	63 927	155 696
UK	3093	12 846	37 084	326 963	379 986

Source: Eurostat

ACTIVITY

1 Draw a pie chart illustrating the length of motorway in each of the major EC states.

2 Suggest reasons why:

a) France has the longest total length (km) of roadways

b) Spain has the shortest total length (km) of roadways. How would you expect this to have changed by the year 2000?

3 Compare the set of figures for Germany with those of France. Why do you think Germany has a considerably shorter total length of roadway, yet has more motorway than France?

4 Compare the set of figures for Italy with those of the UK. What conclusions can you draw from this comparison?

Other features

France:

- many of the motorway (*autoroute*) routes have corresponding national roads (routes national) allowing free access;
- the French government recently introduced a programme to construct a further 2700 km of motorway by 1995.

Germany:

- the well-developed motorway (*autobahn*) system has encouraged the economic development of the provinces and, indeed, of the country as a whole
- not surprisingly, the largest amount of motorway in the EC is supported by a large stock of passenger cars, for in Germany the total number of cars is the highest in the Community.

Italy:

- most motorways (*autostrada*), with the exception of the Salerno-Reggio Calabria and those in Sicily, are toll-paying;
- the development of the *autostrada* in Italy has been significant because the system has greatly improved communications and links with the poorer south. A specific body, ANAS (National Autonomous Road Corporation) is responsible for the planning, construction and management of the *autostrada*;
- the road network in Italy is the system most used by traffic and this has led to a need for more roads, coupled with improved maintenance of existing routes. Italy actually has fewer kilometres of paved road per 1000 inhabitants than the EC average. In regional terms, car ownership in central and northern Italy is estimated as being the highest in Europe.

Spain:

- the government developed a General Highways Plan, to operate between 1984–91, which was designed generally to improve and update road systems.

UK:

- extensive use is made of the various grades of roadway in the UK and the fact that road haulage of goods has been on the increase in recent years, coupled with escalating passenger traffic, has taken its toll on roadways. Thus, long tailbacks on motorways, major road repair work, long lines of traffic cones, and congested cities and towns have become a feature of the UK road transport network;
- problems with road networks are not helped by the statistic that an estimated 66 per cent of British families owned a car in 1988. Furthermore, about 20 per cent of families actually owned two cars.

Air transport

In recent years, air travel in Europe has been increasingly in favour. This trend is likely to become more exagerated in the future and will be assisted by initiatives taken by the European Commission. Having reached agreement on the removal of price-fixing on EC air routes, making it easier for new operators to secure routes, the next phase of the Commission's plan is actually to remove the right of national airlines such as Air France and Lufthansa to dominate routes in their air space. This air liberalisation is likely to have implications for businesses that deal within the Single Market.

ACTIVITY

Read the article 'Air liberalisation' and then answer the following questions:

1. List the advantages and disadvantages of lower fares for Community air travellers.
2. What is meant by 'liberalisation of Community airlines'?
3. Why is the proposal outlined in the article 'seen as vital to the Single Market'?
4. How might the EC implement its intended safeguards?

Air liberalisation

Europe's air travellers are set to enjoy lower fares from next year after EC transport ministers agreed on further liberalisation of Community airlines at a lengthy meeting in Luxembourg on Monday. Under the agreement, carriers from one member state will be free to offer domestic services in any other EC state in direct competition to national carriers so long as the flight forms part of a longer route. The deregulation proposal comes under the Commission's third package of air liberalisation and is seen as vital to the Single Market. Deregulation will take place over four years starting on 1 January 1993. However, certain Community-level safeguards will protect the environment, prevent over-stretching of airport infrastructure and ensure adequate services on lesser-used routes.

Source: *The Week in Europe*, 25 June 1992

Air transport in the major EC states

Member state	*National carrier*	*Major airports*
France	Air France Air Inter	Paris (Orly, Charles de Gaulle, le Bourget), Bordeaux Lille, Marseilles, Nice, Strasbourg
Germany	Lufthansa	Berlin, Koln-Bonn, Dresden, Dusseldorf, Frankfurt, Hamburg, Hannover, Leipzig, Munich, Stuttgart
Italy	Alitalia	Rome (Leonardo da Vinci), Milan (Linate, Malpensa), Pisa, Turin, Venice, Naples, Bologna, Genoa
Spain	Iberia Aviaco	Madrid, Barcelona, Malaga, Alicante, Bilbao, Almeria, Valencia, Santiago
UK	British Airways	London (Heathrow, Gatwick, Stansted), Glasgow, Manchester, Birmingham, Bristol

Inland waterways

France in 1987, it was estimated that there were some 8500 km of navigable waterway in France. Of this total, over 1500 km were considered accessible to craft of 3000 tons. In the same year, the French government set in motion a programme to modernise the navigable waterways, and this included the construction of a canal which would link the Rivers Rhône and Rhine. The port of Paris is France's most important inland waterway port and is also the second largest in Europe. The ANNF (Association Nationale de la Navigation Fluviale) is committed to promoting the interests of those involved in goods transport on French navigable waterways.

Germany inland waterway development is dealt with by the Federal Ministry of Transport (Abteilung Binnenschiffahrt und Wasserstrassen) and this department is responsible for 6700 km of navigable inland waterways. It has also overseen the construction of the Rhine–Main–Danube Canal (linking the North Sea and the Black Sea) which was due to be completed in 1992. In Germany, inland shipping accounts for about 20 per cent of total freight traffic. The freight system of transport is largely based on the Rhine system and the various interconnecting canals that exist.

Italy despite an estimated 2237 km of navigable inland waterway in 1983, the Italian system of rivers and canals is not connected to the Western European system of waterways because of the geographical barrier of the Alps. This makes the waterways system largely redundant as far as EC transport systems are concerned. It is impossible to cross the central spine of Italy via inland waterways. However, Italy does have some notable rivers – the Po being the longest, and the River Tiber, passing through the Italian capital, Rome.

Spain few stretches of navigable inland waterway are used for commercial purposes in Spain and, indeed, the EC statistical service, Eurostat, makes no entry for Spain in its official figures. However, an exception to this is the Guadalquivir River in southern Spain.

UK the 3200 km of inland waterways come under the control and supervision of the National Rivers Authority and British Waterways Board and comprise both river systems and man-made canal networks. Recently, the serious decline of the inland waterways (a transport system that enjoyed its heyday in the 18th century) has been tackled, with many schemes and projects set in place to regenerate such routes. Some projects have included converting stretches of water into tourist attractions and clearing up certain waterways to allow the passage of holiday vessels. Many projects for redevelopment have been at least partially funded by the EC.

Passenger ferries

Important transport services are provided in the five major EC states by the various car and passenger ferries operated by companies such as Sealink, P and O, Sally Line and Scandinavian Seaways which provide vital commercial and leisure links between the UK and Europe.

ACTIVITY

1. Prepare a report for the manager of City Business Forms Ltd which compares the transport systems of the five major EC states. Comparisons should be made under the following headings – road networks, railways, air transport.
2. Attach to your report a set of appendices that detail major roads, main railway stations and principal airports in the five major EC states.

ACTIVITY

Standard EC driving licence

EC transport ministers, meeting in Luxembourg, agreed on a common, standardised, driving licence throughout the Community from 1996 and agreed to introduce common roadworthiness tests for private cars from 1998. The common driving licence means that all national permits will be recognised throughout the EC without any requirement to get a local licence. The Roadworthiness Directive will apply to vehicles registered from 1994. The first test is obligatory after four years and then every two years thereafter, so that the process starts in 1998.

Source: *The Week in Europe*, 27 June 1991

Read the article 'Standard EC driving licence' and then answer the following questions:

1 List the advantages and disadvantages of a common, standardised EC driving licence.
2 How will common roadworthiness tests differ in the future? What implications do these tests have for a UK business such as a courier service?

ACTIVITY Review your progress: 8

1 Explain what is meant by freedom of the press.
2 Match the following newspapers to the relevant EC state:
   a) *El Pais*
   b) *le Figaro*
   c) *La Repubblica*
   d) *Bild*
   e) *Daily Telegraph*
   f) *ABC*
   g) *Corriere della Sera*
   h) *le Monde*.
3 Which of the following EC member states has the largest circulation of daily newspapers?
   a) Spain?
   b) UK?
   c) Germany?
4 Which EC member state has the highest number of TV sets per 1000 inhabitants?
   a) Italy?
   b) France?
   c) UK?
   d) Denmark?
5 What is the 'Television without Frontiers' Directive about?
6 What is the name of:
   a) the German postal service?
   b) the Italian postal service?
7 Which of the EC member states has:
   a) the longest total railway track?
   b) the shortest total railway track?
8 What are French, German and Italian motorways called?

Summary

- There is some variation between the type, style and circulation of newspapers across the EC member states.
- Ownership and organisation of TV and radio broadcasting varies from member state to member state. There are varying degrees of commercial interest in broadcasting.
- Telecommunications are generally operated by national governments in the EC member states.
- The EC has provided few solutions to Community transport problems and member states rely heavily on national governments with reference to transport systems.

Assignment 13

Bradwells Euro Insurance

Bradwells Insurance, based in the Swindon area, has been trading for over 15 years. In response to the opening of the Single Market at the end of 1992, Bradwells have decided to establish a European base in either Northern Italy, Southern Germany or Northern Spain. Before a location is decided upon, a feasibility study is to be carried out which is to consider the following in each of the three favoured areas:

- radio and TV networks
- transport networks
- telecommunications
- the press and advertising.

As part of the feasibility study, you are asked by the European development director of Bradwells to carry out the following tasks.

Task 1

a) For *each* of the three favoured European areas, select three towns or cities where Bradwells could possibly locate their new business. Produce maps of the three favoured areas and mark your selected towns and cities on them.

b) Produce a short, written summary outlining the strengths and weaknesses of the three favoured areas in terms of the location for Bradwells' business.

Task 2

Having identified several possible locations for Bradwells in Task 1, you are now required to suggest *one* town or city that could be recommended to the European development director. Your recommendations should be made in a formal report to the director, that identifies the following:

- population of the selected town or city
- radio and TV networks that could be used to advertise Bradwells in the selected town or city
- national and local press and advertising rates
- availability of telecommunications systems in the area
- transport networks to and from the selected town or city. Include road, rail and air networks
- cultural characteristics of the area/country.

Task 3

Assume that your recommendations for Bradwells' European location are accepted. You are now asked to complete the following.

a) Produce a persuasive circular for existing Bradwells staff asking for volunteers to spend six months setting up the new business in the selected location.

b) Devise a draft press advertisement (in English) for Bradwells Insurance that could be used to promote the new business in your selected location.

9 The infrastructures of the EC member states: 2

Aims

- To consider education and training, social welfare, employment and housing in general within the EC
- To examine the specific policies of the five major EC states in relation to education and training, social welfare, employment and housing
- To encourage the comparison and contrast of further aspects of the infrastructures of the EC member states.

Relevant BTEC Outcome Performance Criteria
5c Policies on education, training, social welfare, employment and housing.

Policies in EC member states

Education and Training

The smaller states
In the smaller EC states, education is generally free and compulsory from the age of 6 (7 in Denmark) up to the age of 15 or 16. The exception is Belgium where education is obligatory up to the age of 18. In Portugal it was estimated in 1988 that only 40 per cent of schoolchildren completed their nine years' education. Indeed, in some rural areas this figure was probably even lower. In partial response to this, the Portugese government has recognised that educational standards must be improved in order to assist the development of the economy. It is interesting to note that education in some states is provided largely by private (and very often religious) bodies. This is true in Ireland where schools receive subsidies from the Education Department and in The Netherlands where some private schools are funded entirely by the Dutch government.

In Belgium, a parallel system of education exists – a Flemish system and a Walloon system. This reflects the cultural differences within that state. An important feature of education in Denmark is the provision for adults which includes training at over 100 traditional folk schools or Folkehojskole.

In terms of primary education, this generally lasts for six years within the smaller EC states. Primary education in Luxembourg includes instruction in German (with instruction in French at secondary level). In Portugal, primary education consists of four years followed by two years' preparatory education.

Secondary education is offered along similar lines in each of the seven smaller EC states. Many states offer a choice to pupils of either a vocational or traditional secondary education. In Belgium pupils attend comprehensive secondary schools, while in Ireland secondary education is divided between secondary, vocational, comprehensive or community schooling. Two-thirds of Danish children receive practical or commercial training in trade or commerce. In Greece, secondary education can last for up to six years, while in Portugal secondary education consists of two three-year cycles plus a one-year pre-professional or pre-university course. In Portugal in 1988, 40 per cent of 12 – 18 year olds received secondary education compared with an EC average of about 75 per cent.

The smaller states all offer higher education at either universities or other institutions. Many offer grants for students, often based on the financial resources of the student. In Ireland, a National Council for Educational Awards issues grants to students, while in The Netherlands, students can apply for scholarships or for interest-free loans from the government. In Belgium, about 20 per cent of students receive government grants, while in Ireland about 33 per cent receive higher education awards. In Portugal, only 11 per cent of school leavers go on to higher education.

The major states

Administration In general, the education systems of the major states are *decentralised* – in practice this means that although central government has some control over the systems (usually broad policy areas), it is deemed more sensible for local administrative units to deliver the systems. Thus, in France, 27 educational districts (academies) administer education from primary right through to higher level. In Germany, the federal nature of the state, and the Basic Law, demands that education be organised in a decentralised way. Each lander is responsible for the local education system, and despite the potential chaos that this would seem to suggest, the systems within Germany are largely compatible with one another. The UK system is known as a national system, locally administered, again reflecting its decentralised nature. Overall responsibility for education, however, remains with the Department for Education and the education minister. This supervisory role is also a feature of the Italian and Spanish systems.

In all the major states, education is provided free and is compulsory. However, the length of compulsory schooling differs from state to state:

Length of compulsory education in major EC states

age	5	6	7	8	9	10	11	12	13	14	15	16	17	18
France		[	—	—	—	—	—	—	—	—	—	]		
Germany		[	—	—	—	—	—	—	—	—	—	—	—	]
Italy		[	—	—	—	—	—	—	—	]				
Spain		[	—	—	—	—	—	—	—	—	—	]		
UK	[	—	—	—	—	—	—	—	—	—	—	]		

(NB: the possibility of raising the school leaving age to 16 is currently being considered in Italy)

Both the UK and Italy operate a national common curriculum for compulsory education – in the UK, this was an integral part of the 1988 Education Reform Act. While a common curriculum was considered to be the priority in the UK, the French identified four main target areas for their system in 1989: a) all should leave school with recognised qualifications; b) 80 per cent of children should achieve the BAC (see below) or equivalent; c) those achieving the BAC should have the right to higher education; d) teaching methods should be reformed.

After the signing of the German unification treaty, a radical restructuring of the education system took place in order to standardise it across the whole of Germany. A particular requirement of the treaty was that qualifications gained in the former East Germany should be recognised as valid in the new, united Germany.

Recent reforms (1990) in Spain, known as the LOGSE, aimed to extend compulsory education to a ten-year period, offering basic education in three cycles.

Pre-school education In some of the major states, provision exists for non-compulsory pre-school education. This is an important part of the Italian system, where about 90 per cent of children attend day nurseries. It is significant in France too – here all children attend the école maternelle (nursery school). Indeed, French parents view this part of the education process very seriously. The UK also makes provision for pre-school education –

often in the form of nursery units attached to primary schools and attended in the morning or afternoon only. One of the features of the UK primary education system has been the increasing demand for nursery places, which is rarely matched by the number of places available.

Primary education In the sense that it provides basic and elementary schooling, primary education is identical in the major EC states. Organisation at this level tends to be similar too, with primary education consisting of cycles (usually two). The duration of the primary stage differs, however – in France, Italy and Spain, it lasts for five years; in Germany four years; and in the UK six years.

French primary education (the basic learning stage) commences at the all-important pre-school stage and continues into the first two years of primary education. The last three years are generally viewed as a period of consolidation and reinforcement.

Such cycles are features of the Italian, Spanish and UK systems too. In Italy, the two cycles result in the primary school leaving certificate (Licenza Elementaire), for which children sit an examination. The Licenza offers access to secondary education. The Spanish primary cycles are known as lower and intermediate, and they form two-thirds of the overall basic general education (EGB). Within these cycles, education is provided by one teacher whose role it is to develop individual basic skills and self-expression. This approach is a familiar element of the UK primary education system. With the exception of some lower and middle schools, UK primary provision tends to be divided into infant and junior cycles, mirroring the systems of other EC states to some degree. Controversial tests at primary level have recently been introduced to the UK, but these do not perhaps have the same status as the Italian Licenza Elementaire.

Note should be made here of German primary education provision, where maturity tests are used to determine whether or not a child is ready for primary school. Those failing such tests can attend nursery school or elementary classes until the required maturity is achieved. Primary education occurs in the Grundschule (elementary school) in Germany and is obligatory for all children during the first four years of their school life.

Secondary education Similarities exist between France and Germany in terms of the type of establishment providing secondary education.

France

- colleges (lower secondary)
- lycées (upper secondary)
- lycées professionnels (vocational secondary).

Germany

- Hauptschule (general secondary)
- Realschule (intermediate secondary)
- Gymnasium (grammar)

These different educational establishments exist to cater for the differing needs of pupils. The French colleges are basically comprehensive schools (like the UK version), which are attended by all pupils after primary education. Lasting for four years and split into the observation and guidance cycles, pupils finish at 15 and then have to spend at least one more year in full-time education, either at a lycée or lycée professionnel. Those attending lycées pursue studies leading to the baccalaureate (BAC) and about 30 per cent of French pupils leave school with this. Similarly, the German system categorises pupils for academic and vocational training.

Education in the Hauptschule lasts for five to six years with pupils then going on to employment (continuing education on a part-time basis for three to four years). In the Realschule and Gymnasium, education lasts for six and nine years respectively. Pupils selecting the Gymnasium route study for the grammar school certificate, the Arbitur, which gives access to universities.

In Italy, pupils take the secondary leaving certificate at the age of 14 and this ends their compulsory education. However, pupils may elect to stay on until they have completed five years' secondary education when they sit the Maturita (higher secondary school certificate), allowing access to higher education.

Before LOGSE, the Spanish secondary system awarded the school graduation certificate (Graduado Escolar) to those pupils successfully completing secondary education, while unsuccessful pupils received the school attendance certificate (Certificado de Escolaridad). The first of these gave access to upper secondary schools and the Bachillerato (BUP). Studies towards the BUP last for three years, and prepare pupils for university and vocational training. The second offered access to the lower level vocational training institutions. Under the new LOGSE, however, a change will occur, for all pupils who complete secondary education will receive the certificate of secondary education, enabling access to the BUP and to intermediate vocational training. This is a shift to the comprehensive type of system that has existed in the UK for some time. Indeed, UK pupils are admitted to secondary school with no reference to ability. Since the switch to the general certificate of secondary education (GCSE), more emphasis has been placed on the assessment of work at school rather than external examination. Pupils take several GCSEs at the end of the secondary period and the results of these may or may not allow access to further education.

About 30 per cent of UK pupils stay on at the age of 16 to study A levels, allowing access to higher education, with many more going on to complete vocational courses such as those offered by BTEC, RSA or City and Guilds.

ACTIVITY

Young people's (15–24) reasons for choice of subjects for study, 1987 (%)

	B	*DK*	*D*	*GR*	*E*	*F*	*IRL*	*I*	*L*	*NL*	*P*	*UK*
Special interest	39	39	27	40	46	41	40	47	55	38	50	61
Leads to desired occupation	43	47	46	43	33	48	44	51	51	48	57	48
Leads to a well-paid job	13	11	20	20	5	21	15	19	29	18	18	20
Offers a better chance of a job	27	20	37	21	23	38	34	39	29	32	20	28
Other people's wishes	10	4	13	9	11	8	11	10	4	5	3	3
Other reasons	8	7	3	1	4	4	5	3	3	13	1	2

Totals more than 100 due to multiple answers

Source: Eurobarometer

1. Produce a bar chart which compares the reasons for choice of subjects for the five major EC states. List the conclusions that you can draw from your bar chart.
2. Consider your own reasons for choosing your current BTEC course. Using the categories given in the table above, rank these reasons in order of importance (where 1 is most important and 5 is least important). How do your reasons compare with the results in the table? Be prepared to give your reasons for ranking your answers as you did.

ACTIVITY

Tongue-tied young Britons

With the exception of ex East Germans and the Irish, young Britons aged between 15 and 24 are worse than the rest of their European counterparts at being able to hold a conversation in any foreign language. A new report on 'Young Europeans' published by the Commission in Brussels found that only 50 per cent of a random sample of young Britons had any knowledge of foreign language. The best result came from young Luxembourgers who spoke an average of 2.7 foreign languages each. They were followed in proficiency by Danes (1.8), the Dutch (1.6) and Belgians with 1.1.

Surprisingly in the ranking of importance of languages young Europeans would like to learn, English has dropped from first to fourth place between 1987 and 1990, and Italian has jumped from fourth to second place. Top ranking choice of languages in the survey was German. 18 per cent of those asked said they did not wish to learn another language.

Source: *The Week in Europe*, 21 November 1991

Read the article 'Tongue-tied young Britons' and then answer the following questions:

1 In your opinion, why do young Britons rank so low in their knowledge of foreign languages and young Luxembourgers rank so high?
2 Suggest measures that could be taken by the UK government to improve knowledge of foreign languages.
3 It would appear from the article that English as a foreign language has lost some of its importance. Why might this be so?
4 Carry out a mini-survey of your European Studies class to discover which students have knowledge of foreign languages.

Post-secondary education All of the major states require some sort of entrance requirement for university education. In France, access to higher education is via the minimum requirement of the BAC, while in the UK, access is usually via A level or BTEC results. The Spanish system makes use of an orientation course preceding university education, whereby students decide which course of study they would prefer. Access to German higher education is via the school leaving certificate, although within this, different qualifications exist – the allgemeine Hochschulreife gives holders access to all higher education institutions without restrictions on the subjects studied; the fachgebundene Hochschulreife gives holders access to a specific subject only; the Fachhochschulreife gives entitlement to study at the Fachhochschule.

Different cycles or stages of university education exist in many of the states. In France, three possible cycles exist including a first degree and a masters degree, while in Spain, three cycles lead to the award of doctor. In the UK, degrees are offered in many disciplines leading to batchelor of arts (BA), batchelor of science (BSc) or BEd (for those wishing to pursue a teaching career). In general, degree courses tend to last for three or four years – in Italy, courses last for at least four years. All of the major states have a good number of higher education institutions, and a recent feature of the UK system is the growing number of universities due to the change in status of many polytechnics and higher education colleges – for example, Leicester Polytechnic became De Montfort University.

A feature of the UK and Spanish higher education systems is the existence of the Open University or UNED (as it is known in Spain). In both countries, these institutions offer flexible, distance-learning, higher education courses on a modular basis over a number of years. Supporting the Open University in the UK is the Open College (established 1987), which offers flexible, open-learning courses in technology, commerce and vocational areas. Business schools are a feature of the Spanish system, particularly in Madrid and Barcelona where training in commerce and business is offered.

ACTIVITY

A Belgian pen-pal of yours wants to come to the UK in order to follow a degree course. Find out whether the pen-pal would be eligible for free tuition and an educational grant, and the steps that should be taken in making an application for higher education. Prepare a set of guidelines to detail this information.

Vocational training Non-school vocational training is offered in all of the major EC states and very often initiatives in this area are a direct response to youth unemployment. Generally, vocational training is the responsibility of the Department of Employment or equivalent government department. In Italy, vocational training is the responsibility of the various regions. Vocational schemes vary among the major states. Both France and Italy still recognise the apprenticeship, but these positions are much less important than they once were. In both cases, apprenticeships lead to vocational qualifications coupled with practical training offered by employers.

Vocational training in the major EC states

France	Apprenticeships	for 16–25 age group. Last for 1–3 years, with practical training.
	Training credit	for 16–25 age group. Individual training courses with qualifications. Includes assessment of previous attainments and of skills acquired.
	Sandwich courses	gives experience in a firm and allows for achievement of vocational qualifications.
Germany	Vocational schools	part-time and full-time offering vocational training.
	Facschule	build on initial vocational training as well as promoting general education.
Italy	Apprenticeships	in arts and crafts and commerce.
	Work training contracts (CFL)	for 15–29 age group. Leads to recognised qualification. Lasts for 40 hours in small and medium firms, and 100 hours in larger ones.
	Vocational training courses	about 20 000 each year in agriculture, industry and services. Ends after 3 years with final exam. 'Qualification certificate' for successful trainees.
Spain	Occupational vocational training (FPO)	for young unemployed with training vocational training regional centres or firms. Aimed at 16–25 age group. Leads to certificate testifying to skills acquired.
	Workshop schools/Skilled craft centres	public work training programmes to combat unemployment. Theoretical and practical training plus compensatory education for those unsuccessful in basic general education.
UK	Youth training	guarantees 2 years' vocational training for those under 18. Usually leads to vocational qualifications and includes work experience/training. Trainees receive 'record of achievement' on completion.
	Further education	colleges also offer broad range of vocational qualifications on full-time and part-time basis.

ACTIVITY

1 You have decided to apply for employment at a Dutch company based in Eindhoven. You are asked to produce a flow chart that illustrates your education to date (inclusive of your BTEC course), showing educational establishments attended, dates and qualifications obtained.

2 You are keen to ensure that your BTEC National Award is recognised in your job application to Eindhoven. Try to find out which Dutch qualification is equivalent to your BTEC award. (You will probably need to visit the college or local library for this information.)

Social welfare

The smaller states

All of the smaller EC states (as with the larger five), offer provision for social welfare. The services and facilities offered by this type of policy, despite the discussion surrounding this controversial area, tend to be taken for granted by many citizens in the EC states.

Medical care

Various ratios between private and public sector hospital beds exist within the smaller EC states. For example, in Belgium in 1985, over 60 per cent of hospital beds were based in the private sector, while the rest were the responsibility of public sector institutions. The type of government in power in the national state probably has much to do with this ratio. Indeed, private health schemes in the UK really only took off when given impetus by the Conservative government – a policy step which is seen as unfair and élitist by the UK Labour party. In addition, many EC states levy charges or require at least part payment for services such as dental treatment and prescribed medicines. This is the case in Denmark where, however, all residents receive free medical treatment.

In Ireland, health provision is administered by eight regional health boards, all coming under the supervision of the Department of Health. As with many of the EC states, the health service is funded by taxation and state subsidy and, interestingly, by proceeds from the Irish national lottery. The Irish government operates a policy whereby patients on low income qualify for free treatment, while others pay a charge which is directly proportional to their income. The Voluntary Health Insurance Board runs an insurance scheme for those not entitled to free treatment. This scheme would appear to be similar in design to schemes in operation in the UK, such as the Birmingham Hospital Saturday Fund.

In Luxembourg, patients pay fixed contributions towards the cost of medical and dental treatment, and for certain medicines.

The Dutch hospital system differs from that of other member states, for clinics and hospitals operate on the basis of a government permit, and traditionally are not allowed to make a profit. However, the recent development of private health care has challenged the notion of medicine being a non-profit making area. Dutch policy dictates that health insurance is compulsory for those who earn a certain amount, but is voluntary for the lower paid. It is estimated that 60 per cent of the Dutch population is covered by state schemes while the rest are insured via private schemes. In The Netherlands, fixed prescription charges operate.

The EC state with the youngest system of health provision is Portugal where a national health service was first developed in 1979. This service aims to provide medical treatment throughout Portugal, financed by the state. The system is administered by the Ministry of Health via a number of regional health boards. Hospitalisation in Portugal is free, but patients pay a proportion of the cost of medicines applied. In addition to the national health service, private medical practices are allowed to co-exist alongside, providing facilities for wealthier Portugese citizens.

ACTIVITY

Number of hospital beds in EC states, 1986 (per 1000 inhabitants)

Member state	*Non-psychiatric hospital beds*	*Psychiatric hospital beds*
Belgium	4.7	2.1
Denmark	5.2	1.7
France	8.7	0.2
Germany	9.6	1.4
Greece	4.0	1.3
Ireland	5.3	3.2
Italy	7.0	0.9
Luxembourg	9.7	2.7
Netherlands	9.6	1.8
Portugal	2.9	0.9
Spain	4.0	0.9
UK	4.6	2.6

Source: Eurostat

1 Using the table above, draw a bar chart which compares the number of non-psychiatric and psychiatric hospital beds for each of the EC member states.

2 a) Which of the smaller EC states has the highest number of non-psychiatric hospital beds? Why might this be so?

b) In your opinion, why does Portugal have the lowest number of non-psychiatric hospital beds in the EC?

c) Compared with the other 11 EC member states, the UK has the fourth lowest number of non-psychiatric beds. Why might this be so?

d) Suggest reasons why Ireland has the largest number of psychiatric hospital beds.

e) France has the smallest number of psychiatric hospital beds. What does this suggest about French medical provision?

Social security

The amount of income that an EC household spends on health has much to do with the financial organisation of the social security system in a particular member state. For instance, in the UK, the National Health Service (NHS) provides all health care. In Denmark, however, the financial balance of the social security system is met by taxation. Households in other EC states contribute by varying degrees. When making comparisons between health care systems across the EC, it is important to bear these differences in mind.

Trends in expenditure on health as a proportion of total household expenditure (%)

	1975	*1980*	*1985*	*1988*
Belgium	8.9	9.8	10.4	11.0
Denmark	2.0	1.8	1.8	2.0
France	7.0	7.7	8.6	9.2
Germany	12.9	13.5	13.9	15.0
Greece	3.9	3.6	3.6	3.6
Ireland	2.2	2.1	2.6	3.4
Italy	4.2	4.8	5.5	6.1
Luxembourg	6.3	7.3	6.7	7.8
Netherlands	11.2	12.1	12.6	12.6
Portugal		4.3	4.6	4.5*
Spain	3.4	3.8	3.6	3.6
UK	0.9	1.0	1.3	1.3

*Figure for 1986

Source: Eurostat

ACTIVITY

1 The table on page 180 shows that Germany spends the highest proportion on health within the EC, while the UK spends the least. In a group discussion led by your tutor, suggest reasons for these statistics.
2 Produce an article (no more than 400 words) for a private health magazine, *Your Health!*, that considers some of the above statistics and then attempts to persuade readers to purchase private health care.

The seven smaller EC states all offer some form of social security system. In general, these systems are administered by the state – in Belgium, the ONSS (Central National Office of Social Security) is responsible, while in many other states there is either a government ministry or department set aside for social security. Denmark, Luxembourg and The Netherlands all place great emphasis on the social security system and these states offer very comprehensive services.

Funding for the various social security systems tends to be provided by national insurance type contributions, usually made by both employer and employee (as in the UK). These contributions may or may not be supplemented by subsidies from the state itself. In Denmark, the system is funded by income tax contributions, supplemented by state subsidy and contributions from local authorities.

The smaller EC states all offer the usual range of benefits that we are accustomed to in the UK. The following benefits tend to be generally offered:

- sickness benefit
- maternity benefit
- disability allowance
- unemployment benefit
- family allowance for each child
- retirement pension.

Most of the smaller states seem to agree that the retirement age for both men and women should be the same. Thus, in most states the retirement age is 65 for both sexes. The exceptions are Belgium where women are permitted to retire at 60 and Portugal where they are permitted to retire at the age of 62.

ACTIVITY

European blow to equal pension rights

The campaign for equal pension rights for men and women in the UK suffered a setback yesterday. The European Court of Justice gave a preliminary opinion that European Community Law does not require equal treatment between men and women in national insurance contributions.

The Advocate-General's opinion in a case brought by the Equal Opportunities Commission is not binding on the full court. In most cases, however, the court upholds the Advocate-General's decision.

The EOC said it was disappointed by the opinion. It had sought a declaration that the UK government was in breach of an obligation in the EC Social Security Directive to give equal treatment in statutory social security. To qualify for a state pension in the UK, men must have paid national insurance contributions for at least 44 years. But for women the figure is 39 years.

After the age of 60 women may not make any further NI contributions. But working men between the ages of 60 and 64 must pay NI contributions from their earnings even if they have already contributed for 44 years.

Source: *Financial Times*, 13 May 1992

Read the article 'European blow to equal pension rights', and then answer the following questions:

1 In what ways is the system described in the article unfair?

2 Do you think that men and women in the UK should have equal pension rights? Give your reasons.
3 What measures should the EC take to ensure that pensions rights are equal in a) the UK and b) the EC as a whole?

The major states

Medical care

As in the smaller EC states, advanced medical care systems exist in all the major states. Hospitals in the former West Germany tend to have a high level of specialist equipment at their disposal. Whether or not medical treatment is administered free of charge really depends upon the system in place in each state.

The majority of the major states offer some form of free medical treatment. The exception is Germany where there is no free national health service, but where treatment costs are covered by comprehensive, contributory insurance funds. In France, medical care is free for those in the lowest income group, while others pay direct for medical treatment and prescribed medicines, and then obtain reimbursement for up to 75 per cent of the total cost of treatment.

In the remaining three major states, the respective national health systems all provide free medical treatment for all citizens. This should be qualified, however, in the case of Spain where treatment is free if it is part of social security provision. It should also be noted here that in Italy and the UK patients have to pay prescription charges (at a flat rate charge in the UK), and fees for sight testing, and dental check-ups and treatment. The French system demands a 'bed and breakfast' charge for hospital patients.

A feature of all medical systems is the extent to which private health care has been introduced. The major states have different ratios of private to public health care. A fairly balanced combination of the two exists in Spain and, in recent years, the UK has witnessed a mushrooming of private health care plans such as BUPA. Indeed, in 1986, it was estimated that five million health care consumers were covered by private schemes (either taken out personally or as part of an employment package).

Social security

Social benefits breakdown in major EC states, 1989 (million ECU)

	France	*Germany*	*Italy*	*Spain*	*UK*
Sickness	60 873	78 722	41 122	13 637	32 023
Invalidity/disability	14 588	24 929	13 506	5 464	15 479
Occupational disease/injury	5 129	8 623	4 279	1 449	1 364
Old age	85 246	85 263	85 450	20 386	62 823
Survivors	18 213	35 957	18 216	6 235	2 015
Maternity	3 996	1 967	1 195	648	1 309
Family	19 752	20 809	7 228	383	15 254
Vocational guidance/mobility	2 790	4 981	120	729	1 960
Unemployment	12 519	13 109	2 857	7 673	7 370
Housing	6 492	2 434	57	347	7 819
Miscellaneous	2 113	8 521	29	114	1 925
TOTAL	231 711	285 315	174 059	57 065	149 341

Source: Eurostat

ACTIVITY

1 Draw a bar chart which compares pensions, sickness benefit and unemployment benefit in each of the five major EC states.
2 What conclusions can be drawn from your bar chart?

All five major EC states offer reasonably comprehensive systems of social security that complement the provision made for health care. Common areas between the different systems include the type of benefits offered to the insured. There are some notable differences between systems and the following profiles of each major state outline arrangements made for the provision of social security.

France the state plays an important role in the social security system which dates back to 1945. It is a very complex system leading to criticisms of it being too bureaucratic. The current system is highly fragmented, consisting of over 500 different schemes.

Many French workers subscribe to non-profit making insurance funds known as 'mutuelles'. There are a large number of schemes, some of which are largely controlled by the 'Partenaires Sociaux' (association of employer and employees). This is especially the case with unemployment and supplementary pension schemes.

The system demands contributions amounting to 5.5 per cent from employees and 12.6 per cent from employers. These help to fund the usual range of social benefits such as sickness, unemployment, maternity, disability (resulting from industrial accident), allowances for large families and war pensions. Sickness benefits and pensions are related to income, age and length of time insured. The latter of these has been suggested as a reason for the escalating costs of the French system. In France, pensions are payable from the age of 60 – for both men and women. These are adjusted every six months according to the cost of living, as is the national minimum hourly wage, introduced by the French government. The minimum hourly wage guarantees workers a certain amount per hour.

ACTIVITY

NATIONAL MINIMUM HOURLY WAGE!

1. With a partner, draw up a list of advantages and disadvantages of a national minimum hourly wage in the UK. Try to consider the issue from the viewpoint of both employee and employer.
2. In a class discussion on the national minimum hourly wage, share your thoughts and opinions with other members of the group. What can you conclude about the implications of this measure for a) UK businesses in general and b) the EC Single Market?
3. Follow up your discussion by conducting a survey of 10–15 people (preferably a cross-section of young people and adults) to determine their opinions about the minimum hourly wage. Collate your results and draw up a set of written conclusions from your survey.

Germany the former West Germany established one of the most advanced and expensive social security systems in the world. It provides comprehensive insurance cover for sickness, accidents at work, retirement, disability and unemployment.

The insurance scheme is administered by autonomous regional and local organisations. The 1990 treaty signed between the old West and East Germany included provisions eventually to establish the system throughout the former East Germany. In the former West Germany, more than 80 per cent of the population was covered by the system. There are several important features of the German social security system.

- *Health insurance* all workers with a monthly income of less than DM4275 are required to be covered by health insurance. Contributions are shared, half and half, by employer and employee. These amount to approximately 13 per cent of gross income on average. This covers all medical attention costs and provides a benefit of 85 – 90 per cent of the worker's normal wage. Insurance cover also provides for expenses beyond medical help such as travelling and so on.

- *Pension Fund* membership of this is compulsory for all employees who receive an income of less than DM5700 per month. Contributions towards the pension fund are made by employers and employees, each paying half, and amounting to 18.7 per cent of gross income. German pensions are the highest in Europe and an individual's pension will depend on the contributions paid and also on the general increase in incomes of the active workforce (the Generationenvertrag). Pensions are index-linked. The age of retirement in Germany is 65 for both men and women.
- *Unemployment insurance* benefits under this insurance cover are administered by a central office, the Bundesamt fur Arbeit. All employees are required to contribute to this scheme, regardless of the amount of income. Contributions amount to 4.3 per cent and are paid, half and half, by employer and employee. If a worker loses their job, they receive up to 68 per cent of their last net income (based on the contributions they have made), but not more than DM2400, for a maximum period of one year. During this time, their contributions to the pension fund and for health insurance will be paid. After one year, unemployment payments reduce to a maximum of 58 per cent of their last net income.
- *Social Aid* the aim of this scheme is to enable all German residents to live with dignity even if they are without income of any kind. It is only paid if no other income is received by the claimant and it is paid out by local authorities.
- *Insurance against accidents at work* under this scheme, employers are required to pay for rehabilitation and damages in cases of accidents that occur in the workplace. In order to cover the risk, employers pay contributions to an insurance scheme known as Berufsgenossenschaften. The level of contribution paid by the employer depends upon the risks involved at the workplace and on the incomes of employees.
- *Women may claim maternity benefit* the level of which is determined by her earnings and there is provision for family allowances for each child.

Italy the main features of Italian social legislation include workers' insurance against industrial accidents and a workers' pension scheme. Benefits such as unemployment, disability, retirement pensions, family allowance and maternity are also available. The Ministry of Labour oversees these benefits through certain organisations.

The Istituto Nazionale per la Previdenza Sociale (INPS) is the organisation responsible for the payment of pensions. These are paid on the basis of assessment of the workers' salary over recent working years. Funding for pension payments is provided by compulsory contributions made by employers and employees. Pensions are generally available for invalids, retirement and survivors. Retirement age for Italian men is 60 and 55 for women. INPS also administers a sickness insurance scheme which pays cash benefits in cases of loss of earnings.

In the case of unemployment benefit, the Italian system operated by INPS is distinctly different from other EC states. Two unemployment schemes for different categories of employee exist. Those most protected by the system are those workers who are employed by large organisations. This group receives the benefits of the casa integrazione guadagni scheme, and receive work-related unemployment benefit amounting to over 70 per cent of the last salary received. This practice applies to short and long-term lay-offs equally. Workers who benefit from this scheme do so because of the political significance of mass dismissals and are therefore advantaged due to the fact that they are employed by a large organisation which perhaps fears the repercussions of laying off so many at any given time.

In the other, less fortunate group, the situation is very different. Those workers who are dismissed from small firms and, indeed, those people who are seeking their first jobs, receive considerably less protection. If registered as unemployed, they receive only a small amount of unemployment benefit and only for a short period of time. This reflects their political 'insignificance'.

Another organisation – INAIL (Istituto Nazionale Assicurazioni per gli Infortuni sul Lavoro) – oversees an insurance scheme which provides benefits for employees who have suffered injuries as a result of accidents in the workplace. This scheme is financed jointly by employers and employees.

ACTIVITY

1 What problems exist with the Italian unemployment benefit scheme?
2 How do you think UK workers would react if the Italian unemployment scheme was introduced in the UK? What does this suggest about a) how workers in Italy and the UK are treated and b) how Italian and UK businesses view their employees?
3 Should the EC intervene with regards to the Italian unemployment scheme? Give your reasons.

Spain the social security system commenced with the 1964 Social Security Law. This aimed to provide a fee-based, social assistance network that would eventually guarantee general benefits, based on the German model. The system was to be financed by contributions from employers and employees.

National insurance is compulsory for all those in employment, including the self-employed. This covers temporary incapacity to work, accident insurance, assistance for dependants, permanent incapacity, widows' pensions, retirement pensions payable at the age of 65 (men and women) and unemployment benefit. As with other EC states, the last of these is determined by previous contributions and availability for work.

Provision exists in the system for early retirement providing the retiree's job is filled by an unemployed person.

UK in 1988, the Department of Health and Social Security (DHSS) was split into two separate departments by the government – the Department of Health and the Department of Social Security. This change reflected the growing importance of both arms of the service. Expenditure in this area represents a large proportion of the UK budget and in 1990/1, it amounted to over £22 million and £52 million on health and social security respectively.

The national insurance scheme is compulsory for most employees and provides funding for the usual range of benefits. Both employers and employees pay earnings-related contributions. Benefits are available for sickness, industrial injury, disability, maternity, retirement pensions, unemployment and child benefit for each child up to the age of 16 (or 18 if in full-time education). Retirement age for UK citizens is 65 for men and 60 for women. Retirement pensions from the state are often supplemented by private occupational pensions.

ACTIVITY

1 Rank the five major EC states in terms of the amount spent on the following social welfare areas:
   a) housing
   b) maternity
   c) vocational guidance.
2 Calculate the percentage of total expenditure of these areas for each of the five major EC states.

ACTIVITY

Provision is made in the EC for people travelling within EC states to have their health care rights transferred. In the UK, this is done by filling in Form E111 (available from post offices).

1 In groups of three or four, obtain a copy of the leaflet 'Health Care for visitors to EC countries'. Prepare a short oral presentation (no more than five minutes) which outlines the procedure for getting assistance in one of the EC member states. The presentation should include the following headings:
   a) where to get information
   b) medical and dental treatment
   c) hospital treatment.

2 Individually, draw up a table which compares the above headings for the five major EC states.

ACTIVITY

Read the article '48-hour week' and then answer the following questions:

1 Why was a political compromise necessary over the issue of the 48-hour week?

2 In your opinion, should the EC be able to enforce a maximum working week of 48 hours? Give your reasons.

3 Do you agree with the suggestion in the article that 'Sunday should be declared a normal day of rest'?

4 On what grounds do you think the UK Social Affairs Minister contested the EC proposals?

5 What are the implications for UK business of the proposed 48-hour week?

48-hour week

Social Affairs ministers are reported to have reached a political compromise in Luxembourg early today over the controversial Commission proposal to enforce a maximum working week of 48 hours for everyone in the Community. Ministers are also said to have found common ground on the suggestion that Sunday should be declared a normal day of rest. UK Social Affairs Minister Gillian Shephard contested both proposals. Final details of the agreement are now being worked out and will be presented to ministers during the UK presidency.

Source: *The Week in Europe*, 25 June 1992

Employment

Statistics for employment make use of terms such as 'active population' and 'non-active' population. In the case of the former, this refers to all people in employment as well as those who are unemployed. 'Non-active' refers to all those people who are not classified as either in employment or as unemployed.

In general, between 1975–88, a steady growth of about 10 per cent in the EC active population was witnessed. A growth in the active population over 14 years of age was mainly due to an increase in the number of women coming on to the labour market.

ACTIVITY

1 List those people who you think would fall into the category of 'non-active' population.

2 Why do you think there has been a general increase in the number of women coming on to the labour market?

The smaller states

Of the smaller member states, significant numbers of people are still employed in agriculture in Greece, Ireland and Portugal. However, in all seven smaller states, the services sector is the most important provider of jobs.

ACTIVITY

Employment by main sectors in smaller EC states, 1989 (%)

	Agriculture	*Industry*	*Services*
Belgium	2.8	28.9	68.3
Denmark	6.0	26.8	67.2
Greece	26.6	27.2	46.2
Ireland	15.1	28.4	56.5
Luxembourg	3.4	31.2	65.4
Netherlands	4.7	26.5	68.8
Portugal	18.9	35.3	45.8

Source: Eurostat

1. What activities come under the services sector, do you think?
2. Suggest reasons why Greece and Portugal have the largest and second largest proportions of people employed in agriculture.
3. What conclusions about employment in the smaller EC states can be drawn from the table?

Trends in government policy

Of the seven smaller states, unemployment rates are highest in Ireland with men appearing to be the worst affected. Rates of unemployment tend to be high at the EC's northern and southern extremities. This is illustrated by Ireland where unemployment rates are the highest of the seven smaller states, with women appearing to be the worst affected. South-east Belgium appears to be another area affected and this may be due to industrial decline.

Within the smaller states, those hardest hit by unemployment tend to be people aged between 20 and 34. Generally, unemployed women are, on average, younger than unemployed men. Exceptions to this are The Netherlands and Luxembourg.

Government employment policies in many of the smaller states have been directed towards dealing with the problem of unemployment which has been widespread across Europe. These policies have incorporated youth training schemes and projects to assist those made unemployed – here the emphasis has been on retraining for new skills in the new jobs created by new technology.

Other common measures across the smaller states have included a gradual reduction in the working week, which does not just result from the need to create jobs, but also from the increased efficiency brought about by modern machinery.

A general trend across the EC member states has been towards the introduction of part-time contracts, allowing employment of more workers and assisting government figures in terms of the unemployed.

ACTIVITY

Unemployment rates in the smaller EC states, 1990

Member state	*Men (000)*	*Women (000)*
Belgium	125	193
Denmark	112	118
Greece	115	182
Ireland	130	73
Luxembourg	1	1
Netherlands	234	301
Portugal	90	132

Source: Eurostat

Consider the table above and then answer the following questions:

1 In general, more women than men are unemployed in the smaller EC states. List the reasons why you think this might be so.
2 Why are there so few people unemployed in Luxembourg?
3 For what reasons do you think fewer women than men are unemployed in Ireland?
4 Why are the figures given in the above table limited?

The major states

ACTIVITY

Employment by main sectors in major EC states, 1989 (%)

	Agriculture	*Industry*	*Services*
France	6.4	30.1	63.5
Germany	3.7	39.8	56.5
Italy	9.3	32.4	58.3
Spain	13.0	32.9	54.1
UK	2.2	29.5	68.3

Source: Eurostat

1 Draw a pictogram that compares the proportion of people employed in the main sectors for the five major EC states.
2 Suggest reasons why:
a) Spain has the largest proportion of people employed in agriculture;
b) UK has the lowest proportion of people employed in agriculture.
3 How would you expect the figures in the table to have changed by the year 2000? Give your reasons.

Trends in employment

Growth of the service sector A very important trend in employment across the five major EC states has been the marked shift in jobs from the traditional manufacturing to the relatively new service industries. In all five major EC states, the service sector is now a significant factor in the economy. In the UK, for example, the number of people employed in service industries rose by 2.1 million during the period 1980–90. In Germany, the service sector accounts for a large proportion of those in employment. Spanish service industries have made the largest recent contribution to employment with a 25 per cent increase in the number of jobs available. In general, the main areas of the service sector that have witnessed this increase have tended to be banking, finance and insurance, and hotel and catering. Public sector service employment has made a significant contribution in France and Germany – partly as the result of government initiatives to reduce unemployment.

Manufacturing decline The expansion of the service sectors in the major states seems to have been paralleled by a marked decline in manufacturing industries. Even Germany, which still has the highest proportion of employees in manufacturing, has experienced long-term decline. Statistics for other countries show a dramatic decline over a period of time – for instance, the UK has experienced a reduction in the number employed in manufacturing industries from 43 per cent in 1955 to 23 per cent in 1990. The number of French people employed in manufacturing fell from a peak of 5.3 million in 1974 to 3.8 million in 1988 – in particular in the coalmining, iron, steel and ship-building industries. Against these trends, it should be noted that Spain (despite suffering decline in the industrial sector in the late 1970s and early 1980s) still has a healthy industrial sector with the construction industry faring particularly well since 1987.

In all cases, the reduction in the number employed in manufacturing industries is partly attributable to the adoption of labour-saving techniques and the continued development of high technology, both of which have assisted the increase in efficiency.

Fewer employed in agriculture Another feature of employment within the five major EC states includes the decline in numbers of those employed in agriculture – less than 4 per cent are employed in agriculture in Germany. In Spain, the figure is rather more (13 per cent of total employment in 1989), yet the trend is similar and this is despite the fact that agriculture is still very significant compared with other major EC states. The exception to this general trend is Italy, which maintains a high proportion of agricultural workers compared with other EC states. This is partly explained by the slow industrialisation of the south and by the labour-intensive nature of agricultural cultivation in Italy.

Importance of SMEs and self-employment The number of small firms providing employment and the number of self-employed provides a further trend worth noting. In the German industrial sector, for example, small and medium enterprises (SMEs) with less than 1000 employees provide 60 per cent of all jobs with larger firms providing 40 per cent. In Spain, the number of self-employed has remained relatively stable, while the UK has witnessed a substantial increase in self-employment – in June 1990, 12.3 per cent of the workforce were self-employed. Self-employment has been positively encouraged by successive Conservative governments in the UK.

ACTIVITY

In small groups, consider the following questions and then be prepared to discuss them with the rest of the class:

1. In your opinion, what role has new technology played in the decline of traditional manufacturing in the major EC states?
2. For what reasons might German small and medium enterprises (SMEs) be able to provide more jobs than larger firms?
3. How can governments encourage people to become self-employed?

Government employment policy

In recent years, the focus of many governments, and particularly those of the major EC states, has inevitably rested upon possible measures to combat unemployment. This has meant that much government policy has been channelled in this direction. Yet, although EC states share this problem, each government is faced with specific issues within the overall picture. For example, limited unemployment in most of northern and central Italy contrasts with high and rising unemployment in the south. In France and Spain, the unemployment rate for women is significantly higher than that for men. This contrasts with the UK, where the official unemployment rate is normally higher for men than women. A common factor within the major EC states, however, is the level of youth unemployment. Let us consider some of the employment measures taken by individual EC governments.

France as in the other EC states, France has now accepted that unemployment is likely to be a feature of the economy for some time to come. The government has recognised that the crisis in jobs is at least partly a structural problem – that is, due to changes brought about by technology for example. Youth unemployment has been particularly highlighted by French governments and much money has been injected into campaigns to provide work for school-leavers. Unfortunately, these have met with limited success – almost 40 per cent of all unemployed people are in the 16–25 age group.

Suggestions to improve the employment situation have included a possible reduction in the working week which would enable more jobs to become available. This idea has been welcomed by French trade unions, but has yet to come about.

Measures taken by the government have included legislation to make it easier for firms to hire temporary staff with short-term contracts of up to one year. Many firms such as Peugeot took advantage of this measure, but the insecurity that it brought led the French government to control short-term contracts more strictly. Other initiatives have included:

- expansion of public sector employment;
- government aid to firms in difficulty;
- training schemes;
- early retirement schemes;
- reduction of social charges for employers.

Germany forecasts of high unemployment rates for some time to come have been aggravated in Germany by the process of reunification. Inefficient industries in the old East Germany, forced to close in a market economy, have had no alternative but to lay off workers. Furthermore, demographic factors, such as population booms working their way through to the labour market, have helped to contribute to the number of unemployed. Various short-term solutions have been attempted by German governments including:

- reduction in hours in the years before retirement;
- job-sharing schemes;
- working hours to suit the demand for a product.

In addition, the federal employment agency has given cash to cities and the lander to assist in job-creation schemes. More importantly, in 1985 the government introduced legislation making it easier for firms to hire staff on short-term contracts of up to 18 months (as in France).

A particular consequence of unemployment in Germany has been increased German prejudice against the various 'guest' workers such as the Turks.

ACTIVITY

1 With a partner, list the advantages and disadvantages of the short-term contract from the following viewpoints:
   a) the government
   b) the employer
   c) the employee.
2 In what ways can the European Community become involved in employment issues such as short-term contracts? Is Community intervention desirable or not? Offer reasons for your opinions.

Italy until the 1980s, the Italian government had to deal with workers who had a militant reputation, and who often resorted to disruptive and costly strike action. But since the defeat of the trade unions in the Fiat strike of 1980, they have been much more on the defensive. Italian unions have experienced similar conditions to their European counterparts – dwindling membership (fuelled by unemployment) and a host of other problems have meant that they have had to concede ground on issues such as flexibility, and have been forced to accept government reforms in the shape of wage-index systems. Government policy, as in other major states, has succeeded in curbing the power of the trade unions.

The Italian government faces a particular employment problem which is not so pronounced in other states. This problem is the one of *dualism* – in effect, a poor south and a much richer north. In the south, government employment policy has largely been centred on the development of infrastructures. The hope has been here that if infrastructures could be encouraged to develop, then jobs would be created. Indeed, the south has a particularly high-quality *potential* labour force – for example, of the 758 000 young unemployed in the south, 45 per cent have diplomas or degrees. The government has introduced a new regional fund for the south – the Azienda per il Mezzogiorno, a series of measures designed to boost the region. However, there is some doubt as to the extent that this will assist employment in the south.

A number of issues still need to be tackled by the Italian government in terms of employment policy and these include:

- more investment in the south to enable full use of the labour force;
- a balancing up of graduates in the disciplines needed. Graduates generally do not have the type of degrees that industry wants;
- the tendency to view part-time work as a way of reducing the size of the workforce and to reduce labour costs, rather than as a means of supporting full-time employment.

Spain in the 1980s, Spanish employment divided into two clear periods – one of huge destruction of jobs and a second, distinct recovery of employment. The newly democratic Spain that emerged in the late 1970s brought recognition of trade unions and employers' organisations. Legislation introduced in 1980 brought greater flexibility and the possibility of part-time contracts. The Spanish government has also introduced other employment measures over time including:

- policies designed to adapt labour force qualifications to new job requirements;
- the introduction of employment promotion programmes in firms, sponsored by the government in the late 1980s, which created many thousands of temporary and part-time jobs;
- special employment programmes aimed at the young unemployed, coupled with training provided by the National Institute for Employment.

The continuing industrialisation of Spain means that the government has to be aware of changes in employment patterns, and to be able to step in and take action in an attempt to rectify problems.

ACTIVITY

Age of employees with temporary contracts in major EC states, 1988 (%)

	Under 25	*25–44*	*45–64*	*Over 64*
France	60.7	33.0	6.1	0.2
Germany	66.2	26.2	7.5	0.1
Italy	34.2	44.6	20.0	1.2
Spain	43.9	41.8	14.1	0.2
UK	38.9	41.0	16.5	3.6

Source: Eurostat

Gender of employees with temporary contracts as % of total employees in major EC states, 1988

	Men	*Women*
France	7.3	8.5
Germany	10.4	12.5
Italy	4.6	8.0
Spain	20.5	20.6
UK	4.7	7.5

Source: Eurostat

1 Decide which of the following statements can be deduced from the above tables:

a) most employees with temporary contracts tend to be in the under 25 age group;

b) there are fewer employees with temporary contracts in the 45 – 64 age group because it is unlikely that any of these have just come on to the labour market;

c) in terms of temporary contracts, men tend to be affected more than women;

d) temporary contracts are much more a feature of the Spanish employment scene than they are in other major EC states.

2 Using the figures in the tables only, decide which major EC state would appear to offer the best employment opportunities for you. Give your reasons.
3 Draw out a set of written conclusions from the two tables. Rank order these conclusions in order of importance as you see them.

UK a feature of British employment policy during the last 12 years or so has been the effective curbing of trade union power. As in other major states, this has been made possible by the levels of unemployment that have been witnessed. Unemployment as an issue in its own right has been very significant, reaching over three million in 1984. This has led the British government to respond in a variety of ways.

- The encouragement of small businesses (including those people made redundant from their previous job) by the use of an enterprise allowance. This has had the effect of creating new jobs, although many small businesses have been forced to 'go under' in subsequent years.
- A commitment to training and retraining by a variety of measures, including the Training and Enterprise Councils (TECs). It is through the TECs that business enterprise training, youth training and employment training are now offered.
- The provision of 'Job Club' places for the unemployed.

The problems of the UK government in relation to employment policy and issues have been aggravated by other policies such as the proposed closure of coal pits, which has, in some ways, rekindled a degree of public sympathy for affected workers. The re-emergence of the threat of industrial action or strikes in many cases underlines these problems.

ACTIVITY

Weekly hours, earnings and labour costs in the EC, 1989

Member state	*Basic weekly hours*
Belgium	38
Denmark	37.5
France	39
Germany	37.9
Greece	40
Ireland	40
Italy	40
Luxembourg	40
Netherlands	38
Portugal	40
Spain	40
UK	39

Source: BDA

Earnings and labour costs of manual workers in industry, 1989

Member state	*Hourly earnings (£)*	*Hourly labour costs (£)*
Belgium	4.80	8.70
Denmark	7.30	8.70
France	4.10	7.70
Germany	6.00	10.70
Greece	2.00	3.20
Ireland	4.30	6.10
Italy	4.10	7.70
Luxembourg	5.30	7.70
Netherlands	4.90	8.70
Portugal	1.00	1.70
Spain	3.50	n.a.
UK	4.80	6.80

Source: Eurostat

Consider the above tables and then answer the following questions:

1 Draw bar charts to illustrate:
 a) the basic weekly hours of the 5 larger states
 b) the hourly earnings of the 12 member states
 c) the hourly labour costs of the 12 member states.

2 What sort of factors contribute to labour costs?

3 Why do you think there is such a difference between the lowest hourly labour cost and the highest?

4 One of the cornerstones of the Rome Treaty is the free movement of labour. Based on the hourly earnings figures, what trends do you think might develop in terms of migrant workers?

5 a) Should the EC introduce a standard wage for certain categories of jobs? Give your reasons.
 b) State in which jobs you think a standard wage could be introduced.

Housing

Within the EC, two major patterns of housing can be identified. These are as follows:

- in some member states, many households opt for the *ownership* of a one-family house;
- in other member states, many households opt to live in rented flats or other accommodation.

In general, the dwellings that EC citizens occupy vary greatly in terms of amenities and facilities that they enjoy. For statistical reasons, the EC classifies these in terms of whether or not occupants have appliances or equipment such as telephones, freezers, televisions and dishwashers.

The smaller states

A number of key features of housing can be identified within the smaller EC states.

- Within the seven states, in Ireland and Greece, over 70 per cent of dwellings are owner-occupied. At the other end of the scale, The Netherlands has only 40 per cent of owner-occupied dwellings.
- Where construction of new dwellings is taking place in the smaller states, the larger proportion seems to be in states such as Greece, Denmark and The Netherlands. A decade earlier, in 1978, construction of new dwellings had been a chief feature of housing policy in Belgium and Luxembourg.
- Greece has the highest proportion of new housing, however (for our purposes, those built since 1970), with 37 per cent. Ireland and The Netherlands follow Greece, while at the bottom of the scale is Belgium where only 16 per cent of homes have been built since 1970, despite the fact that construction of new homes had been a feature of policy ten years earlier.
- In the 1980 census, the lowest proportion of dwellings with bathrooms was in Portugal (58 per cent). The highest percentage of dwellings with bathrooms was recorded in The Netherlands (95.9 per cent), followed by Denmark.

ACTIVITY

Types of housing unit in smaller EC states, 1982 (000)

	B	*DK*	*GR*	*IRL*	*LUX*	*NL*	*P*
One-family houses	2512	1175	2896	835	79	3372	1788
Flats	1148	853	–	40	45	1569	981

Source: Eurostat

1 Why do you think only one figure has been recorded for Greece?
2 For what reasons do you think Ireland has such a low proportion of flats?

Irish housing policy

As a means of illustrating the housing policy of one of the smaller EC states governments in some detail, the following case study considers the measures taken by the Irish government.

Basic housing policy statement

The basic aim of housing policy is to ensure that, as far as the resources of the economy permit, every household can obtain a house of good standard, located in an acceptable environment, at a price or rent it can afford. A secondary aim is the encouragement of owner-occupation. An important principle in the operation of housing policy is that the primary responsibility for the provision of housing rests with the individual. Those who can afford to do so are expected to provide housing for themselves, if necessary with some assistance from the government and local authorities. Households unable to house themselves from their own resources depend largely on local authorities to provide them with accommodation. The development of the voluntary housing sector to meet social housing needs, particularly special category needs such as the elderly and the homeless has been an important feature of housing policy in recent years and this sector is likely to grow in significance in the coming years.

Source: Irish government

In bringing about its policy on housing, the Irish government has identified a number of important policy instruments. These are as follows.

Irish housing policy instruments

Policy area	*Instruments*
Owner-occupation	a) New house grants (IR£2000) available to first-time occupiers of new dwellings of a certain size. b) Mortgage subsidies to allow first-time buyers to break into the housing market. c) Mortgage interest relief – tax allowances in respect of interest payments on mortgages for property. d) A low level of residential property tax – levied at 1.5% of the excess value of the property over IR£91 000. e) Relief from stamp duty on new houses.
Home ownership by low-income groups	a) 'Surrender' grant scheme of IR£5000 paid to local authority tenants who surrendered their property in order to purchase their own homes. b) 1988 Tenant Purchase Scheme – this allowed for tenants to purchase their local authority homes at discounted prices.
Private rented sector	a) Tax incentives to encourage the provision of new, refurbished or converted property for private rented accommodation.
Local authority	a) The policy of selling local authority dwellings to tenants at reasonable prices has resulted in there being less than 10% of housing stock being held by local authorities.

Source: Irish government

ACTIVITY

Read the case study on Irish housing policy and then answer the following questions:

1 What are the main principles behind Irish housing policy?
2 According to the policy statement, what is likely to be the major trend in housing in the future?
3 The Irish government has encouraged the sale of local authority (council) houses at reasonable prices to tenants. With a partner, list the advantages and disadvantages of such a policy.

4 In your opinion, would it be better to rent or purchase a property in Ireland? Give your reasons.

The major states

As with the smaller EC states, a number of features of housing in the 'big five' can be identified.

- Spain has over 70 per cent of dwellings which are owner-occupied, while Germany only has some 40 per cent.
- In the major states, a comparison of 1988 figures with 1978 reveals that an overall decline in the construction of new dwellings has occurred, with the exception of Italy.
- In the 1981/2 British census, it was revealed that over 50 per cent of dwellings in the UK were built before 1945. There is also a high proportion of dwellings in traditional industrial areas of the UK and France that were built before 1945. This is not the case in Germany, which has a lower proportion of older dwellings due to the damage suffered during the Second World War. In particular, the areas around Madrid, Rome and Sardinia stand out as having housing stock of more recent origin.
- In terms of the breakdown between one-family houses and flats, the major five EC states reveal the following:

Types of housing unit in the major EC states, 1981/2 (000)

	France	*Germany*	*Italy*	*Spain*	*UK*
One-family houses	10 291	11 394	5 484	3 835	19 635
Flats	9 147	12 403	12 058	6 635	

Source: Eurostat

- The vast number of dwellings in the UK (98 per cent) and Germany (92.3 per cent) are equipped with bathrooms or showers on the premises. Of the major states, the highest proportion of dwellings with central heating systems are in Germany.

Amenities in homes in the five major EC states, 1981/2 (%)

Amenity	*France*	*Germany*	*Italy*	*Spain*	*UK*
Bathroom/shower	85.2	92.3	86.4	85.3	98.0
Internal WC	85.4	96.0	87.8	n.a.	97.3
Central heating	67.6	70.0	56.5	22.5	n.a.

Source: Eurostat

ACTIVITY

Consider the two tables above and then answer the following questions:

1 For what reasons might there be more people living in flats than in houses in Germany and Italy?

2 Draw bar charts to illustrate the amenities in place in homes in the major EC states. What conclusions can you draw?

3 a) Why does Germany have the largest proportion of central heating in homes?
b) Why does Spain have the lowest proportion of central heating in homes?

Housing policy in the major states

Most of the major EC states' governments have wanted to encourage home ownership via the instruments of their housing policies. The status of owning your own home appears to be a desirable one almost universally. Certain member states' governments have positively encouraged this move – for example, in the UK the sale of council houses to tenants at reasonable prices has brought many more people into home ownership for the first time.

Each of the major EC states has particular problems relating to housing, demanding different solutions. A consideration of these specific problems and the measures adopted to tackle them follows.

France as late as the 1960s, the French housing shortage was considered to be 'national disgrace number one'. With the necessary measures put into effect to increase the number of homes available, the problem is now largely solved. Now, housing is plentiful and comfortable in France, but prices have increased dramatically – the average share of family income spent on rents and mortgages has increased from 3.4 per cent to over 25 per cent, bringing France into line with the UK and Germany. An offshoot of this growth in the supply of housing has been that French expectations of housing have risen. No longer are French people tolerant of the overcrowding that was a feature of the 1960s – now they demand larger and better-built properties.

The tempo of building that resulted from the humiliation of the 1960s has now slowed, and this was partly brought about by economic depression and political measures taken by the government. However, a new shortage of homes occurred in the mid 1980s, which was partly brought about by the decay of old buildings. The response to this by the French government has been to adopt a policy of *rehabilitation* rather than demolition. This policy has led to two major trends in France:

- more people wanting to move back to city-centre living;
- more people wanting their own individual houses within commuter range of their jobs.

ACTIVITY

1 Explain why you think French expectations of housing have risen in recent years.
2 List the reasons why you think:
   a) more people in France want to move back to city-centre living
   b) more people want individual homes within commuter range.
3 Would you be attracted to/do you like living in a city? Give your reasons.

Germany nobody would deny that the 'economic miracle' witnessed in post-war Germany was a striking feature. Part of this recovery was a very effective rehousing programme – as we have already seen, over 70 per cent of today's Germans live in houses built since the Second World War. Homes are generally better-equipped and more sturdily constructed than the European average, and of a better quality. Today, most Germans live in a comfortable rented flat or in a house that they own.

However, the German government has had specific housing problems to face, and these particularly relate to low-income groups and young families. In the case of the former, the government has operated a policy of subsidising 'social' housing for groups with low incomes. This type of housing has been built mostly by semi-public agencies and co-operatives, with the rents controlled by the lander. In addition, for some years now, the federal government has operated a system of rent-topping grants paid to poorer tenants on a means test basis, to help with payment for accommodation.

In the case of the other group, namely young families, problems still exist for the supply of good, cheap flats is exceeded by the demand and a government priority is to try to assist these groups. This lack of supply is in some ways aggravated by the lack of public housing in the old East Germany. That which does exist is allocated mostly by local councils – but many newly-weds have to wait some two years before they can obtain accommodation.

Germans prefer to buy their properties if possible, but one of the reasons that so many rent is because German building societies require a minimum deposit of 30 – 40 per cent for a mortgage.

Italy unlike some of the other major EC states, there is no equivalent to the building society in Italy. This has meant that mortgages at cheap rates of interest and over a reasonable amount of time have been in short supply. This would seem to push people towards renting accommodation. It could also be argued that rented accommodation is even more difficult to come by. This sort of situation has led to a total of seven million 'illegal' buildings being constructed in Italy since the end of the Second World War. Many of these buildings have been constructed by emigrants who return home to the south and invest their earnings in their home, building it up stage by stage until the whole project is completed.

One of the government's major problems with housing in Italy is the crisis that exists in terms of lack of homes. This is especially the case among the poorer citizens who inhabit the larger cities.

Spain the Spanish government did not recognise the need for a separate housing ministry until the late 1950s, and, from the outset, it became clear that it would be unable to build and manage a massive stock of state-owned rented accommodation like the council houses in the UK. This was due to the fact that the economy was unable to support such expense.

Measures taken by the government, however, included a national housing plan which ran from 1961 – 76, that succeeded in introducing four million new dwellings. Of these new homes, about 50 per cent were provided by the private sector and the rest was subsidised housing. Government subsidies offered on accommodation are based on the rate of interest of the loan and not the actual price of the accommodation.

The overriding concern of successive Spanish governments has been the quest to find ways of diverting the cheapest accommodation towards the neediest sections of the population. This has been attempted by introducing various government plans, designed to restrict cheaper accommodation to those on the bottom rung of the social ladder. In addition to this, socialist governments have introduced measures to make it easier for families on low incomes to acquire their first home.

Despite these measures, about 230 000 Spaniards are still without a home of their own. In an attempt to deal with this problem, the Spanish government has offered incentives to developers who produce cheap and low-level accommodation. The idea of this is partly to reverse the trend of high-level flats which are seen to have detrimental effects on the families that are resident in them.

UK as a direct consequence of government policy in the UK, the pattern of housing tenure has changed. The trend has been for an increase in owner-occupied properties, with owners purchasing their property by way of a mortgage from the building societies (the largest source of mortgage funds), coupled with a decline in privately rented accommodation. This is in keeping with the ideals of many of the other major EC states – to allow as many people as possible to own their own homes. Between 1971 – 90, owner-occupied properties rose from 50 per cent to nearly 70 per cent, underlining the government's commitment to this policy. The promotion of home ownership still remains a central theme in UK government housing policy. Although house construction is undertaken by public and private sectors, most are built by the latter for sale to owner-occupiers.

Public housing in the UK is provided by some 460 local housing associations. Another theme in government policy has been to allow the housing associations to become the main providers of new housing in the subsidised rented sector. In this, local authorities who were once major suppliers of rented accommodation, are being encouraged to view their role as 'enablers', working with the housing associations and the private sector to increase the supply of low-cost housing for rent, without providing it themselves. The traditional role of councils in providing accommodation has therefore been significantly altered.

ACTIVITY

We have seen that most of the major EC states wish to encourage citizens to purchase their own homes and that this is often central to a government's housing policy.

1 With a partner, list the reasons why you think governments wish to encourage owner-occupation of homes.
2 In a class discussion, consider the following statement: 'The sale of council houses in the UK is an underhand way of the government releasing itself from its housing reponsibilities.'

ACTIVITY **Review your progress: 9**

1 How long is compulsory education in:
   a) Italy?
   b) Spain?
   c) Germany?
   d) Belgium?
   e) Greece?
   f) Portugal?
2 Explain what is meant by the following:
   - LOGSE
   - BAC
   - Licenza Elementaire
   - UNED.
3 What are the main features of vocational training in the major EC states?
4 List the social benefits that are common to EC member states.
5 How do the Italian and UK social security systems differ?
6 Explain what is meant by the term 'non-active population'.
7 What are the major trends in employment in the major EC states?
8 Which EC state has:
   a) the highest hourly labour cost?
   b) the lowest hourly labour cost?
   c) the shortest working week?
9 Why does Germany have such a low proportion of older dwellings?
10 What have been the key aims of housing policy in the major EC states?

Summary

- The education systems of the EC states reveal some similarities, although there are some marked differences between them.
- Vocational training is an important educational issue in EC member states and is often seen as a means of tackling youth unemployment.
- EC member states share common social benefits, but some marked differences exist between the various systems.
- In employment policy, most EC member states' governments have witnessed similar trends and, in particular, the problem of how to deal with unemployment.
- Housing policy among the five major EC states has common areas. A majority of the states want to promote home ownership. In some cases, a shortage of adequate housing is still a problem.

Assignment 14 European education

A group of foreign students from a country within the EC are visiting your college on an exchange trip. In preparation for their visit, you have been asked to investigate various aspects of life in their country. In particular, you have been asked to research the education system. In this respect, carry out the following tasks:

Task 1 Select an EC member state on which you could carry out research.

Task 2 a) Prepare an oral presentation to be given to fellow students that deals with the education system of your chosen country. The presentation should deal with such aspects as:

- primary education
- secondary education
- post-16 education (further and higher)
- vocational training.

Use appropriate visual aids to illustrate your presentation.

b) Produce a written evaluation (no more than 250 words) of how you thought your presentation went.

Task 3 Prepare a handout for use during your presentation, which summarises the various qualifications that exist in the country that you have selected.

Task 4 Draw up a table that illustrates how the qualifications in the country you have selected compare with equivalent UK qualifications.

Assignment 15 A question of industrial location

Scenario

You are part of the 'location investigation' team for a major Japanese car manufacturer, Tokami. Your team has been given the following brief by the company management: 'Compare the infrastructures of European Community states, evaluate them and make a recommendation to the board of Tokami as to where it should build its next major production unit.'

Task 1 Prepare a comparative survey in the form of a report which deals with the following:

- transport systems
- education and training
- social and medical care
- employment and housing.

Your report should consider one of the four groups listed below only:

Group 1	*Group 2*	*Group 3*	*Group 4*
UK	Italy	France	Netherlands
Denmark	Luxembourg	Greece	Germany
Spain	Portugal	Ireland	Belgium

The report should be contributed to by all members of the team.

Task 2 Your team is to present its case to the Tokami board, some of whom will be sent to manage the operation. Your presentation should cover the following:

- why your team has made its recommendations
- the cultural and social advantages of your recommended location for Tokami's executives and managers who will work there.

All members of your team must contribute to the presentation.

10 International trading patterns

Aims

- To consider the international trading patterns that the EC is involved in
- To highlight the importance of the EC in world trade
- To distinguish between intra-Community trade and external trade, and identify the major countries involved
- To review the major trade flows between the EC and other countries, and trade groupings
- To examine the range of goods and services available, and their value to the EC balance of payments.

Relevant BTEC Outcome Performance Criteria
1b Major international trade agreements
6a Impact of external trade on balance of payments
6b Volume and flow of international trade
6c Trends in trade

Some facts and figures about EC trade

In 1987, 60 per cent of EC member states' exports went to other member states, with the remainder going to the rest of the world.

The EC has a balance of trade *surplus* with other industrialised economies in Western Europe and with all other industrialised nations except the USA and Japan.

The EC's major competitors are the USA and Japan, and comparing the three in terms of total population, the importance of the EC as a trading bloc can be seen:

EC home market	340 million consumers
USA home market	240 million consumers
Japan home market	120 million consumers.

As an importer, the EC is slightly less important than the USA, but as an exporter it was responsible in 1986 for 19 per cent of world trade, compared with 13 per cent and 12 per cent in the USA and Japan respectively.

These figures and the undeniable significance of the EC as the most important trading group in the world reveal the achievement of one of the major hopes of the creators of the Community – that the EC would be able to compete effectively with the USA and Japan.

EC trading patterns

Under the Common Commercial Policy the Commission has developed some form of trade or economic co-operation agreement with nearly every country in the world. These agreements differ in the following ways:

- some may be concluded with individual states (for example, the trade agreement of 1985 with the People's Republic of China);
- some may be concluded with *groups* of countries like the Lomé Conventions, which take in 69 countries;
- some are narrowly based (for example, a trade agreement which takes in only a few commodities);

- some are more broadly based, like the current European Economic Area with the seven EFTA states.

Trade patterns affecting the EC differ from country to country and are also dependent upon the state of economic development of the partners concerned. A number of patterns exist:

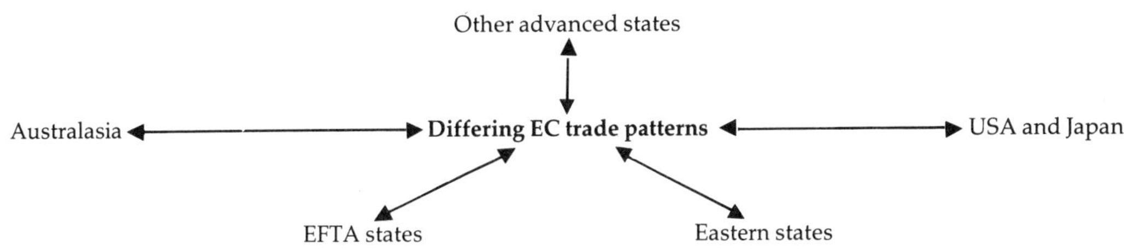

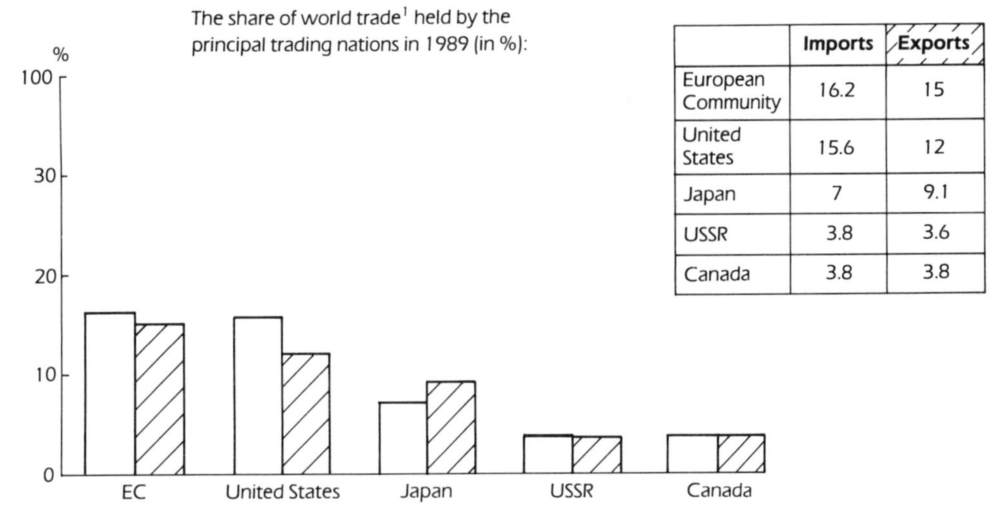

	Imports	Exports
European Community	16.2	15
United States	15.6	12
Japan	7	9.1
USSR	3.8	3.6
Canada	3.8	3.8

Source: Eurostat

▶ *10.1 Europe, world partner*

Different EC trade patterns

Countries/area	*Pattern of trade*
USA and Japan	Despite being the EC's most important trading partners, no formal trading agreements with either the USA or Japan exist. Generally, the US government supports European integration, but many US farmers are concerned about EC competition. Trade patterns with Japan differ for Japanese competition has aggravated the problems of industries such as steel, plastics, radio and TV, and others. In response, both the EC and the USA have resorted more and more to 'one-off' measures to protect their own industries.
Other advanced countries	The EC has close links with Australia and New Zealand, who both have major interests in agriculture. The exports of both states were affected by the UK's entry into the EC (being Commonwealth states). As a result, both have been keen to improve access for their agricultural products, and to counter the effects of EC exports on the world market.
EFTA	This is the EC's other major trade partner. In many ways, a special relationship exists, for the agreement on the European Economic Area will eventually extend the free trade area to EC and EFTA states.

The relationship is underlined by the fact that former EFTA states are now EC members (the UK for example), and current EFTA members are seeking EC membership (Sweden and Austria among others).

Eastern states	Patterns of trade between Eastern and Western Europe had been increasing rapidly since the 1960s. This was due to the great emphasis placed on co-operation with the West by Eastern European governments. The aims of Eastern European government have been to remove EC obstacles to trade and to secure attractive credit facilities with the West, and industrial co-operation. Much of this has been speeded up by the break-up of the Soviet Communist bloc.

ACTIVITY

We have suggested that Japanese competition in markets such as those for cars, electrical products and radio/TV has aggravated the problems of industries within the EC and the USA.

1. If the Japanese provide such stiff competition, why have companies like Nissan or Mitsubishi been allowed to locate in the UK?
2. Why do Japanese products provide such stiff competition?
3. Identify any Japanese companies that are located in your area or region. What effect have these companies had on the local economy and community?

ACTIVITY

The Common Agricultural Policy has been a major source of disagreement between the EC and the USA. The USA is a large exporter of food and US farmers have resented the European export subsidies on agricultural products which are a feature of the CAP.

US wheat subsidies

In a swift reaction to the White House announcement last week that US wheat will receive export subsidies, the Commission issued a five-point statement showing concern that traditional EC wheat markets may be threatened. The Commission's strongly-worded response commented that the US declaration was not conducive to promoting fruitful EC/US commercial relations. The Commission is considering the measure's compatability with the 'stand still' accord on agriculture agreed within the Uruguay round of GATT. External Affairs Commissioner Frans Andriessen met US Trade Secretary Carla Hills in Brussels on 1 September to discuss GATT and the newly-negotiated free trade area between USA, Canada and Mexico. They restated the aim of concluding GATT talks by the end of the year.

Source: *The Week in Europe*, 10 September 1992

Read the article 'US wheat subsidies' and then answer the following questions:

1 Why do you think the US decided to grant export subsidies to its wheat farmers?
2 Do you think the EC's response to this action is reasonable considering the level of EC export subsidies?
3 What sort of effect is the US retaliatory action likely to have on trade relations with the EC?

ACTIVITY

Hit list smaller than wine industry feared

Yesterday's US trade measures against European exports, targeting white wine, corn gluten and rapeseed oil, will enrage the French government, but were less widespread than the French wine and spirits industry had feared.

The threat of 200 per cent tariffs is more punishing than expected, but after targeting $350 million of EC farm exports from an initial hit-list of $2 billion, many of those preparing against sanctions will live to export to the US another day. French cheese makers are unhurt, as are producers of Cognac and other liqueurs. French mineral water exports, epitomised by Perrier, are untouched, as are Germany's small sugar confectioners and apple juice makers.

France exported a mere FFr470 million of still white wine to the US last year. Within that, the main wines were white Burgundies, worth FFr291 million, followed by white Bordeaux, worth FFr120 million, then cheap white *vin de pays* worth FFr33 million.

The damage will be spread around hundreds of small to medium producers and wine merchants when export sales are suffering in their main markets.

Source: *The Financial Times*, 6 November 1992

Selected US food imports from Europe (1989–91 average)

France		*Germany*		*EC*		*World total %*	
Cheese	$38.4m			Cheese	$134.50m	Cheese	–91.00
		Confectionery	$38.2m	Confectionery	$104.40m	Confectionery	52.33
Waters	$13.2m	Apple Juice	$45.4m				
Wine	**$272.0m**	**Wine**	**$41.3m**	**Wine**	**$558.80m**	**Wine**	**51.65**
Brandy	$68.3m	Animal feed	$27.7m				
Liqueurs	$166.7m			Liqueurs	$333.70m	Liqueurs	62.78
Wheat gluten	**$2.1m**	**Wheat gluten**	**$4.5m**	**Wheat gluten**	**$11.80m**	**Wheat gluten**	**46.10**
Rapeseed	**$1.5m**	**Rapeseed**	**$12.5m**	**Rapeseed**	**$21.58m**	**Rapeseed**	**46.00**
Total	**$613.9m**	**Total**	**$236.2m**	**Total**	**$2,018.30m**		

Figures in bold are products targeted

Source: Agro Europe

Read the article 'Hit list smaller than wine industry feared' and then answer the following questions:

1 What measures did the USA take against European exports?
2 Why do you think the USA decided to take such measures?
3 What are the intended effects of the measures?
4 Look at the table 'Selected US food imports from Europe' and draw bar charts to illustrate the quantities of wine, wheat gluten and rapeseed oil imported by the USA from France, Germany and the EC as a whole.
5 Why do you think the USA may have decided to target products such as wine, wheat gluten and rapeseed oil?

Trade within the EC

The series of trading patterns between member states is known as *intra-Community* trade. These have grown much faster since 1958 than trade with non-members of the EC. For example, between 1958–86, trade between EC members grew by 36 times, whereas trade with non-members during the same period increased by only 16 times.

Intra-Community trade is very important for member states and it makes the Community an attractive proposition for outsiders (such as the EFTA states). For most member states, intra-Community trade accounts for over half of their total trade. Some member states are extremely dependent upon this – in particular, the Benelux states and Ireland. By contrast, the UK is the least dependent – in 1986, her exports to EC member states accounted for only 47 per cent of her total exports, with about 50 per cent of her total imports coming from other member states.

ACTIVITY

1 With a partner, list down those goods that you think the UK may import from other EC member states.
2 For what reasons, do you think, are Ireland and the Benelux states most dependent upon intra-Community trade?

EC external trade

One of the benefits to consumers of being a member of the EC is that the number and range of products have greatly increased over the years. This means that the type of import entering the EC has changed. When the Community was first established, it mainly imported raw materials, using these to process into consumer goods. Now, an increasing proportion of imports are of either a semi-finished nature or are manufactured articles. By 1986, more than 50 per cent of Community imports were manufactured goods in either a finished or semi-finished state.

Commodities that have been subject to much variation in EC trade have been oil and natural gas. Some comes from sources within the EC (for example, the North Sea), but most is purchased on the world market where the price traditionally fluctuates widely. This sort of variation has meant that the volume of EC trade has tended to fluctuate, as oil and energy prices have moved up and down.

Major EC trade flows

ACTIVITY

Consider the table on page 205 and then answer the following questions:

1 Which of the following statements is true?
   a) The volume of EC exports to the rest of the world exceeded the volume of imports to the EC from the rest of the world
   b) The volume of EC imports from EC states exceeded the value of EC exports to EC states
   c) The volume of EC imports from non-EC states exceeded the volume of EC exports to non-EC states.

2 Draw conclusions from the EC's trade with:
a) EFTA
b) USA
c) Japan
d) ACP states
e) Eastern Europe.

The trade[1] of the 12 in 1989

	Imports from	*Exports to*	*Balance[4]*
World	1 073 552	1 043 289	−30 263
Intra-EC	624 488	625 722	–
Extra-EC	446 716	413 010	−33 706
of which:			
EFTA	102 589	107 968	+5379
Other West European	13 436	14 947	+1511
US	83 660	78 020	−5640
Japan	46 337	21 130	−5207
Other industrialized countries	24 871	26 653	+1782
ACP[2] plus overseas departments and territories	21 888	26 617	+4729
Other developing countries	115 225	104 580	−10 645
Eastern Europe (state trading)	28 992	25 870	−3122
Other state trading	9715	7216	−2499
Miscellaneous	2347	4557	+2210
Trade with specific country groups included in extra-EC category above			
Mediterranean basin	37 174	40 699	+3525
OPEC	40 843	35 031	−5812
Latin America	26 047	15 109	−10 938
ASEAN[3]	15 173	14 110	−1063

Notes:
1. Million ECUs.
2. Lomé Convention countries – i.e. ex-colonial dependencies.
3. Association of South-East Asian Nations.
4. Exports minus imports.

Source: Statistical Office of the European Communities, *External Trade Monthly Statistics*, 1990, no. 12.

Trade agreements and commercial treaties

We saw in Chapter 2 that GATT is a major trade agreement that the EC is involved in. Other treaties exist too, although individual member states are no longer able to sign *commercial treaties* with other states, where reductions or the abolition of customs duties are involved. This is because the EC is responsible for concluding these agreements on behalf of all member states. Individual member states do sign international agreements on commodities, where they agree to purchase certain amounts of wheat for example, from producer countries as a whole. Here, each importing country is committed by the agreement to buy the specified amount, but without stating the actual producer country. So, an importing state would buy say, 100 000 tonnes of wheat, but would not know which of the producer countries they had actually traded with.

Member states may also conclude individual co-operation agreements with other countries, although these are usually with developing states which were once part of their colonial empires (for example, France with Senegal). Such agreements may have a commercial aspect but are generally mutually beneficial. This sort of agreement is allowed under EC rules, although the Commission has the right to be informed about them.

The EC as a whole also negotiates on detailed issues in the United Nations Conference on Trade and Development (UNCTAD). For example, the idea of the Generalised System of Preferences (see Chapter 2) was discussed, negotiated and agreed during the second UNCTAD in 1968.

ACTIVITY

Read the article 'Cuban/EC trade' and then answer the following questions:

1 Why did President Bush wish the EC to veto the Cuban Democracy Act?
2 How might such a veto damage trade between the EC and the USA?
3 What reasons did the EC offer for not going along with the veto? Do you agree with these reasons? Why?

Cuban/EC trade

The EC urged US President Bush again last week to veto the Cuban Democracy Act under which the US is seeking to speed up Cuba's transition to democracy by imposing a reinforced trade embargo on US and Cuban trading partners. An EC statement pointed out that the sanctions would be in conflict with international law, as well as damaging to international shipping and EC trade with the US. While the EC expressed its support for peaceful transition to democracy in Cuba, last Thursday's statement said it could not accept US unilateral moves which restrict EC commercial and economic relations with any foreign nation.

Source: *The Week in Europe*, 15 October 1992

The EC balance of payments

The EC's trade in goods and services, or *international trade*, is set down as two sets of figures and is known as the balance of payments. This divides into two parts:

- the current account;
- the capital account.

The current account

This consists of actual trade – imports and exports. The current account balance shows the excess national income from the rest of the world if it is *positive* or the income transferred to the rest of the world if it is *negative*. Trade is split into a number of categories:

Goods | Services | Investment income | Labour income | Government transactions | Unilateral transfers

Trade categories

Trade division	*Explanation*
Goods	These are recorded at their frontier value.
Services	Transport (goods and passengers, port services). Travel (expenditure of people visiting abroad). Other services (technical assistance, professional services, construction services, communication services).
Investment income	Dividends and interest on capital invested abroad or paid on capital invested in nation states.
Labour income	Income of workers employed in one economy and resident in another.
Government transactions	Expenditure of embassies and armed forces stationed abroad. Non-market transactions of public bodies.
Unilateral transfers	Migrant workers' pensions and social security benefits, government subsidies, international aid.

The capital account

This records the variation in an economy's financial assets and liabilities in relation to the rest of the world. The account is designed to record all movements of capital entering or leaving an economy and present them in an analytical way.

The range of goods and services

Trade in goods is extensive within the EC. The following table shows the range of goods and their respective values in terms of imports and exports:

EC trade by product in 1990

	Imports		*Exports*	
	(Mio ECU)	*(%)*	*Mio ECU*	*(%)*
Agri-food products	35 655	7.7	30 595	7.2
animals, meat, fish	9 900	2.1	4 604	1.1
fruit and vegetables	10 258	2.2	3 199	0.8
coffee, tea, spices	4 886	1.1	1 602	0.4
cereals, dairy products, eggs	2 115	0.5	8 512	2.0
beverages, tobacco	2 537	0.5	7 677	1.8
other	5 959	1.3	5 001	1.2
Non-energy raw materials	37 944	8.2	8 846	2.1
cork, wood, pulp	13 432	2.9	–	–
metal ores	8 756	1.9	–	–
other	15 756	3.4	–	–
Energy products	70 491	15.2	11 185	2.7
petroleum and petroleum products	59 997	13.0	10 130	2.4
Chemicals	30 366	6.6	48 553	11.6
organic chemicals	8 378	1.8	10 293	2.5
medicines and drugs	4 960	1.1	8 811	2.1
plastics	6 514	1.4	9 154	2.2
other	10 514	2.3	20 295	4.8
Machinery and transport equipment	132 164	28.6	169 749	40.4
road transport equipment	20 310	4.4	38 334	9.1
other transport equipment	13 905	3.0	14 370	3.4
engines and generators	11 563	2.5	15 189	3.6
machine tools	26 483	5.7	60 544	14.4
other data-processing, telecommunications equipment, etc.	59 903	12.9	41 312	9.8
Miscellaneous manufactures	132 499	28.6	130 720	31.1
clothing, footwear, bags	25 490	5.5	16 656	4.0
furniture	2 660	0.6	5 013	1.2
precision instruments	15 554	3.4	14 671	3.5
other	88 795	19.2	94 380	22.5
Products not broken down, including gold	23 601	5.1	20 166	4.8
Total	**462 720**		**419 814**	

Source: Eurostat

The value of goods

We can consider the relative value of different types of goods by studying products imported and exported to and from EC member states. Comparing these figures with those of the USA and Japan helps to illustrate the importance of the EC as a trading group, and the significance of certain types of goods.

Imports by commodity classes – 1989 (Mio ECU)

Importing country	*Total imports*	*Food, beverages and tobacco*	*Mineral fuels, lubricants and related materials*	*Crude materials, oils and fats*	*Machinery and equipment*	*Other*
EUR 12	**1 073 552**	**108 841**	**86 701**	**69 689**	**349 269**	**459 052**
Belg./Lux.	93 008	8 442	6 895	6 492	23 051	48 128
Denmark.	24 723	2 859	1 758	1 201	7 520	11 385
Germany	244 679	23 415	18 530	16 967	74 572	111 195
Greece	14 683	2 256	935	836	4 526	6 130
Spain	61 599	5 763	7 127	5 024	24 029	19 656
France	182 861	16 907	15 333	8 546	67 628	74 447
Ireland	15 687	1 657	867	505	5 849	6 809
Italy	138 963	16 708	13 303	12 945	39 687	56 320
Netherlands	101 550	12 171	11 257	6 678	29 618	41 826
Portugal	17 145	1 705	1 824	1 199	6 272	6 145
United Kingdom	178 654	16 958	8 872	9 296	66 518	77 010
USA	429 677	24 676	50 913	15 710	191 341	147 037
Japan	191 320	28 102	39 795	29 118	25 511	68 794

Exports by commodity classes – 1989 (Mio ECU)

Exporting country	*Total exports*	*Food, beverages and tobacco*	*Mineral fuels, lubricants and related materials*	*Crude materials, oils and fats*	*Machinery and equipment*	*Other*
EUR 12	**1 043 289**	**104 136**	**34 752**	**35 306**	**393 781**	**475 314**
Belg./Lux.	90 851	8 330	3 129	2 966	23 020	53 406
Denmark.	25 942	6 812	770	1 498	6 630	10 232
Germany	308 682	14 240	3 818	6 625	150 251	133 748
Greece	6 883	1 767	374	802	227	3 713
Spain	42 265	6 039	1 873	1 882	14 979	17 492
France	167 994	23 908	3 413	6 774	66 575	67 324
Ireland	18 753	4 512	88	793	5 958	7 402
Italy	127 799	7 615	2 438	2 242	47 105	68 399
Netherlands	105 090	20 658	10 077	7 393	23 123	43 839
Portugal	11 498	815	391	1 244	2 187	6 861
United Kingdom	137 532	9 440	8 381	3 088	53 726	62 897
USA	330 171	31 979	8 954	25 683	135 058	128 497
Japan	249 817	1 497	867	1 852	175 783	69 818

Source: Eurostat

ACTIVITY

Consider the tables above and then answer the following questions:

1 Decide how important in EC trade the following are:
a) food, beverages and tobacco
b) machinery and equipment.

2 Draw bar charts to illustrate total imports and exports for the EC12, the USA and Japan. What conclusions can you draw?

3 Write an article (no more than 350 words) for the trade section of your local newspaper which summarises the most important findings from the tables.

EC trade in the future

We have already seen how the EC plans to move to economic and monetary union, and has set out a timetable to achieve the three stages of EMU. When this becomes a reality with the ECU in place as a possible single currency, then the EC will have a monetary zone which should be able to rival the dollar and the yen. This would bring certain advantages to the EC's customers, it is argued:

- the costs of transactions arising from the use of different currencies when buying and selling on different EC markets, will be reduced. This should help to stimulate further trade with the EC;
- customers could hold some of their reserves in ECUs, cushioning the impact of dollar fluctuations, as and when these occur;
- some countries may choose to link their own currency to the ECU, especially those who have the EC as a major trading partner

Much depends upon the successful implementation of economic and monetary union. Once political and national differences are ironed out, the future for Community trade seems bright, for it should be able to trade much more like a single state than a set of individual ones.

ACTIVITY Review your progress: 10

1 The EC home market is second only to that of the USA. True or false?
2 What is meant by 'intra-Community' trade?
3 Explain briefly why the USA is opposed to EC export subsidies on agricultural products.
4 Which of the following statements is incorrect:
   a) Member states are no longer able to sign commercial treaties with other states
   b) Member states can agree to purchase stocks of products from producer countries as a whole
   c) Member states may not conclude individual co-operation agreements with former colonial states.
5 Is the flow of EC trade greater with EFTA or with the USA?
6 What are the two parts of the EC's balance of payments?

Summary

- The EC is involved in a number of different but important trading patterns.
- The EC is a significant actor in world trade, and this is demonstrated by the flow of goods and services.
- An extensive range of goods and services are available within the EC.
- When discussing EC trade, the distinction between intra-Community trade and external trade must be made.
- The prospects for increased EC trade are favourable, and economic and monetary union should further promote these prospects.

Assignment 16 The trade fair and exhibition

You are employed by a research agency which has been asked to run a stand dealing with EC trade matters at a major trade fair and exhibition. In preparation for the exhibition you decide to do the following.

Task 1 Draw up a large-scale map of the world and indicate the major trading groupings. Use a key to illustrate the flow of goods and services between the EC and its major trading partners.

Task 2 Produce an 'EC Trade Background Sheet' (on no more than three sides of A4 paper) which deals with the following:

- intra-Community trade
- EC external trade
- an explanation of the EC's balance of payments
- the benefits of trade with the EC.

Task 3 Choose one of the EC's major trading partners and produce a booklet covering such aspects as:

- value of trade with the EC
- the major goods and services traded
- trade agreements or treaties which exist between the chosen partner and the EC
- other useful information on the trading relationship.

Appendix 1: Glossary of European Community acronyms

Acronym	*Meaning*	*Purpose (if not self-explanatory)*
ACP	Africa, Caribbean and Pacific	68 Third World countries associated with the EC by the Lomé conventions
AGRIMED	Mediterranean Agriculture	Agricultural research
ARION	Programme of study visits for education specialists	
ASEAN	Association of South Eastern Countries	Group of six south-east Asian countries: Malaysia, Brunei, Indonesia, Thailand, Singapore, Philippines
BCC	Business Co-operative Centre	EC body aimed at helping SMEs to co-operate across Community boundaries
BES	Business Expansion Scheme	
BEUC	European Bureau of Consumers' Unions	
BRITE	Basic Research in Industrial Technologies in Europe	EC framework programme covering research projects in the advanced materials area
BTR	Basic Technological Research	Long term technical research
CAD/CAM	Computer Aided Design/Computer Aided Manufacture	
CAP	Common Agricultural Policy	Community action in the area of agriculture
CARICOM	Caribbean Community and Common Market	
CCC	Consumer Consultative Committee	Representation of consumer opinions
CCT/CET	Common Customs Tariff/Common External Tariff	Tax or duty on goods entering the EC
CEC	Commission of the European Communities	
CEDEFOP	European Centre for the Development of Vocational Training	
CEN	European Committee for Standardisation	Standards body including EC and EFTA states
CENELEC	European Committee for Electrotechnical Standardisation	Standards body including EC and EFTA states
CERD	Committee for European Research and Development	Committee of independent scientific experts
CERN	European Nuclear Research Centre	
CFP	Common Fisheries Policy	Community action in the area of sea fishing and total catches
CID	Centre for Industrial Development	
COGECA	General Committee for Agricultural Co-operation in the EC	
COM	Commission of the EC proposals for legislation	Abbreviation for Commission documents
COMETT	Community Action Programme in Education and Training for Technology	Promotes high technology co-operation between member states

Acronym	*Meaning*	*Purpose (if not self-explanatory)*
COPA	Committee of Agricultural Organisations in the EC	Committee representing the farmer's viewpoint
COREPER	Committee of Permanent Representatives	Ambassadors of the EC member states to the Community
CPC	Community Patent Convention	A body of EC law concerning patents and procedures
CRONOS/ EUROSTAT	EC Statistical Data Bank	EC statistics service providing useful data about the EC and member states
CUC	Central Accounting Unit	
DC	Developing Countries	
DG	Directorate General	1 of the 23 departments of the European Commission
EAC	European Accident Code	
EAEC	European Atomic Energy Community	Energy body formed in 1957 which aimed to encourage a civil nuclear industry in the EC
EAGGF	European Agricultural Guidance and Guarantee Fund (FEOGA)	The farm fund which finances the CAP. One of 3 EC structural funds
EC	European Community	The association of 12 member states
ECJ	European Court of Justice	EC institution that ensures the equal application of EC law
ECSC	European Coal and Steel Community	Formed in 1951 with 6 original members: France, Italy, Germany, Belgium, Luxembourg and The Netherlands
ECU	European Currency Unit	The basket of 12 EC currencies used in matters relating to EC expenditure
EEA	European Economic Area	The free trade area agreement between the EC and EFTA states
EEC	European Economic Community	
EEIG	European Economic Interest Group	Association of companies from different member states in joint business ventures
EFTA	European Free Trade Association	Group of 6 countries which has economic links with the EC (*see* EEA)
EIB	European Investment Bank	Independent organisation responsible for granting loans in the EC
ELEC	European League for Economic Co-operation	
EMF	European Monetary Fund	Fund which provides a reserve asset
EMS	European Monetary System	System aimed at stabilising exchange rates between EC member states
EMU	European Monetary Union	Community action in the area of economic and monetary policy
EP	European Parliament	
Erasmus	European Community Action Scheme for the Mobility of University Students	
ERDF	European Regional Development Fund	Fund designed to correct regional imbalances in the EC. One of the 3 structural funds
ERM	Exchange Rate Mechanism	The instrument for linking EMS currencies
ESA	European Space Agency	EC body promoting space exploration
ESC (ECOSOC)	Economic and Social Committee	Committee comprising EC employers, trade unions and commercial interests
ESF	European Social Fund	EC fund that assists with training and retraining. One of the 3 structural funds
ESPRIT	European Strategic Research Programme in Information Technology	EC programme aimed at improving co-operation in the IT industry

Acronym	*Meaning*	*Purpose (if not self-explanatory)*
ETUC	European Trade Union Confederation	Body covering trade unions in West European countries
EUA	European Unit of Account	The predecessor of the ECU
EURATOM	European Atomic Energy Community	(*see* EAEC)
Euronet-Diane	Direct information access network for Europe	
EUROSTAT	EC's Statistical Office	(*see* CRONOS)
EUROTECNET	EC Action Programme in the field of vocational training and technological change	Programme taking account of technological changes and their impact on work, employment and qualifications
Eurydice	The Education Information Network in the EC	Body providing useful data on the education systems of the EC member states
FIPMEC	Internal Federation of Small and Medium-sized Enterprises	
FEOGA	Fond Europeen d'Orientation et de Garanti Agricole	(*see* EAGGF)
GATT	General Agreement on Tariffs and Trade	International agreement on trade involving the EC, the USA and other states
GRT	Gross Registered Tonnes	
GSP	Generalised System of Preferences	Tariff preference scheme which operates in favour of less developed states
IMF	International Monetary Fund	The reserve assets of the international monetary system
IMP	Integrated Mediterranean Programmes	EC programme to assist lesser developed regions of the Community in the Mediterranean area
ISO	International Organisation for Standardisation	International body responsible for setting common standards
IT	Information Technologies	
LDC	Least Developed Countries	A list of the world's poorest states compiled by the United Nations
LINGUA	EC Action Programme to promote Foreign Language Competence	EC programme aimed at teaching and learning of foreign languages
MCA	Monetary Compensatory Amounts	A system of border subsidies affecting the normal prices of cross-border agricultural products
MEP	Member of the European Parliament	
MFTA	Medium-term Financial Assistance	A loan facility available under the European Monetary System
MS	Member States of the EC	
OECD	Organisation for Economic Co-operation and Development	Group of 24 states who meet to discuss the economic policies of industrialised countries
OJ	*Official Journal*	Daily EC publication printed in all official Community languages
PETRA	EC Action Programme for the vocational training of young people and their preparation for adult and working life	Vocational training and development programme
PSTN	Public Switched Telephone Network	
RAP	Research Action Programme	Common EC research scheme
R&D	Research and Development	

Acronym	Meaning	Purpose (if not self-explanatory)
RPI	Retail Price Index	
SEA	Single European Act	
SEM	Southern and Eastern Mediterranean Countries	
SITPRO	Simplification of Trade Procedures	Office concerned with EC trade procedures
SME	Small and Medium-sized Enterprises	Businesses employing up to 500 people
SPRINT	Strategic Programme for Innovation and Technology Transfer	EC programme aimed at allowing the transnational sharing of technology
STMS	Short Term Monetary Support	Credit mechanism under the European Monetary System
TAC	Total Allowable Catch (Fisheries)	
TRIS	EC Network of Training Programmes for Women	
UA	Unit of Account	(*see* EUA)
UN	United Nations	International body consisting of many countries of the world
UNCTAD	United Nations Conference on Trade and Development	
UNESCO	United Nations Educational, Scientific and Cultural Organisation	
UNICE	Conference of Industries of the EC	Consists of employer federations of the EC and EFTA
VAT	Value Added Tax	Member state contributions form part of 'own resources' income
WHO	World Health Organisation	A United Nations body operating in the area of world health

Appendix 2: Useful addresses and telephone numbers

European Documentation Centres (EDCs)

There are EDCs in the following public and college libraries.

Aberdeen Library
Telephone: 0224 272587

Bath Library
Telephone: 0225 826826

Belfast Library
Telephone: 0232 245133

Bradford Library
Telephone: 0274 383402

Cambridge Library
Telephone: 0223 333138

Cardiff Library
Telephone: 0222 874262

Coventry University Library
Telephone: 0203 838295

Dundee Library
Telephone: 0382 23181

Durham Library
Telephone: 091-374 3041/3044

East Anglia Library
Telephone: 0603 56161

Edinburgh Library
Telephone: 031-650 2041

Essex Library
Telephone: 0206 873181

Exeter Library
Telephone: 0392 263356

Glasgow Library
Telephone: 041-339 8855

Hull Library
Telephone: 0782 621111

Kent Library
Telephone: 0227 764000

Lancaster Library
Telephone: 0524 65201

Leeds Library
Telephone: 0532 335040

Leicester Library
Telephone: 0533 522044

London Library
Telephone: 071-755 5555

London School of Economics and Political Science Library
Telephone: 071-955 7273

Loughborough Library
Telephone: 0509 222343

Manchester Library
Telephone: 061-275 3751/3764

Nottingham Library
Telephone: 0602 484848

Oxford Library
Telephone: 0865 277201

Reading College Library
Telephone: 0734 318782

Salford College Library
Telephone: 061-745 5000

Sheffield Hallam University Library
Telephone: 0742 532126

Southampton College Library
Telephone: 0703 595000

Surrey Library
Telephone: 0483 509233

Sussex Library
Telephone: 0273 678440

Ulster Library
Telephone: 0265 44141

University of Central England in Birmingham Library
Telephone: 021-331 5289

University of North London
Telephone: 071-607 2789

University of Northumbria
Telephone: 091-227 4136

University of Portsmouth Library
Telephone: 0705 843240

University of Wolverhampton Library
Telephone: 0902 322300

Warwick Library
Telephone: 0203 523523

Wye College Library
Telephone: 0233 812401

European Institutions

Commission: United Kingdom

Commission for European Communities
Jean Monnet House
8 Storey's Gate
London
SW1P 3AT
Telephone: 071-222 8122

Commission for European Communities
Windsor House
9–15 Bedford Street
Belfast
BT2 7EG
Telephone: 0232 40708

Commission for European Communities
4 Cathedral Road
Cardiff
CF1 9SG
Telephone: 0222 371631

Commission for European Communities
9 Alva Street
Edinburgh
EH2 4PH
Telephone: 031-225 2058

Commission: European Community

Commission of the European Communities
Brussels Office
rue de la Loi 200
1049 Brussels
Telephone: 010 322 235 1111

Commission of the European Communities
Luxembourg Office
Batiment Jean Monnet
rue Alcide de Gasperi
Kirchberg
Luxembourg
Telephone: 010 352 43011

European Parliament: United Kingdom

European Parliament
London Information Office
2 Queen Anne's Gate
London
SW1H 9AA
Telephone: 071-222 0411

European Parliament: European Community

European Parliament
Brussels Office
97 rue de Belliard
1040 Brussels
Belgium
234 2000

Other institutions: European Community

Council of Ministers
Secretariat
170 rue de la Loi
1040 Brussels
234 6422

Economic and Social Committee
2 Rue Ravenstein
1000 Brussels
512 3920

European Court of Auditors
29 rue Aldringen
118 Luxembourg

European Court of Justice
BP96
Plateau de Kirchberg
Luxembourg

National Embassies

Information on the activities of individual member states within the EC may be obtained from the national embassies listed below.

Belgian Embassy
103 Eaton Square
London
SW1H 9AB
Telephone: 071-235 5422

Royal Danish Embassy
55 Sloane Street
London
SW1X 9SR
Telephone: 071-333 0200

French Embassy
58 Knightsbridge
London
SW1X 7JT
Telephone: 071-235 8080

German Embassy
23 Belgrave Square
London
SW1X 8PZ
Telephone: 071-235 5033

Greek Embassy
1a Holland Park
London
W11 3TP
Telephone: 071-727 8040

Irish Embassy
17 Grosvenor Place
London
SW1X 7HR
Telephone: 071-235 2171

Italian Embassy
14 Three Kings Yard
Davies Street
London
W1Y 2EH
Telephone: 071-629 8200

Embassy of Luxembourg
27 Wilton Crescent
London
SW1X 8SD
Telephone: 071-235 6961

Royal Netherlands Embassy
38 Hyde Park Gate
London
SW7 5DP
Telephone: 071-584 5040

Portuguese Embassy
11 Belgrave Square
London
SW1X 8PP
Telephone: 071-235 5331

Spanish Embassy
24 Belgrave Square
London
SW1X 8QA
Telephone: 071-235 5555

For information on the UK's participation in the EC, contact:

European Community Unit of Foreign and Commonwealth Office
King Charles Street
London
SW1A 2AH

National Tourist Offices

Information on the culture, geography and industries of member states of the EC may be obtained from the various national tourist offices listed below.

Belgian Tourist Office
38 Dover Street
London
W1X 3RB
Telephone: 071-499 5379

Danish Tourist Information Office
Sceptre House
169/173 Regent Street
London
W1R 8PY
Telephone: 071-734 2637

French Government Tourist Office
178 Piccadilly
London
W1V 0AL
Telephone: 071-491 7622

German National Tourist Office
Nightingale House
65 Curzon Street
London
W1Y 7PE
Telephone: 071-495 3990/91

Greek National Tourist Organisation
4 Conduit Street
London
W1R 0DJ
Telephone: 071-734 5997

Irish Tourist Board
150 New Bond Street
London
W1Y 0AQ
Telephone: 071-493 3201

Italian State Tourist Office
1 Princes Street
London
W1R 8AY
Telephone: 071-408 1254

Luxembourg Tourist Office
36/37 Piccadilly
London
W1V 9PA
Telephone: 071-434 2800

Netherlands Board of Tourism
25–28 Buckingham Gate
London
SW1E 6LD
Telephone: 071-630 0451

Portuguese National Tourist Office
22/25a Sackville Street
London
W1X 1DE
Telephone: 071-494 1441

Spanish Tourist Office
57–58 St James's Street
London
SW1A 1LD
Telephone: 071-499 0901

Appendix 3: Bibliography

Books

Arbuthnott, H. and G. Edwards (1992) *A Common Man's Guide to the Common Market* (2nd edn), Macmillan.

Eurostat (1991) *A Social Portrait of Europe.*

Eurostat (1991) *Basic Statistics of the Community* (26th edn).

Central Statistical Office (1992) *Britain 1992 – An Official Handbook.*

Randlesome, C. (ed.) *et al.* (1991) *Business Cultures in Europe*, Butterworth Heinemann.

Kent, P. (1992) *European Community Law*, M and E/Pitman.

Somers, F. (ed.) *et al.* (1991) *European Economies – A Comparative Study*, Pitman.

Scott, A. (1992) *European Studies*, Pitman.

Eurostat (1992) *Europe in Figures* (3rd edn).

Gray, T. (1992) *Europeople*, MacDonald.

Ardagh, J. (1988) *France Today: France in the 1980s*, Penguin.

Ardagh, J. (1987) *Germany and the Germans*, Penguin.

Eurydice (1991) *Structures of the Education and Initial Training Systems in the Member States of the European Community.*

Kerr, A. (1987) *The Common Market and How it Works* (3rd edn), Pergamon.

Nevin, E. (1990) *The Economics of Europe*, Macmillan.

Swann, D. (1992) *The Economics of the European Community* (7th edn), Penguin.

The Economist (1988) *The Economist Business Guides: France, Germany, Italy, Spain and the UK.*

Goodman, S.F. (1990) *The European Community*, Macmillan.

Lintner, V. and S. Mazey (1991) *The European Community*, McGraw-Hill.

Budd, S.A. and A. Jones (1991) *The European Community: A Guide to the Maze* (4th edn), Kogan Page.

Bailey, R. (1983) *The European Connection*, Pergamon.

Nugent, N. (1989) *The Government and Politics of the European Community*, Macmillan.

Haycroft, J. (1987) *The Italian Labyrinth: Italy in the 1980s*, Penguin.

Minshull, G.N. (1990) *The New Europe* (4th edn) Hodder and Stoughton.

Hooper, J. (1986) *The Spaniards*, Penguin.

Europa (1992) *Western Europe.*

Willings Press Directory (1992).

Booklets and pamphlets

Apart from the range of European Community pamphlets and leaflets for which a catalogue is available from the London office of the Commission, several other useful sources exist:

'Barclays Bank Guide to the Member States of the European Community' (1990).

UK Office of the Commission and the European Parliament (July 1991) 'Europe at a Glance'.

Department of Trade and Industry (DTI) (1991) 'Influencing Decisions in the European Community'.

DTI (quarterly) *Single Market News.*

DTI (1991) 'Target Europe – The Single Market'.

DTI (March 1992) 'The Single Market – A Guide to Sources of Advice.

Commission London Office (Weekly) *The Week in Europe* information sheet.

McLaughlin, N. (Conservatives in the European Parliament) (1992) 'Understanding Europe – A Classroom Guide to the European Community'.

Index